THE BOOK OF THE KNIGHT OF THE TOWER

MANNERS FOR YOUNG MEDIEVAL WOMEN

Rebecca Barnhouse

THE BOOK OF THE KNIGHT OF THE TOWER

First published in 2006 by
PALGRAVE MACMILLAN™
175 Fifth Avenue, New York, N.Y. 10010 and
Houndmills, Basingstoke, Hampshire, England RG21 6XS
Companies and representatives throughout the world.

PALGRAVE MACMILLAN is the global academic imprint of the Palgrave Macmillan division of St. Martin's Press, LLC and of Palgrave Macmillan Ltd. Macmillan® is a registered trademark in the United States, United Kingdom and other countries. Palgrave is a registered trademark in the European Union and other countries.

ISBN-13: 978–1–4039–6991–0
ISBN-10: 1–4039–6991–4

Library of Congress Cataloging-in-Publication Data

Barnhouse, Rebecca.
   The book of the knight of the tower : manners for young medieval
women / Rebecca Barnhouse.
      p. cm.
   Includes bibliographical references and index.
   ISBN 1–4039–6991–4
   1. Young women—Conduct of life. 2. Christian women—Conduct of
life. 3. La Tour Landry, Geoffroy de, 14th cent. Livre du chevalier de La
Tour Landry pour l'enseignement de ses filles. I. La Tour Landry, Geoffroy
de, 14th cent. Livre du chevalier de La Tour Landry pour l'enseignement
de ses filles. II. Title. III. Series.

BJ1681.B33 2006
170.82—dc22   2005057424

A catalogue record for this book is available from the British Library.

Design by Newgen Imaging Systems (P) Ltd., Chennai, India.

First edition: June 2006

10 9 8 7 6 5 4 3 2 1

Printed in the United States of America.

CONTENTS

FOREWORD

In 1372 a French knight compiled a book of stories to teach his daughters how to be good wives and good Christians. The book was popular in his own century and the next, in France, in Germany, and in England. In the fifteenth century, William Caxton translated it into Middle English and used the technology he had recently introduced to Londoners to print an edition of the book. Instead of an aristocratic audience, merchants were his main clientele, people who read the book to discover how to behave more like knights and ladies, and how to make their daughters attractive marriage partners. They also read the stories for the same reason a modern audience might: for what medieval writers called *sentence and solas* — to learn and to be delighted.

The Knight of the Tower's stories have long been available to scholars, but not to general readers and undergraduate students, for whom this book was written. To give readers a sense of the people who would have read this book in the Late Middle Ages, I have reconstructed the daily habits of two families: the knight's, and a London woolmerchant's.

About Geoffrey de la Tour Landry and his first wife, Jeanne de Rougé, much more is known than about the rest of his family, who survive only as names in manuscripts. Thus I have imagined the ages, activities, and sometimes even the thoughts and speech of their daughters and sons, as well as some of their servants. The fifteenth-century family of London merchants is invented in all but name; there really was a wool merchant named Robert Goodwyn, but I have recreated all of the details about him and his family, including their ownership of a copy of Sir Geoffrey's book.

My purpose in these inventions is to give modern readers a feel for the kinds of people who might have read Sir Geoffrey's book in the fourteenth and fifteenth centuries, as well as a sense of how and why their reactions to his stories might have differed from ours. These families—especially the young women who were (or, in the case of the Goodwyn sisters, who might have been) the recipients of copies of *The Book of the Knight of the Tower*—serve as guides to the late medieval era.

Acknowledgments

I owe thanks to many people who have helped me with this book. In London, the staff of the British Library graciously allowed me access to manuscripts and early printed books. In France, I found unprecedented generosity and kindness. Françoise Rouquié and Daniel Delpech took the most amazing care of a complete stranger who had boarded the wrong train. They gave me a bed for the night, fed me a gourmet meal in their country farmhouse, got up very early the next morning to drive me to the station, and made sure I was on the right train. Later, a young man in the Chemillé tourist office drove me to La Tourlandry when there was no public transportation available. And in Lyons, Monty Laycox was a superb host.

Closer to home, I am grateful to Youngstown State University for granting me a sabbatical, to the librarians at Maag Library for their unstinting and professional assistance, and to Palgrave Macmillan's anonymous reader for thoughtful comments about my manuscript. Thanks also go to Lisa Carl, who housed me in Chapel Hill as I was starting this project, and to Cynthia Brincat, who put up with me during a research trip to Chicago.

Most of all, my deepest thanks are due to the three people who read, commented on, asked questions about, and supported this book from the very beginning: Sid Brown, Allison Wallace, and Nancy Barnhouse. To them, and to my father, I dedicate this book.

PART I

THE KNIGHT AND HIS BOOK

Chapter 1

The World of the Book

Shining Knights and Ladies Fair—Sir Geoffrey and His Family

I saw my daughters coming towards me. I wanted them to turn to honor above all other things, for they were young and small and lacking wisdom and reason. . . . I wanted to make them a little book to read so they might learn and study and understand the good and evil that has already happened, in order to keep them from that which is yet to come.

So writes Sir Geoffrey de La Tour Landry, a fourteenth-century French knight, about his daughters Jeanne, Anne, and Marie. In this world, where so many temptations stand between his daughters and salvation, he knows he must teach them to live virtuously, to behave according to their station, to obey church law, and to avoid what he calls the "blame, shame, and defame" that might mar their reputations and their chances for good marriages. He sees them only rarely, so how best to teach them? He decides to compile a book for them, as he has already done for his two sons, to teach them to be virtuous. With the help of priests and scholars, he gathers stories of good women and bad and tales from many sources that will help his daughters "turn to good." Search the Bible, he tells his helpers, listen to stories of kings, read chronicles of France, of Greece, of England, of many strange lands, and when you find a good example, copy it. To these tales, Sir Geoffrey adds stories from his own life, about great lords and ladies he has known, soldiers he has heard about, and the deeds of members of his own family.

What was it that a fourteenth-century father, a country nobleman from Anjou near the great Loire River, wanted his daughters to know? Sir Geoffrey was a soldier, and he knew that soldiers sometimes acted dishonorably toward women. Since he couldn't always be there to protect his daughters, he wanted them to know how to preserve their reputations. Above all, he wanted each one to be a devout Christian and to wake every morning remembering that God has made her. He wanted his daughters to wear appropriate clothing, to avoid sin, and to exhibit the right kind of behavior to their future husbands, behavior that rarely agrees with modern ideas about how to live.

The degree of subservience expected of medieval wives seems unbelievable to the twenty-first-century reader, but Sir Geoffrey's opinions are hardly remarkable for his time. In his view, obedience to one's husband is expected, and wifely disobedience is harshly reproved, sometimes with beatings. A husband's cruelty is something a wife should bear with patience and humility, whereas a wife should offer only gentleness and understanding to her husband. Further, faithless wives deserve terrible punishment, even death, yet they should tolerate their husbands' infidelities with good cheer. All of these ideas are reinforced in Sir Geoffrey's stories, as are standard medieval ideals of Christian piety. Nevertheless, it becomes evident throughout his book that Sir Geoffrey treated his own wives and daughters with courtesy, love, and respect.

A *chevalier banneret* who consorted with nobles close to kings, but hardly a *grand seigneur*, Sir Geoffrey was often away from home fighting; however, one scholar notes that he had more passion for family than for war.[1] During the Hundred Years War, he fought with the army of Charles de Blois at the Battle of Auray in 1364 (they lost), and sent men to the Siege of Cherbourg in 1378. In one record, he is noted for his expensive brown horse, the sine qua non for a knight. Jean Froissart, the great chronicler of the Hundred Years War, and Sir Geoffrey's almost exact contemporary, describes some of the campaigns Sir Geoffrey fought in. Both Froissart and Sir Geoffrey mention many of the same people, such as the famous soldiers Charny and Boucicaut the elder, and Jean, Duke of Normandy, who later became Jean le Bon, King of France. Like Froissart, Sir Geoffrey writes about aristocrats, people of his own social station and higher. Little about the common rabble seeps into either author's work.

When Sir Geoffrey wasn't involved in military campaigns, there was the business of being a wealthy Christian to attend to: in addition to La Tour Landry in Anjou, Sir Geoffrey was the lord of four other estates,[2] and he was the benefactor of an Augustinian monastery. In exchange for the land he bestowed on them, the monks must have promised to say masses for Sir Geoffrey after he died, because some 400 years later, at the time of the French Revolution, they were still including the souls of Sir Geoffrey and his wife Jeanne de Rougé in their prayers.[3] Jeanne also had a chapel built; she and Sir Geoffrey knew these acts would serve them well at that final hour when God's judgment was upon them.

Jeanne de Rougé, Sir Geoffrey's first wife, grew up in a wealthy and influential family in Brittany, which borders Anjou. Her father knew King Jean le Bon, and he counseled Jean's successor, Charles V. The marriage, Jeanne's second, took place in the 1350s and brought Sir Geoffrey prestige as well as wealth in the form of new estates to manage. After Jeanne died in the 1380s, Sir Geoffrey married another wealthy widow, Marguerite des Roches.

Of the children of Jeanne and Geoffrey, we know only a little, but what we do know connects the family with great events. One son, Charles, fought at the battle of Agincourt in 1415. He is listed among the multitude of French princes, lords, and knights who died on St. Crispin's Day, when Henry V and his English archers prevailed so overwhelmingly against the superior French forces. Another of Jeanne and Geoffrey's sons, Arcades de la Tour, accompanied Joan of Arc on her divine mission to have the French Dauphin crowned king at Rheims in 1429.[4]

Jeanne and Geoffrey's daughters, Jeanne, Anne, and Marie, were the recipients of *The Book of the Knight of the Tower*, but we will never know their reactions to it, since no such record exists. Even the illustrations of their father giving them his book are stylized portraits made in the century after they lived. These manuscript illustrations show the two older daughters standing behind their mother. Marie, the youngest daughter, may not have been born when her father compiled his book, and nowhere in its pages does he mention how many daughters he has.[5] In one miniature of the family, the two Jeannes, mother and elder daughter, wear magnificently adorned clothing befitting their station: furred and intricately cut sleeves and collars on their rich gowns, and bright headdresses of red and blue. Only Anne dresses simply in a gray gown and no headdress. All three women stand in a walled garden filled with flowering trees. Before them sits their father, wearing equally expensive and fashionable attire, a blue coat that exposes his scarlet hose, and a stylish lavender headdress.[6]

Of the girls' lives, only sketchy details survive. Marie must have been much younger than her brother Charles, because she married his stepson. (Charles took as his second wife Jeanne Clerembault, who later became not only his wife but his stepsister, when her mother, Marguerite des Roches, married Sir Geoffrey.) Jeanne and

Anne ventured further from the family in their liaisons, but in the end the two sisters married two brothers. Their father was surely pleased by their engagements, since his new sons-in-law were the sons of King Charles V's chamberlain and counselor, Louis Vicomte of Rochechouart.[7] But there, with marriage, the story of Jeanne and Anne falls silent—did they have children? We don't know that any more than we know when they died. Of their father we know more: he was at least seventy-five years old when he died around the year 1405.

But these are mere dates and facts. What of the real Tour Landry family, their joys and sorrows? Into what patterns were their daily habits stitched? We can construct a broad picture of their lives based on what we know of their times. The five children of Sir Geoffrey and Jeanne de Rougé wouldn't have grown up together after the boys reached the age of eight or so. Let us imagine Charles and his oldest sister Jeanne being about the same age, followed by Arcades, Anne, and, several years later, little Marie. By the time Marie is born, her brothers have been sent to live with Pierre, Lord of Craon, where they first become pages, serving at table, helping the knights dress themselves, running errands, delivering messages, and learning the rudiments of knighthood: riding, handling weapons, playing chess, singing, and dancing. They would get to show off these skills—and Craon's livery, of which they were immensely proud—on the rare occasions when they saw their sisters, perhaps once or twice a year. When he was fifteen, Charles graduated from page to squire. Arcades must have envied the time his brother spent polishing the armor of Sir Bertrand, who had just been made a knight. Charles carried Sir Bertrand's weapons to jousts and tournaments, made sure his horse was well looked after, and as he took care of his knight, he learned the very real skills he would need in deadly battles against the English. By the time Arcades became a squire, three years later, Charles was getting ready to become a knight himself.

While their brothers were off learning to be soldiers, the girls would have watched other boys, the sons of neighboring nobles, learning those same skills from Sir Geoffrey and his knights. We can guess at how they, too, might have passed an afternoon, although we have to imagine the details. Jeanne, at sixteen, would be too old to be interested in the pages her little sister Anne whispered to her about as they sat sewing after the midday meal, but one of the squires might have caught her interest. You can see her shrugging off thirteen-year-old Anne's chatter and moving to an open window where she can watch the squires in the tilting yard, riding with lances toward the mechanical dummy that slaps them when they miss. She can tell which one is Robert, her favorite, by the black hair peeking from under his practice helmet. She wishes she could give him a favor to carry the way ladies do at tournaments, but she's never even talked to him, and besides, her father would have her beaten if he found out. She wonders if her parents have a husband in mind for her, and if they do, if it's someone she's met, if he's handsome, if he has black hair and shapely, slender legs like Robert does.

In their parents' chamber, snuggled into the wet nurse's arms, Marie suckles, happily oblivious to pages, squires, knights, and husbands. Her mother sweeps into the room and the wet nurse nods the only kind of curtsey Marie's bulk will allow her. Jeanne de Rougé smiles and cradles Marie's head in her hand, mindful that after three stillbirths, this child is healthy. She offers a quick prayer to the Virgin, in whose honor her daughter is named, before she sweeps out again, followed by Dame Isobel, one of her ladies-in-waiting. As she enters the girls' chamber, she glances at the window where Jeanne sits staring out, her embroidery forgotten on her lap. Anne looks up guiltily and then becomes a suddenly industrious seamstress, but her sister is still dreaming of Robert wearing her favor on his helmet and dancing with her after the feast that follows the jousting. In a voice louder than is strictly necessary, Jeanne de Rougé commands the girls' attendant, Dame Agnes, to bid the priest to come read stories of saints to the ladies as they sew. Jeanne turns, red-faced, and picks up the embroidery that's fallen from her lap.

Whereas we have to imagine the lives of his family, we can say much more about Sir Geoffrey himself. Between the lines of his book, in his morals, and in his comments about himself, he reveals a great deal about the kind of man he must have been in middle age. Like most people, he was full of contradictions. Deeply moral, deeply pious, he was also more than a little concerned with his worldly honor and his material wealth. A soldier all his life, he disapproves of frivolous, flirtatious behavior, but some of his stories seem frivolous and some of his own behavior flirtatious. As a young man he rejected a young lady's hand in marriage because she wasn't demure enough. Yet he bantered with her, drawing her into his love game. Perhaps he was testing her. In Sir Geoffrey's world of double standards, it's acceptable for a man to act in ways that a woman can't even consider, lest she lose her honor and all her prospects for a suitable marriage.

As pious as Sir Geoffrey was and as much as he wanted to focus on spiritual matters, celebrity awed him. He drops the names of famous soldiers whenever he has a chance, even when their morals are suspect. Sometimes he seems guilty of the sin of pride when he connects himself to great earthly events and people, instead of keeping his focus on his soul.

Sir Geoffrey wants his daughters to be chaste and honorable, yet some of his stories promote chastity and honor by means of some rather shocking plots full of sex and violence. Or at least they seem shocking to us. Tastes change, so perhaps this isn't a contradiction for Sir Geoffrey any more than it is for Chaucer to have a nun among his pilgrims listening to the Miller's rude story about the lusty games of Alison, her husband John, the student Nicholas, and Jolly Absolon, the parish clerk.

Sir Geoffrey finds most women to be filled with sin by their very nature, yet he portrays his wife as warm and wise, nothing like the wicked women of so many of his tales. And he doesn't think of his daughters as evil. He seems genuinely fond of them and hopes they will avoid the follies of their sex. If they live well in this transitory life, there is hope that they will be together for eternity in the Heavenly City of Jerusalem. At least one of his daughters left this world before he did, but the book he wrote for her lived on through the centuries.

I Wanted to Make Them a Little Book— Sir Geoffrey's Manuscript for His Daughters

The original manuscript of Sir Geoffrey's book for his daughters no longer survives, but copies of it do. Other people borrowed Sir Geoffrey's manuscript and employed scribes to make copies for their own families. Still other people borrowed those manuscript copies to make more copies of the book, sometimes binding Sir Geoffrey's stories together with other tales of saintly or sinful women. This copying continued long beyond Sir Geoffrey's lifetime, because the book was popular in the fifteenth and sixteenth centuries, in both handwritten and printed form. Twenty-one manuscripts survive today, housed mostly in Paris, but also in Brussels, Chantilly, The Hague, London, Turin, Vienna, and Breslau.[8] Many of these manuscripts were expensive copies, written on vellum, opening with a miniature painting of the knight, his wife, and his daughters, and ornamented throughout with initials in gold, red, and blue. Others were much cheaper productions, written on paper, containing no elaborate decorations, and indicating that upper-middle-class readers, not just the nobility, bought copies. Of the nobility, powerful men owned manuscript copies of Sir Geoffrey's book, including the dukes of Burgundy in the fourteenth and fifteenth centuries, and in the fifteenth, Philippe le Bon and Jean, Duc de Berry (who also owned the famous *Très Riches Heures*).[9] France wasn't the only place where the book took hold. Sir Geoffrey compiled his book in 1371, at the same time Chaucer was writing in England and Boccaccio in Italy. Someone—we don't know who—translated Sir Geoffrey's text from French into English about fifty years later, during the reign of Henry VI, who was crowned king of both England and France, and whose queen, Marguerite d'Anjou, came from the same region of France as Sir Geoffrey's family. When William Caxton printed his own translation in 1483, he probably didn't know this English version existed.

The book also found an audience in Germany, thanks to a certain Marquard vom Stein, the Landvogt of Montbéliard, who translated it into German for his own two daughters, Elsa and Jakobea, in the year 1460. Like Sir Geoffrey, Marquard vom Stein was a soldier first, a literary man second, but he made the text his own, translating "freely, compressing, expanding, transposing, or interpolating material at will," according to his modern editor, Ruth Harvey.[10] Every now and then he misunderstood Sir Geoffrey's French: did *marrie* mean "married," as he translated it? No—it meant "out of temper." The difference was an accent over the final *e*, but medieval manuscripts don't contain anything like the standard punctuation we're accustomed to nowadays, and Marquard's copy would not have included accents. He unwittingly created a comical passage when he misunderstood a phrase about a woman being thrown from a horse "head first" to mean that the poor lady was beheaded.[11] The German translation, like the French version, was known and read outside Marquard vom Stein's household, and it was printed several times in the fifteenth and sixteenth centuries, ornamented with decorative borders and woodcuts—some possibly by Albrecht Dürer.[12]

Even after the Reformation, the book remained popular in Germany, but the Catholic elements, an integral part of Sir Geoffrey's book, had to be removed. In sixteenth-century editions from Strassburg, a stronghold of the Reformation, references to the Mass, the saints as intercessors, and the doctrines of confession and purgatory were replaced by Protestant-approved ideas, such as prayers directly to God and the teachings of Saint Paul. "And, not surprisingly," Ruth Harvey writes, "all notion of merit acquired by good works—a theme strongly stressed in the original—is rejected, though the emphasis on punishment for bad ones remains undiminished."[13]

By the sixteenth century, however, there were those in England who found Sir Geoffrey's words distasteful for reasons other than religious ones. One writer, Master John Fitzherbert, says, "the knyght of the toure . . . hath made bothe the men and the women to knowe more vyces, subtyltye, and crafte, than euer they shulde haue knowen, if the boke had not ben made." An early-nineteenth-century scholar held a similarly negative opinion, calling the book "a compilation of dull divinity, and unpardonable indelicacy."[14] Delicacy, however, was hardly valued in the fourteenth and fifteenth centuries, as any reader of *The Canterbury Tales* can attest—think of the jokes about sex and flatulence in the Reeve's and Miller's tales, for example. The compiler of the 1808 catalogue of manuscripts in the Harleian collection, now in the British Library, was slightly more generous in his assessment of the first Middle English translation of the book. He describes the manuscript as "An Imperfect Treatise, in old English, containing Counsels to young Ladies & other Women how to govern themselves, by following Vertue & eschewing Vice." He goes on to say,

> it appeareth that the design of the book was good; but the Legendary Stories are so numerous and idle, as much to impair the Reputation of the Performance. However, one Use may be made even of them; they serving to make one laugh at the extreme ridiculousness of gross Popery: and the book may be also further consulted about Habits & Fashions; and the Significations of certain Words now obsolete & not easily understood.[15]

Despite these later opinions, the book retained its popularity in both Germany and England a hundred years after Sir Geoffrey first compiled it, just when the advent of printing meant books no longer had to be laboriously (and expensively) copied by hand.

Begun and Finished in One Day—William Caxton's Version

In the epilogue of the first book printed in English, a history of Troy, William Caxton explained why he printed it. Many people wanted copies, but copying the whole book by hand not only wore out his pen, "mine hand [was] weary and not steadfast, mine eyes dimmed with overmuch looking on the white paper." His spirit faltered at the task, so he learned how to use moveable type. The result? This book "is not written with pen and ink as other books are," he tells his readers, but all the copies "were begun in one day and also finished in one day."[16]

In 1476, Caxton brought this new technology to England from the Low Countries and opened a printing press at a shop in the almonry near Westminster Abbey. Printing caught on quickly, revolutionizing Europe the way computers and the Internet have been changing the world 500 years later. But as with so many changes, buyers are conservative. They like what they're accustomed to, and in Caxton's day they were accustomed to manuscripts. For many years printed books coexisted with manuscripts the way typewriters and computers shared office space in the late twentieth century until computers edged most of the typewriters out. The earliest books printed with moveable type, called incunabula (literally, books "in the cradle"— you can just see these young volumes being rocked to sleep), look very much like manuscripts. In fact, it was customary for Caxton and his assistants to add hand painted rubrics, the red letters that indicate new chapter beginnings, to their printed books. Of the six remaining complete copies of Caxton's edition of *The Book of the Knight of the Tower*, one in the British Library contains capital letters marking new chapters, drawn by hand in red pigment, perhaps by an illiterate apprentice. Most of the initials he is to add after the book is printed are indicated by rubricator's marks—he looks at the tiny "L" and draws a large red "L" in the space left for it. Where the rubricator's mark is missing, the apprentice has guessed, and badly. At Chapter 53, for example, a lovely red M begins the text where an F was obviously needed to begin the phrase "Fayre doughters."[17] In the other surviving copies of Caxton's edition you can see the rubricator's marks, but no rubrics were ever filled in.

What you can't see in the printed copies are glowing miniature paintings of Sir Geoffrey speaking to his daughters, as you can in several manuscripts. Although some early printed books did contain hand-wrought decorations and miniatures, making them look even more like manuscripts, the ones Caxton printed to sell to bourgeois London citizens needed to be cheaper than that.

In the fifteen or so years before his death, Caxton printed editions of about a hundred books including *The Canterbury Tales*, Malory's *Morte Darthur*, and a variety of historical, religious, and moral works. Because French books were particularly fashionable in London, because they would *sell*, Caxton translated several of them himself— including *The Book of the Knight of the Tower*. He printed it for "yong gentyl wymen," by which he meant girls of well-to-do families. A businessman, Caxton thought he could sell enough copies to the nobility and to upper-middle-class families with aspirations toward gentility to make it worth his while to both translate and print the book. Some copies did make it into the hands of these families, as we know from the inscription in one book which reads in Latin, in the highly orna-mented hand of an unprofessional scribe, a man whose pen flourishes indicate the pride he took in his purchase—*and* in his handwriting: "This book belongs to Thomas Lane of Gloucester, Gentleman." Another book-owner, "John Goodyere, of Monken Hadley, gentleman" lists among his possessions in his will, "a boke of the Knyght of the Tower in printe."[18]

We can construct the sort of family who might have bought a copy of Caxton's book by looking at medieval records. Robert Goodwyn was an acquaintance of the Cely family, London woolmerchants. Of the Celys we know a great deal because a collection of their letters and business documents from the 1470s and 1480s survives. We know, for example, that they had no daughters. Of the Goodwyns, however, we know nothing besides the name, so let us invent an older son, Richard, who at twenty-two is learning the wool trade, sometimes serving as an agent for his father in Calais. John, eighteen, is at Oxford studying to be a clergyman and his parents have high hopes that he will raise the family's status by obtaining a good benefice. Meanwhile sixteen-year-old Katherine and her fifteen-year-old sister Elizabeth remain at home with their mother and the servants, Joan and Lucy. Their brother John has taught them to read and both girls are able to sign their names, although neither they nor their mother know how to write, a common state of affairs in fifteenth-century England.[19]

Like other woolmerchants, the Goodwyns are wealthy enough to own a London house and a country estate, and they spend some time at each during the year. And like Sir Geoffrey, Robert Goodwyn is often gone from home, although instead of fighting, he is buying wool in the Cotswolds, shipping it to London and then on to Calais where he sells it. When business is good, he surprises his daughters with luxury items such as rings, pieces of velvet, small silver knives to wear at their belts and use at meals—and Caxton's courtesy book. He and his wife hope that their daughters will marry well, perhaps to country knights or to men whose rank in the Merchants of the Staple will bring honor to the Goodwyn family. And so, Robert Goodwyn, having seen a nobleman buying a copy of the book for his daughters, purchases his own copy of *The Book of the Knight of the Tower*. Not only does the mere fact of owning it increase his family's status, making them more like that nobleman's family, the book might also teach

Katherine and Elizabeth courtly manners, perhaps increasing their prospects for good marriages. When he brings it home, the girls and their mother aren't the only ones excited about the book; their friends and neighbors are pleased and a little envious, as well. After all, books of courtesy and instruction were just as popular in fifteenth-century London as they had been in fourteenth-century France, and some of the Goodwyn's neighbors will surely be invited to hear portions of it read aloud for an afternoon's entertainment.

Medieval Bestsellers—Books of Courtesy and Instruction

What Sir Geoffrey did when he compiled his book was nothing new or surprising. Courtesy books, or books of manners and advice, were common, as were books of instructions written by parents for their children. Sir Geoffrey wrote two of them, one for his sons and one for his daughters. Although the book for his sons no longer survives, he alludes to it several times in his daughters' book, telling them about stories he included in it. Perhaps it was similar to one of the guides to chivalry that circulated in Europe in the Late Middle Ages, written by knights such as Ramon Llul, Raoul de Hodenc, and Geoffroi de Charny. Sir Geoffrey may have known Charny, whom he mentions in his book for his daughters, and even if he hadn't read it, he had probably heard of Charny's *Book of Chivalry*, which tells young knights how to conduct themselves both on and off of the battlefield. It even includes a short section addressed to young ladies, who are told to distinguish themselves through their clothing, since they aren't able to do so in tournaments the way men are.[20]

Sir Geoffrey's book for his daughters discusses far more than fashion, as do other works for women. Within a span of thirty-five years, three important courtesy books for women were written in France: Sir Geoffrey's in 1372, a book called *Le Menagier de Paris* (*The Parisian Book of Housekeeping*) in about 1394, and Christine de Pizan's *Livre des Trois Vertus* (*Book of the Three Virtues*) in 1405. Because the three books share some stories as well as ideas about spirituality, fashion, and behavior, a look at the other two can help us better understand *The Book of the Knight of the Tower*. Each book addressed a different audience: Sir Geoffrey wrote for country aristocrats, the author of *Le Menagier de Paris* wrote for his wealthy but bourgeois Parisian wife, and Christine de Pizan addressed a young princess. But the late fourteenth century was a time of changes in social class, and a book for a princess was exciting reading for both the nobility and the bourgeoisie. Although *Le Menagier de Paris* survives in only three manuscripts, suggesting that it wasn't widely copied and owned in the fourteenth century, both Sir Geoffrey's and Christine's books were frequently copied, and at least once, the two were bound together in one manuscript. What binds all three books together, metaphorically at least, is the education of young women.

Le Menagier de Paris

In the 1390s, about twenty years after Sir Geoffrey wrote his book, and at about the same time that Chaucer was composing his *Merchant's Tale* about the marriage of doddering old January to bright young May, an older Parisian merchant took as his bride an orphaned teenager of higher social rank than himself. He was in his fifties, she was fifteen. Expecting to die before her, he knew she would probably marry again. His own honor depended on what kind of a wife she would make the second time around, and to that end, he wrote a book to teach her not only how to be a good Christian, but also how to be a good housewife. Although both wife's and husband's names have been lost over the years, he is often called the Householder of Paris, and his book survives as *Le Menagier de Paris*, which means something like *The Parisian Book of Housekeeping*.[21]

   In the tradition of both Sir Geoffrey and Christine de Pizan, the Householder was concerned foremost with the salvation of his wife's soul. Like Sir Geoffrey, the Householder uses exempla, or stories with morals, to illustrate many of his points, some of them taken from his own experiences. Like Christine, he also includes practical information about how to conduct a household. But his focus on the practical goes much further than Christine's does. For example, he includes a wide variety of recipes — one for an omelet with fifteen herbs and sixteen eggs, three for ink, six for getting rid of fleas, and one for catching and preparing frogs. He tells his wife how to manage her servants and hired men (laborers will always try to cheat you, so bargain for the price beforehand); which markets to send her servants to for meat, for fish, for vegetables, for firewood; when and how to plant her garden (although he doesn't expect her to dirty her own hands doing so); and how to get stains out of clothing.

   While Christine addresses her book mostly to princesses and Sir Geoffrey writes for the daughters of a knight, the Householder of Paris is bourgeois, not aristocratic. Although wealthy, he is not as high on the social ladder as Sir Geoffrey, and nowhere nearly as lofty as the royals Christine addresses. He tells his wife about meals the Duke of Berry serves, but he hears about these feasts from the Duke's servants rather than experiencing them firsthand as a guest.

The great difference in age between the Householder and his wife causes him to address her almost as paternally as Sir Geoffrey addresses his daughters. In his prologue, he tells his young wife that he is writing this book because she has asked him not to correct her in front of others, but to wait until they are alone in bed to explain her faults to her patiently. So far, he says, she hasn't done anything wrong, but this book will help her in the future, especially since she has neither father nor mother nor kin to help her, and since she is now far from the land of her birth.

We can get a picture of what Sir Geoffrey's daughters might have been like when the Householder tenderly describes his wife doing things young women like to do: tending roses and violets, making chaplets of flowers, dancing, and singing. The Householder may be bourgeois, but his refined tone marks him as more genteel in taste and style than Sir Geoffrey.

Christine de Pizan's *Livre des Trois Vertus*

Christine de Pizan (1365–ca. 1430), a very unusual French noble-woman, was the first Western woman to make her living by the pen, a necessity after she was left a widow with three children, a mother, and a niece to provide for. (Being born into the nobility didn't necessarily mean being born into wealth.) In *Livre des Trois Vertus* or *The Book of the Three Virtues*, Christine first addresses princesses before adding comments for ladies-in-waiting, the wives of merchants and artisans, nuns, and even prostitutes. Unlike Sir Geoffrey, Christine doesn't tell many stories to illustrate her suggestions. Instead, her short chapters of advice are "dictated" to her by Reason, Rectitude, and Justice, personified as the Three Ladies of Virtue. They begin, just as Sir Geoffrey and the Householder of Paris do, with proper ways to honor God. Then the book treats honor and reputation, modesty and moderation, and other things ladies need to know.

The first and largest part of Christine's book focuses on princesses and other ladies of very high nobility. Girls of Jeanne, Anne, and Marie de la Tour's station are not addressed until part two, in several chapters about ladies living on manors. It is their responsibility to know how to manage their estates while their husbands are away, or should they become widows, Christine says, and she ought to know, having been widowed at twenty-five. As the book progresses, Christine descends the social ladder, ending with chapters about chambermaids, prostitutes, laborers' wives, and finally, the poor. Like the highest-ranking princesses, all women must be concerned foremost with their souls and with honoring God. Only after addressing these spiritual matters does Christine move on to worldly honor and reputation, fashion, envy, and modesty.

In Christine's book, upper-class men seem to have one primary concern in life: the seduction of women. She urges women to be careful not to elicit such responses from men. They should keep themselves away from men's company as much as possible and dress and behave in such modest and moderate ways that they can never be blamed themselves. Not *all* men are bad; Christine alludes to a few wise priests and virtuous husbands. However, the general impression she gives is one of a man hiding behind every castle wall awaiting his chance to seduce a lady. She dedicates large portions of her book to discussions of adulterous affairs and the careful ways that chaperones, ladies-in-waiting, and servants should respond to their mistress's involvement in them.

Christine's advice is frank and straightforward. Having seen her own fortunes rise and fall, having been embroiled in several lawsuits after her husband died, in which men tried to separate her from her property, she knows the value of rank and of reputation just as well as she knows about the salvation of the soul. She knows what she needs to do to keep herself and her family in a good position, and it's probably no coincidence that Reason and the other Ladies of Virtue tell princesses—and the lesser souls the book is addressed to—to read books of advice about behavior and manners, presumably books just like *The Book of the Three Virtues*. Christine doesn't expect all women to read, however. In fact, she recognizes that the laboring classes may never know of her book—her Three Ladies of Virtue say, in their remarks to poor women, "remember our lessons addressed to you, if it happens to reach your ears."[22]

Because Christine seems to share many of the values of modern Americans in the way she lives independently, writing books to support herself and her family, it's easy to forget how alien many of her ideas are to modern experience, particularly those about social class. For Christine, all people are far from being created equal. Princesses, she tells her audience, gain more merit when they are charitable than lesser women do. Laborers and servants have low morals by nature, and they are lazy and dishonest. These medieval attitudes, and the similarities between her book and other conduct books, reveal that, despite her singular literary powers, Christine is indeed a woman of her time, shaped by her social milieu just as much as Sir Geoffrey is by his.

The *Miroir des Bonnes Femmes*

There is no mistaking the attitudes in the *Miroir des Bonnes Femmes* as anything but medieval. One of Sir Geoffrey's sources, one that he sometimes copied wholesale, *The Mirror for Good Women* was compiled in the last half of the thirteenth century by a Franciscan friar and it remained popular through the sixteenth century. The writer collected stories, many of them from the Bible, to teach women how to be good. The friar would have used these stories in his sermons to teach the common people, the way other friars did. And, like other friars, he changed biblical stories to emphasize the vices and virtues of the women he was writing about. According to the scholar who discovered the connection between *The Mirror* and Sir Geoffrey's book, the friar who wrote *The Mirror* "was not averse to distorting the letter or spirit of the Bible in order to add evidence to his arguments on the goodness or badness of a woman." For example, in one biblical story where Saint Peter does something wrong, the writer of *The Mirror* makes the fault lie with two maidservants, not Peter.[23]

Sir Geoffrey must have owned a manuscript of *The Mirror* because he took many biblical stories directly from it, and he added details and comparisons to tales that *The Mirror*'s compiler had already embellished.[24] Sometimes he loosely paraphrases stories from *The Mirror* in order to make them suit his own needs better. The fact that he stole stories shouldn't bother us—it's what you did in the Middle Ages. Instead of trying for the most original plot, you repeated stories you had heard elsewhere, improving on them by adding details or slightly changing the ending to please your audience. Petrarch took the story of Patient Griselda from Boccaccio, and Chaucer got his version from Petrarch. Later, Shakespeare wandered freely in the garden of plots other writers had left for him. It's what writers did and nobody thought there was a problem with it any more than modern audiences fault Jane Smiley for retelling the Lear story in *A Thousand Acres*. After all, even *King Lear* wasn't original to Shakespeare—he got it from an earlier English chronicle. So when

Sir Geoffrey took stories from *The Mirror*, whether he changed them or not, he was following in an established tradition.

One scholar believes that many of the manuscripts of *The Mirror* were probably intended for traveling preachers, not for women, since they're small enough to be carried around and they have no decorations.[25] And while it's true that friars would have used this kind of compilation as they composed their sermons, another scholar, Kathleen Ashley, has examined fifteenth- and sixteenth-century copies owned and used by Burgundian families and discovered that both men and women have left their signatures of ownership in the books' margins. Clearly, priests weren't the only ones who used the books. Ashley also finds that some of the families who owned copies of *The Mirror* used the margins to record family history, events such as births, deaths, and marriages. This is hardly surprising, since books were often used this way in the Middle Ages: you recorded important information in the margins of books, which were expensive and well cared for. (The custom has persisted across the centuries and many modern families own bibles with their family history recorded in ballpoint pen on the opening leaves.) Ashley's discovery is important, however, because it demonstrates what kinds of people owned and used courtesy books.

Other Conduct Books

The literature of courtesy and conduct was popular throughout Europe, and England is no exception. Middle-class women are the subject of a fourteenth-century poem written in Middle English, "How the Good Wife Taught Her Daughter." Like instructions for all classes of women, it's concerned with the daughter being a good Christian (rain is no excuse for not going to church, and once you're there, don't gossip with your friends), and a proper wife (speak to your husband meekly and help him conquer his anger). One scholar has argued that the wife of a middle-class family would have read the poem to her maidservants, not her daughters, since the servants wouldn't have had their mothers around to teach them how to behave.[26]

These books were not for women only—not by any means. William Caxton knew a good sell when he printed it, and *The Book of the Knight of the Tower* was only one of the courtesy books he printed. His *Book of Curtesye*, a seventy-six-stanza poem, was sometimes known as "Lytyl Iohn" (or Little John), since it started with those two words, indicating its audience: boys and young men of the upper classes. The poem also exists in several manuscript versions with some slight variations, but all of them teach boys the kinds of things they need to know to behave themselves upon rising, at church, at the table (whether serving or eating at it), and among other people. A great many verses focus on table manners: boys shouldn't undo their belts if they get too full, they shouldn't gnaw on bones like dogs, and they shouldn't say unkind things about people who aren't there.

The poet reminds Lytyl Iohn and his fellows of the importance of entertaining others by learning to dance and sing, to play the lute and the harp. He's particularly concerned that they read *all* of the books of Chaucer, whom the poet says is the father and founder of ornate eloquence who illuminated all of Britain (and whose works, should you need a copy, Caxton printed and sold). Concerning behavior toward women, the poet gives only one stanza, but he makes it sound important. "I warn you specially," he writes, "to hold womanhood in awe, to serve them well, to obey their commandments, to speak to them pleasantly, and to be diligent in pleasing them and revering them."[27]

The Book of Good Manners, which Caxton printed for William Pratt, a mercer, or cloth-trader, instructs readers about the Seven Deadly Sins, the virtues, and the manners appropriate for each of the three estates (those in the church, the aristocracy, and the common people).[28] *The Game and Play of the Chess*, another of Caxton's translations, "explains the chessmen and their moves in terms of human society and assesses the morality of various ways of behaving."[29] Several of Caxton's books focus on dying well, that is, with a healthy soul.

Other conduct books also survive, some written specifically to instruct people about the duties of particular stations: that of the chamberlain, for example, or the page. Books of courtesy for pages focused more on etiquette than on moral instruction, since pages had to serve adults of a high social status as they learned to become gentlemen themselves. Don't belch as if you have a bean in your throat like a peasant in a cottage, they're warned, and don't spit over the table or into the washbasin that's brought around the table. Pages shouldn't pick their teeth with their knives, or bring dirty knives to the table, or throw their bones on the floor. "Make neither the cat nor the dog your fellow at the table," one treatise reads, and almost all of them warn young men not to stick their food in the saltcellar.

Conduct books were a medieval bestseller, just as self-help books are today. A book such as Sir Geoffrey's had the added bonus of including good stories, a point William Caxton no doubt had in mind when he printed it: complete in one volume, stories *and* advice on how to behave. The medieval ideal for literature was that it both teach and delight—and *The Book of the Knight of the Tower* does just that.

Le Livre du Chevalier de la Tour Landry pour l'enseignement de ses filles

Where does Sir Geoffrey's book fit among all these other books of rules, of courtesy, and of conduct? Squarely in the middle. Like the books written by Christine de Pizan and the Householder of Paris, Sir Geoffrey's book has a first-person narrator, Sir Geoffrey himself, who speaks directly to his daughters. Unlike these two writers, Sir Geoffrey relies almost entirely on stories to make his points.

Readers hear Sir Geoffrey's own voice in his prologue, where he explains why he is writing the book, and in the first few chapters, where he speaks directly to his daughters about how and when to pray. Then he turns from direct address to stories as his teaching method. But even within the stories, his personality reveals itself. He often inserts comments for his *chieres filles* at the beginnings and endings of his tales. Sometimes the morals he takes from the stories are a little bit surprising. Sometimes it's as if he wants to teach a particular lesson but can't find a story that fits it exactly. Instead, he uses an example that's close, and then slaps his moral onto the end, showing his daughters exactly what he wants them to take from the tale.

His personality comes through much more vividly, however, when he tells stories from his own experience, or tales about people he knows. These stories reveal details about aristocratic life in fourteenth-century France. When they suddenly appear in the midst of more generic stories, these personal reminiscences turn the book into a glimpse of the lives of a real medieval family. Sir Geoffrey's family was fond of minstrels, for example, and Sir Geoffrey himself idolized military men, whose names he works into his stories. He talks about women he knows who dress foolishly, and women who act with decorum in dicey social situations. We hear about a young gentlewoman Geoffrey considered marrying, and the discussion he had with his father on the way home from visiting her. These kinds of gem-like pictures enliven his book, revealing the people behind it.

The organization of Sir Geoffrey's book seems haphazard to us, and he may have simply added chapters when he found a new story he wanted to include. After his prologue, he turns his attention to the relationship he wants his daughters to have with God. Chapters about praying, fasting, confessing, and attending Mass make up the first section of his book, reminding us of the absolute importance of Christianity in medieval Western Europe. Then this sense of a plan vanishes. A chapter about being obedient to your husband is followed by one on the importance of giving alms, and the chapters after that focus on the dangers of wearing new fashions, going to social gatherings, and again, fashion and clothing. Sir Geoffrey includes a long section on sin, illustrated with biblical stories of wicked women, and then a group of stories about good women. The next set of chapters is generally about how to be a good woman and a good Christian, and how to guard your reputation and avoid shame. It's followed by a fictional debate between Sir Geoffrey and his wife on the subject of courtly love. Another group of stories about appropriate conduct follows, and the book ends with eight chapters about the advice Cato, the Roman moralist and senator, gave to his son and how the son treated that advice—he ignored it, to his peril.

In all, Sir Geoffrey's book has 144 chapters, not counting his prologue. The chapters range from a paragraph to a few pages, and the stories they tell cover a wide range of medieval genres. Some of them are funny, some serious, some grisly. Always as he tells his tales, Sir Geoffrey winds together ideas about the worldly and the spiritual, the body and the soul, this world and the next. He may be a fervent Christian who fears the pangs of hell, but he is also very much a man of the world who desires its rewards for himself and for his daughters.

The Retelling

Over half of Sir Geoffrey's stories appear in the following pages, along with my own comments and discussion to place them within their literary and historical context. Like the printed editions in the British Library, we begin with William Caxton's Prologue, then Sir Geoffrey's, before moving on to the stories. The first nine of Sir Geoffrey's tales appear in the order he uses. After that, I have rearranged his chapters, organizing them around larger ideas. Although I've kept groups of stories together whenever I can, I have omitted some chapters, and abridged or summarized others. Repetition is a hallmark of the book. Often, within the same page, a story will be told and then summarized. Because this kind of repetition is so prevalent, I've condensed considerably. My retelling follows the time-honored medieval tradition of translating not word for word, but according to the sense. My intent is to make the book as enjoyable for modern audiences as it was for Sir Geoffrey's daughters and for Caxton's customers.

I have retold the stories not from Sir Geoffrey's French version but from William Caxton's translation into Middle English. Caxton's prose style can be tedious to modern readers, but usually his translation follows the Knight's words slavishly. Like Marquard vom Stein, Sir Geoffrey's German translator, Caxton sometimes mistranslated, for example when he wasn't sure whether *lange* meant "l'ange" (angel), or "lange" (tongue), causing a few odd passages in his text.[30] Sometimes he left out parts that might annoy his English readers, such as a sentence from the French book suggesting that English women are immoral. Sometimes he added a patriotic comment—for example, when Sir Geoffrey mentions Paris as a place for scholarship, Caxton adds "Oxford and Cambridge."[31] His Middle English can be cumbersome, especially when the subordinate clauses get piled one upon another with no main clause to give the reader a resolution. Sometimes it can even be hard to find the subject of his sentence. And the word "and" seems to begin every sentence, and join every phrase and clause to the next.

You can see a little of Caxton's Middle English in his chapter headings, which I have left intact, with their unfamiliar contractions like *thexample* for "the example." No spelling standard existed in fifteenth-century England, so Caxton can spell the same words in different ways without being incorrect. Nor is there a standard system of punctuation—he uses a slash (called a virgule) where we might use either a comma or a period. He might capitalize a name— such as God—but just as often, he doesn't. And although he uses plenty of direct speech, quotation marks are a thing of the future for him; I have supplied them, along with paragraphs and phrases such as "she said" for clarity.

Other English versions of Sir Geoffrey's book do exist, but none in Modern English. In 1930, G. S. Taylor published a slightly modernized version of the book, to which D. B. Wyndham-Lewis contributed an introduction. An earlier version also exists. At the turn of the twentieth century, Gertrude B. Rawlings added modern punctuation to about half of Caxton's text, which Garth Jones illustrated. Noting, "the only salient point in which the literature that the Knight of the Tower thought fit for his daughters differs from that which would be set before young gentlewomen to-day, lies in its outspokenness, which sometimes amounts, according to modern notions, to obscenity," Rawlings omitted what she considered "the coarser and the more tedious chapters." She spares her readers stories about monks fornicating in churches and the tale of the fat prior's affair with the ropemaker's wife. Rawlings's editorial comments reveal more about Victorian attitudes than medieval ones:

> The feminine iconoclast of to-day will note that the Knight of the Tower takes for granted, without stooping to argument, the superiority of spear over spindle, and gather that then, as now, the sexes consisted of the fair and the unfair, though she will also observe that in a few follies and weaknesses not yet quite obsolete, such as an extravagant love of finery, or the inability to keep a secret, some old-fashioned women still resemble their mediaeval ancestresses.[32]

Our own reactions to Sir Geoffrey's stories can be just as telling as Gertrude Rawlings's. We may puzzle over the courtly love debate, we may bristle at the class or gender expectations, we may laugh at the descriptions of clothing, or be moved by what Wyndham-Lewis calls the book's "deep, but not dark piety."[33] However we respond, we reveal just as much about ourselves and our times as Gertrude Rawlings does about hers—almost as much as Sir Geoffrey reveals about his own attitudes and expectations for this life and the next.

Part II

The Book of the Knight of the Tower

Chapter 2

The Prologues

Because I am Ignorant—Caxton's Prologue

Those who have died before us have left as a memorial their wisdom about how we should conduct ourselves in this present life. They have given us knowledge, wisdom and understanding, and good rules to be governed by. Above all this book is a special work of instruction by which all young gentlewomen especially may learn to behave themselves virtuously, both in their virginity as well as in their wedlock and widowhood, as the book will plainly tell.

This book has come into my hands at the request and desire of a noble lady who has brought forth many noble and fair daughters who have been raised and taught virtuously. Because of the great love she has always had for her fair children and still has, she wants them to know more about moral behavior so that they may always be virtuous themselves. To this end, she has asked me to translate this book out of French into our common English so it may be better understood by all who shall read it or hear it read. Therefore, at the lady's request, and according to the small skill that God has sent me, I have endeavored to obey her admirable wish.

In this work I find many virtuous instructions from authentic histories and good examples for all kinds of people in general, but especially for ladies and gentlewomen who are the daughters of lords and gentlemen. For this book all the gentlewomen living now and hereafter should praise and thank the author, and also the lady who caused me to translate it. They should pray for her long life and welfare, and when God calls her from this transitory life they should pray that she may reign in heaven everlastingly, where there is joy and bliss without end.

Because this book is necessary for every gentlewoman of any estate, I advise every gentleman or woman with children who desires them to be brought up virtuously to get and have this book. Then their children may learn how they ought to govern themselves virtuously in this present life, by which they may better and more quickly come to honor and a good reputation. And I ask all of those who learn anything from this book which makes them wiser or better to give praise and thanks to the aforesaid lady's request and also to pray for her. And if they find any fault in the translation into our English tongue, that they blame me because I am ignorant and not an expert in such work, although I have dabbled before in such translations (which I confess are imperfect because of my ignorance). Therefore I humbly beseech my good lady to pardon me for my simple and rough translation. If anything within it gives her pleasure, then I'll think my labor is well employed, and I humbly ask her to receive this little book kindly. And I shall pray to almighty God for her long and good life, and to send to her after this short and transitory life everlasting life in heaven, Amen.

And to all others who find any faults of mine, I ask for their charity that they will correct and amend them, and in doing so they will deserve the thanks and merit of God, to whom I shall pray for them.

William Caxton added prologues to many of the works he printed. In large part, they were advertisements. Not only did they link his works with important patrons, the way blurbs by famous writers function on today's book covers, they also identified the audience and purpose, the way the paragraph on the front cover flap of a modern hardback does. In this preface, Caxton urges every gentleman or woman who has children and who wants them to be brought up virtuously to buy his book. If they do, their children will learn to govern themselves "in this present life, by whiche they may the better and hastlyer come to worship and good renommee"—that is, the more quickly they will come to honor and to a good reputation, and then, one assumes, to a profitable marriage to somebody with lots of money and heady social connections. What loving parent could deny a child these necessities? The book is clearly indispensable!

Caxton's prefaces often refer to a patron who has asked him to print the book. Some of them were noble, such as the lady at whose desire he printed *The Book of the Knight of the Tower*, and the "gentle and noble esquire" who requested that he print *The Book of the Order of Chivalry*.[1] Others came from the merchant classes, such as "a special friend of mine, a mercer of London named William Pratt,"[2] and "the honorable and worshipful man Hugh Bryce, alderman and citizen of London."[3] The mercers, aldermen, and citizens of London made up that rising middle class with aspirations to gentility that Chaucer makes so much fun of in his General Prologue to *The Canterbury Tales*—the self-important guildsmen whose wives insist on being called "madame" and who bear silver knives at their belts despite laws decreeing that folk of their status use brass (forks not yet being commonly found on the dinner table, people carried their own knives to use as cutlery). Chaucer maintained his standard of living by serving the king and wrote poetry on the side, whereas for Caxton bookmaking was bread and butter. Chaucer could afford to poke fun at the people who might read his work; Caxton couldn't. And besides, it wasn't in his nature. Caxton was a man of his time, a tradesman impressed by those whose station exceeded his.

In the case of *The Book of the Knight of the Tower*, his unnamed patron, the "noble lady which hath brought forth many noble and fayr doughters," may have been very far above him. One modern scholar argues that she was Queen Elizabeth Woodville, the widow of Edward IV, who had five daughters. Because she was out of favor at court, the argument goes, Caxton didn't name her for political reasons,[4] entirely plausible when you consider how volatile the political situation was in late-fifteenth-century England. One of the first books Caxton printed was a little something that Anthony Woodville, Earl Rivers — the queen's brother — translated. Earl Rivers acted as regent when the young Edward V and his brother were imprisoned in the Tower of London. For his service to the crown, Richard III had the Earl beheaded.[5] As much prestige as Earl Rivers's name brought to Caxton's early career as a printer, it could hardly help business to be associated with him when he fell from favor.

Patronage didn't necessarily imply a financial investment; the noble lady might lend only her approval of the book in order to increase the sales potential. Whoever she was, Caxton tells us that she wants her daughters to own the book so they'll have examples of virtue, and stories and lessons for all kinds of people, but especially for "ladyes and gentilwymen, daughters to lordes and gentilmen." If such a noble woman (maybe even a queen) wants her daughters to own this book, the preface implies, shouldn't your daughters have a copy, too? If you were a member of the rising middle class with money and social aspirations, you might be particularly moved by Caxton's argument, and by the noble lady's patronage, to buy a copy for your own unmarried daughters for whom you had high hopes.

Robert Goodwyn, our London woolmerchant, might well hope that the two daughters we have imagined for him would raise the family's station by marrying the sons of knights — or at least wealthy merchants' sons. If Katherine and Elizabeth are to take their places in the exalted social circles he has in mind for them, they'll need to know about proper etiquette. And where better for them to learn than in a book that Mr. William Caxton says is necessary for all gentlewomen of any estate? Wool sales having gone well this year,

Robert Goodwyn betakes himself to the crowded alley beside Westminster Cathedral to seek out Caxton's shop. There he purchases a copy of *The Book of the Knight of the Tower*, much to the satisfaction of his wife Alice and his daughters Katherine and Elizabeth, who turn its thick, rag-paper pages carefully, running their fingers over the red initials marking each new story, excited by the prospect of new tales to entertain them.

On a cold English afternoon, Katherine, the eldest, a quiet, sober young woman of sixteen, reads the book aloud to Elizabeth, her irrepressible fifteen-year-old sister. Gathered in the new sitting room of which their father is so proud—it was part of the hall until he had it made into a separate chamber last year—are the girls' mother, her maidservant Joan, the young servant girl Lucy, and their neighbor Mary Rawson, the daughter of a glover not quite as successful as Robert Goodwyn. They all crowd toward the wheeled brazier, the only warmth in the room, as they darn, hem, and embroider. For light to read by, Katherine relies on the newly glazed window behind her (another sign of her father's wealth) and the candle at her side.

The book measures about nine by fourteen inches, a comfortable size for Katherine to hold in her lap, and the rubrics as well as the wide margins on each page and the blank spaces between stories help her keep her place in the text. After each tale, Katherine stops reading so they might all reflect on the Knight's words. Mary, the neighbor, reports that the Riche family, with their four marriageable daughters, owns a copy of the same book, and the women speculate about who else might have a copy. When Katherine reads Caxton's preface, all of them wonder aloud who the noble lady is who requested that he translate it. Each of them has an opinion, and Dame Alice even suggests that it's Elizabeth Woodville. None of them mentions the tone of humility Caxton takes in the preface; they hardly notice it.

To us, Caxton's voice makes him sound about as humble as Uriah Heep and just as convincing. He says he's ignorant, he's bad at translating, he's sure to have made mistakes—yet you should still buy his book! We shouldn't take much of his modesty seriously, because he's using a standard medieval literary device, the humility formula. "My wit is short," Chaucer writes in the General Prologue to *The Canterbury Tales*. The modesty formula is one Chaucer's audience, like Caxton's, would recognize. Caxton says he's no expert and has only dabbled in translating, but by the time he printed *The Book of the Knight of the Tower* he had already translated at least nine other major works and printed an edition of *The Canterbury Tales*.

Unlike his modesty, Caxton's piety probably isn't in question. Like Sir Geoffrey's, Caxton's is real. Although he asks readers to pray for the long life of his patron, in the same sentence he acknowledges that even a long life on earth is short in comparison with the eternal afterlife.

Before turning to Sir Geoffrey's prologue, Caxton prints a long table of contents, itself entitled, "Here follows the table of the rubrics and the chapters of the book of precepts and instructions that the Knight of the Tower made for his daughters." I've left it out. Since the book has *C xliiij*, or 144 chapters, each with its own title, I've only included the titles within the text—Caxton prints them there, too. After the table of contents comes Caxton's translation of *The Book of the Knight of the Tower*, beginning with Sir Geoffrey's prologue. Compared to Caxton's prologue, it has a more literary, less commercial tone. Unlike Caxton, who needed to sell this book to make a living, Sir Geoffrey's living came from his birth into the landed aristocracy. He wrote with only his daughters, not profit making, in mind.

Blame, Shame, and Defame—Sir Geoffrey's Prologue

Here begynneth the book whiche the knyght of the toure made. And speketh of many fayre ensamples and thensygnementys and techyng of his doughters
(Here begins the book which the Knight of the Tower made. It contains many fair examples to teach his daughters)
Prologue
In the year of our Lord 1371, at the end of April, I sat in a garden under a shadow, all mourning and pensive. But I rejoiced a little in the music of the wild birds, who sang in their own language—the blackbird, the song thrush, the throstle and the nightingale, who were happy and joyful. This sweet song gave me spirit and made my heart enjoy everything, so that I started to remember the times that passed during my youth. Then love held me firmly in his great service so that for hours I would be glad and happy, and many other times full of sorrow, like many a lover. But I have been compensated for my sufferings, since the fair and good lady has been given to me—she who knows everything about honor, goodness, and conduct. The beautiful lady seemed to me the flower of all that's good. I delighted in her so much that I made songs and lays, roundels, ballads, virelays, and new songs in the best way I knew how. But death, who spares no one, has taken her, and I have suffered sorrow and heaviness for more than twenty years. The heart of a true lover shall in no time nor day forget love, but will remember it forever.

And then, while I was pensive, I saw my daughters coming towards me. I wanted them to turn to honor above all other things, for they are young and small and lacking wisdom and reason. And therefore they ought to be taught and courteously chastised by good examples, as did a queen—a queen of Hungary, I think—who fairly and sweetly chastised her own daughters and taught them (it's told in a book she wrote).

When I saw my own daughters coming toward me, I thought about when I was young and rode with my fellow soldiers in Poitou and in other places. I remembered the things the soldiers said about their encounters with ladies and damsels, whose love they asked for. If one lady wouldn't listen to their prayer, another soldier would ask for her love without even waiting. And the men didn't care what answer the ladies gave them, because they had neither fear nor shame, being so hardened and accustomed to acting this way. They spoke well, using fine language to deceive the ladies and damsels. They brought them news, sometimes true, sometimes lies. Because of them, many ladies were dishonored—and all for no cause or reason.

In all the world there is no greater treason than to deceive gentlewomen or to cause them dishonor. Yet many gentlewomen have been deceived by the great oaths the men use and so I often argued with them, saying, "You over-false men, how may the gods allow you to live when you forswear yourselves and hold no faith?" But none of them amended their ways.

I fear that some men are still like this now. Therefore I concluded that I would have a little book made wherein I would have written the lives, manners, and deeds of reputable women who are honored for their virtues and bounty. After their deaths they will be renowned and praised until the end of the world, and people will take good example of them. By way of contrast I would have included in the book the vices and wrongdoings of evil women so that the evils they are guilty of may be avoided by those who might err but who are not yet blamed, shamed, and defamed.

I thought about my beloved daughters, who seemed so young and small, and I wanted to make them a little book to read so they might learn and study and understand the good and evil that has already happened, in order to keep them from that which is yet to come. For there are those who laugh with you, but mock and lie about you behind your back. It's a hard thing to know the present world.

Thus I left the garden and found two of my priests and two clerics. I told them I wanted to make an exemplar for my daughters to learn from, to read and understand how they ought to govern themselves, and to keep themselves from evil. I had the priests and clerics read to me the Bible, stories of kings, chronicles of France and England, and many other strange histories, and from them I made this book. I didn't want it in rhyme, but in prose in order to condense it, and also so it would be easier to understand. The book is for the great love that I have for my daughters, whom I love as a father ought to love them. My heart will have perfect joy if they turn to good and honor, serve and love God, and have the love and the grace of their neighbors and of the world. And because, according to God and nature, every father and mother ought to teach their children in order to turn them from the evil way and to show them the right way both for the salvation of their souls and the honor of their earthly bodies, I have made two books, one for my sons and the other for my daughters. As they read, they will retain some good example about fleeing from evil and retaining the good. For it may happen that sometime a good example will come to their minds when they are with others who are speaking of these things.

In his prologue, Sir Geoffrey mingles fact with fiction in confusing ways. In the opening paragraph he says he mourns a dead lady, which has led some readers to assume that his wife has died, leaving behind motherless daughters in need of advice. It may make a compelling story, but Jeanne de Rougé, the mother of Jeanne, Anne, and Marie, was alive and well in 1371, when the book was begun, not dying until some time after 1383. Then who is the dead woman? Perhaps Sir Geoffrey refers to a lady he idealized in his youth. Perhaps there's no lady at all, and he's merely echoing the kind of literature he knows in order to make a start—after all, many fourteenth-century works begin with prologues set in springtime gardens. While birds sing joyously, the narrator—like Sir Geoffrey—suffers from love-longing or feels melancholy over a lady's death.

However, the meeting with his daughters in the second paragraph need not have been fictional. One of the most common forms of recreation for medieval ladies and gentlemen was to walk in the gardens of manor houses and castles. Full-time gardeners looked to the upkeep of sweet-smelling herbs, flowering fruit trees, and carefully placed seats, some of them benches made of grassy earth constructed around small trees where young men and women could have the kinds of intimate conversations that Sir Geoffrey worries about his daughters having. In one miniature painting in a manuscript of his book (reproduced on the cover of this book), Sir Geoffrey is shown sitting on just such a bench, pointing his index finger at his wife and daughters as he reads to them from a scroll in his lap. A low garden wall surrounds all four family members.[6]

Nor need we doubt the existence of the queen of Hungary who wrote a courtesy book for her daughters, the one Sir Geoffrey mentions in the second paragraph of his prologue. Although it doesn't survive today, such a book was known in the fourteenth century—Elizabeth of Bosnia wrote one for her daughters before she died in 1382.[7]

From this point forward, we can probably take the knight's words at face value. We know he rode with other soldiers in his youth, and indeed, he continued his military activities throughout much of his life. His stories about his own experiences demonstrate the truth of his statement that some men still deceive gentlewomen.

We can also believe him when he says he had two priests and two clerics working for him. The household of a wealthy knight such as Sir Geoffrey needed many people to keep it running, from the laundresses and seamstresses to the male cooks, the men who kept the stables, the huntsmen, the minstrels, and the aristocratic servants who took care of the family's rooms and their clothing: pages, chamberlains, and ladies-in-waiting. Household priests and clerics would say daily masses in the private chapel, hear confessions, and act as secretaries, writing letters and keeping the household accounts. With the number of estates Sir Geoffrey maintained and the amount of time he was gone at war, his retainers had plenty to keep them busy.

Although we have to imagine the bustle of activity that kept the household running in the fourteenth century, Sir Geoffrey's tower, his moat, and even his family name still survive in the tiny town of La Tourlandry, not far from the city of Angers, and about twenty-five kilometers south of the Loire River, with its mighty medieval châteaux. When you enter the village from the north, climbing a narrow highway to a promontory overlooking verdant fields, a blue sign proclaims your arrival: Main Street is still called Rue Geoffroy de la Tourlandry.

Take a right, walk a few hundred yards to the church and the town hall, and take another right on Rue Abbé Vincent, a narrow brick street running between the church yard and the cemetery, and you'll end up on a dirt lane where an old clock tower, burned down during the Revolution but subsequently rebuilt, stands in a shady park. And just around the corner is the château. Although the current château has the date 1808 above its gate and a silver Renault in its driveway, you can still feel the antique flavor of the place in the dark moat, the grassy path running in front of it, and the ivy-covered stone wall surrounding a pasture where a brown horse with a white nose whisks flies away with his tail. Through a door in the wall, a short, round tower is barely visible, different from the rest of the architecture, perhaps part of the *tour* of Sir Geoffrey's name.

Standing on the edge of this hilltop village, the château commands a view of the surrounding countryside, the fields dotted with spring buttercups, grazing cows, and distant towns, their church steeples rising like castles. Adjacent to the château and just across the lane is a little wooded park with low, mossy stone benches and hundreds of birds singing songs of spring and sunshine, like the joyful blackbirds, song thrushes, and nightingales of Sir Geoffrey's prologue. It's easy to picture his daughters lifting their skirts to stroll here amidst the buttercups and cow parsley on a spring afternoon, "all mourning and pensive" over some squire who hasn't visited as he promised he would, but comforted by the "songs of the wild birds." The horse's whinny, the buzz of a honeybee, church bells ringing the quarter-hour, the wind through the treetops, and the calling of crows are the only sounds that compete with the wild birds' songs, and a visitor can escape entirely into the fourteenth century—that is, until a lawnmower revs its engine at the house next door.

And then you're brought back to the present, to a village with a street named "Rue de l'Industrie," whence come the sounds of machinery. But the past is embedded in La Tourlandry, in the moated château, in birdsong and wildflowers, and in streets called "Rue de la Quintaine" and "Allee de Maille," with their reminders of young knights practicing their aim against the quintain and blacksmiths rolling the rust from coats of mail in sand-filled barrels. And just outside of the village is the "Chemin des Demoiselles," perhaps a tribute to Jeanne, Anne, and Marie de la Tour Landry.

Like the fragments of fourteenth-century life still visible in La Tourlandry, echoes of rhyme and metrical lines still linger in Sir Geoffrey's prologue, indicating that he first wrote it in verse. Anatole Montaiglon, his nineteenth-century editor, printed some of the prologue as verse, and you don't have to read Old French to see the end-rhymes when Sir Geoffrey writes about the singing birds reviving his spirits:

> Mais un peu je me resjouy
> Du son et du chant que je ouy
> De ces gents oysillons sauvaiges
> Qui chantoient dans leurs langaiges[.][8]

By his own admission, Sir Geoffrey also composed songs and lays, roundels, ballads, and virelays, hardly unusual for a French nobleman of his time. But after the prologue, the rest of his book contains no vestiges of verse. He feels compelled to mention his use of prose because poetry was the more common medium in fourteenth-century France. He defends his choice, saying that prose is shorter and easier to read.

The choice of prose might have been innovative, but a collection of moral stories wasn't. In a time when books were so expensive that even a wealthy household might own only two or three, this kind of collection provided variety. Some of these books were informal miscellanies that might include both short poems and long stories, prayers, a sermon or two, and perhaps a medical recipe to cure the bite of a mad dog. Others, like this one, followed a controlling idea. One fifteenth-century manuscript contains not only *Le liure que fist le Cheualier de La Tour pour lenseignement de ses filles*, as the British Library catalogue identifies it, but also French versions of the Book of Melibee and Dame Prudence and the tale of Patient Griselda (both known to English-speaking audiences from *The Canterbury Tales*), and an eighty-eight-line poem by Jean de Meun, one of the authors of *The Romance of the Rose*. The purpose of the collection is summed up at the end of Patient Griselda's tale, whose colophon begins, "Here ends the story of the mirror of married women, known for her high and marvelous virtues of patience, obedience, true humility and constancy."[9]

Like the miscellaneous nature of Sir Geoffrey's book, the kinds of sources he used wouldn't have surprised a medieval audience in the least. He mentions the Bible, stories of kings, and chronicles of various lands, and he includes bawdy tales and saints' lives as well, the types of stories his contemporaries would have been accustomed to finding side by side. Only one feature distinguishes *The Book of the Knight of the Tower* from other miscellanies: the compiler's personal comments and stories.

In his prologue, Sir Geoffrey describes one impetus for writing his book: the wicked ways his fellow soldiers treated women — deceiving ladies with fine language to get their love, and feeling no shame when they dishonored women. If only his book for his sons had survived so we could compare the reasons he wrote it. Did he warn Charles and Arcades to avoid treating women the way other soldiers do? Or did he assume that soldiers would act that way no matter what? With his fellow soldiers, Sir Geoffrey seems to have easily given up his efforts at reform; despite his reproofs, "none of them amended their ways," he says. Instead, throughout his daughters' book he makes it the responsibility of women to guard themselves against male treachery in order to protect their social and spiritual well-being.

Christine de Pizan takes a similar stance in her *Book of the Three Virtues*; assuming men will be wicked, she counsels women to guard themselves vigilantly to avoid blame, never even reading a letter privately unless it's from their husbands, lest someone accuse them of having affairs. One of the ironies of Christine's attitude, and Sir Geoffrey's, in which men are portrayed as treacherous and untrustworthy, is that the antifeminism so prevalent in the later Middle Ages, and reflected in many of Sir Geoffrey's stories, assumes that all women, at least the ones who aren't saints, are sinful. But unlike Geoffrey Chaucer, whose Wife of Bath is well aware of all the arguments antifeminist writers use against women, Sir Geoffrey de la Tour Landry never recognizes the irony implicit in his words. He's a father concerned about his daughters' social and spiritual well-being, not a poet out to please a court audience with his wit and humor. And as the next chapters indicate, his daughters' spiritual salvation requires that they learn how to avoid worldly blame, shame, and defame.

CHAPTER 3

TURN YOUR HEARTS TO GOD — PRAYER

For the writer of the 1808 *Catalogue of the Harleian Manuscripts in the British Museum*, the Middle English translation of Sir Geoffrey's book serves "to make one laugh at the extreme ridiculousness of gross Popery." But for most people living in Western Europe in the fourteenth and fifteenth centuries, Roman Catholicism was the only game around. The most important thing in life was your relationship to God — in theory, at least. And the most important part of that relationship was your ability to achieve salvation. Where would your immortal soul spend all of eternity? Heaven, one hoped, and without a several-thousand-year delay in Purgatory, suffering the torments appropriate for your particular sins. Those who made it neither to Heaven nor to Purgatory suffered the all too real horror of eternal damnation, and from this Sir Geoffrey wanted to protect his daughters' souls. He begins his book with chapters focusing on ways to honor God and his theme of salvation winds through every tale, much as Roman Catholicism wove medieval society together.

If in some ways Sir Geoffrey reminds us of people we know today, in other ways he couldn't be more alien. Our pluralistic society, with its diverse ideas about religion and morality, with its varieties of religious practices, bears little resemblance to the Western medieval landscape, where one church reigned supreme, where life ordered itself according to that church's teachings so deeply that people were scarcely aware of it. Business and commerce provide the metaphors for American life (we often call ourselves consumers, not citizens; "the bottom line" is important in education and other arenas of our lives; we talk about a "marketplace of ideas" or someone being "morally bankrupt"; and when our lawmakers return to Washington after a recess, we say they are "open for business" or they're back to "business as usual"). In a similar way, the Church determined much of medieval life, from the way dates were remembered to the intricacies of local politics. And always, the promise of eternal bliss and the fear of eternal damnation were present, and devils were real and walked abroad.

Nevertheless, Sir Geoffrey's spirituality has a certain mercantile quality. He gives to God and therefore he expects certain things in return—prayers answered a hundredfold, he often says. As befits their station as his daughters, Jeanne, Anne, and Marie can also take part in this quid pro quo arrangement: I pray, therefore I get. What they get, according to their father, is not just spiritual rewards. His fifteenth-century London counterpart, Robert Goodwyn, had a similar stance toward his religion. As a modern scholar says of a family of London woolmerchants, "They took it for granted that the deity had a benevolent interest in their daily affairs, crediting [for example] their opportune withdrawal of money from Bruges bankers to divine prompting."[1] Often, Sir Geoffrey's stories emphasize the worldly, material rewards prayer can bring, and this emphasis would also have appealed to Robert Goodwyn and his daughters, Katherine and Elizabeth. The sincerity of Sir Geoffrey's devotion isn't in doubt, but the depth of his spiritual understanding is, despite the two priests and two clerics who were assisting him in compiling his book.

Like Sir Geoffrey, both Christine de Pizan and the Householder of Paris begin their books with chapters about a lady's relationship to God. According to Christine, we should love God because of his goodness and his blessings, and we should fear his justice, "which leaves nothing unpunished."[2] Punishments are a large part of Sir Geoffrey's world. Throughout *The Book of the Knight of the Tower*, both spiritual and worldly concerns result in gruesome punishments as well as pleasant rewards, as we see in the stories in this chapter.

Here foloweth the book of thensygnemens and techynges of the knyght of the Toure. And first how god ought to be honoured aboue all thynges.
(Here follow the lessons and teachings of the Knight of the Tower. And first, how God must be honored above all things.)

It's a right and noble thing to see the old stories about our predecessors which were written to give us good examples, and to instruct us about their good deeds and how to avoid the evil that they avoided.

My very dear daughters, I am much older than you and have seen the world longer than you have, so I'll teach you about the world according to my own knowledge, which isn't large. Because of my great love for you, I want you to turn your hearts and your thoughts to God, to fear and serve him. Doing so will bring you happiness and honor in this world as well as in that other world, for certainly all the true happiness, honor, and all of a person's good name comes from God and from the grace of his holy spirit. All things happen according to his pleasure and rule, and he returns a hundredfold all the service done to him. Therefore, my dear daughters, it is good to serve such a Lord.

In his insistence that his age and experience make him much more knowledgeable than his daughters, Sir Geoffrey sounds like a modern father. But he seems to undercut his own claims to authority with the same kind of traditional medieval modesty formula that Caxton uses in his Prologue when, in the same sentence, he says his knowledge isn't large. He doesn't necessarily think that, but it was what you said in the Middle Ages. Besides, compared to God, humans and human knowledge were minuscule, and humans needed to acknowledge that in their daily prayers.

How the matyns and houres ought to be said
(How matins and hours ought to be said)

Because the first work that man and woman must do is to adore and worship our Lord and to say his service, as soon as you wake up you ought to acknowledge him as your Lord and maker and remember that you are his creature. Say your matins, hours, and prayers, and give thanks and praise him. Those who are in holy orders should say *laudate dominum omnes gentes Benedicamus patrem et filium cum sancto spiritu*, or something similar which praises God. It is better to thank and bless our Lord God than to ask him for things. The requesting, the demanding, and the giving of rewards and praise is the office of the angels, who always give thanks, honor, and praise to God. We should thank God instead of asking things of him because he knows better than we do what is good for a man or woman.

Before going to sleep, we ought to pray for those who are dead. Also, we should pray for those who pray for dead men. And don't forget the blessed and sweet Virgin Mary, who prays for us night and day. Commend yourself to the holy saints of heaven, and when that is done, then you may go to sleep.

It may appear from the Knight's advice that his older daughters, Jeanne and Anne, spent a great deal of their time praying. This would be true in an ideal world; monks and nuns, for example, spent the major part of their day in prayer. Formally, they participated in services seven times a day, during the canonical hours of matins, prime, terce, sext, nones, vespers, and compline, and at other times they might engage in private devotions. Some of them might have other obligations, like the Augustinian friars of Cornuaille, who, in exchange for land and other riches, added these words to the first Mass they celebrated each day after Sir Geoffrey's first wife died: "We pray for peace and for Monsieur de la Tour et Madame Jeanne de Rougé, our founders, that God give them good life and that they acquire the joy of paradise, and to her [the deceased Jeanne] the glory of God."[3]

Lay people would have been well aware of the seven canonical hours because they would have heard the church bells summoning the members of religious orders to prayer. When Sir Geoffrey's family stayed at their château in Bourmont, an estate Jeanne de Rougé brought with her to the marriage, the sounds of bells tolling from two nearby priories, Notre Dame de Beaulieu and Saints Peter and Paul at Freigné, would have floated across the fields, telling the girls the monks were at their prayers.[4] At midnight, they might have stirred in their beds when bells called the monks to matins. Unlike the monks, trudging across the cold stone floors into the choir to sing another service, Jeanne and Anne could roll over and go back to sleep.

Before the late fourteenth century, most lay people would have thought of time in canonical language—that is, until clocks became common. William Caxton's late-fifteenth-century English still echoes this vocabulary. In a story in the next chapter, he includes both the word *terce* (literally, the third hour after sunrise) and his translation of it, *midday*, to indicate time. Later, he uses the word *nones*, by which he probably means noon, although literally it means the ninth hour after sunrise, corresponding more closely to three p.m. than to twelve noon. The words for the canonical hours also indicated the prayer services or the particular devotions that accompanied those services, as we see earlier when Sir Geoffrey tells his daughters to say their matins.

Even if they didn't pray seven times daily, the schedules of young laywomen like the Tour Landry girls would have followed a pattern just as regimented as that of a modern woman who rises every day to run two miles, shower, eat breakfast, and make it to the office by 8:30. The daily schedule Christine de Pizan describes for a princess is heavy with spirituality. According to Christine, a princess should pray immediately upon awakening and then go to Mass. As she leaves the chapel, she should give alms to the poor people waiting outside (the way Christine says it, it sounds as if the poor have been rounded up to stand outside the chapel when the princess leaves it). On some days, she might stop to listen to their requests.

Holy matters finished just for the moment, the princess meets with her counselors on counsel days, before having her midday meal in the hall. During the meal, however, it's back to saving her soul: she and her household listen to the story of a good person or else a discourse on some moral subject. After the tables are removed, grace is said. Then the princess receives any visitors, and finally, the meal ends when spices are passed around to sweeten the diners' breaths.

The meal is followed by time spent resting in her chamber, and then the princess and her ladies might do some needlework, perhaps embroidering altar cloths or a surplice for the priest. Still in the chamber, they have some sort of entertainment (which might well have included a religious story), and then it's time to go to the chapel for vespers, unless, Christine says, the day is very busy with secular cares. In this case, the princess might say her prayers privately with her chaplain.

Following vespers, or evensong, she and her ladies walk in the garden for their health, and during this time, people who need to might see her. Then supper, and bed. But before she sleeps, the princess should again pray to God.

Christine notes that there might be some moderate amusements added to this schedule—hunting with a hawk by the river, for example. But even so, the pattern of the princess's day, like that of Sir Geoffrey's daughters, begins and ends with prayer. Christine gives an example of a particular prayer a lady might say when she wakes up: "Lord, I beseech thee to guard us this day from sin, from sudden death and from all evil mischance, and also protect all our relatives and friends. To those who have passed on, pardon, and to our subjects peace and tranquillity. Amen, Pater Noster."[5]

In fifteenth-century England, Richard III's mother, Cicely, Duchess of York, spent even more of her day in religious activities. She said matins with her chaplain when she rose at seven, then heard Low Mass (a simplified Mass celebrated by only one priest and one helper, with no singing) in her chamber before she ate. After eating, she went to the chapel for two more Low Masses. Then came the main meal of the day, accompanied by a reading from some religious work. Like the princess Christine describes, Cicely followed the meal by giving audiences to people and taking a short nap. Then it was back to prayer until "the first bell for Evensong, at which she had a drink of wine or ale. Her chaplain said Evensong with her; at the final bell for Evensong, she went to her chapel to hear it sung." At supper, there was a discussion of the religious text Cicely had heard during the main meal of the day, and then she and her gentlewomen took some kind of entertainment, perhaps like Christine's princess, walking about in the garden. And like Christine's princess, Cicely ended her day at around 8 p.m. with prayers.[6]

Minus the duties specific to royalty, this kind of schedule could fit the lives of aristocratic girls such as Jeanne and Anne and later, baby Marie, if they wanted to be as pious as Cicely, Duchess of York. Morning, midday, and evening prayers would also be appropriate for members of the bourgeoisie, such as Katherine and Elizabeth Goodwyn. The Householder of Paris presents his wife with four prayers she can say either when she hears the matins bells calling the monks to prayer at midnight, or when she wakes up in the morning. Two of the prayers are to God, two are to the Virgin Mary, the "day star brighter than the sun and whiter than the snow."[7] The Latin prayer Sir Geoffrey quotes above for those in holy orders to say—*laudate dominum omnes gentes Benedicamus patrem et filium cum sancto spiritu*—is actually two prayers, although he seems to have gotten them confused. The first phrase, from *laudate* through *gentes* is the opening line of Psalm 116, "Praise the Lord, all nations." His daughters would have been familiar with the words from their psalters, and they would also have heard them in the liturgy, where they would be followed by a prayer beginning, *Gloria patri et filio et spiritu sancto*, or "Glory be to the father and the son and the holy spirit." Sir Geoffrey may have been thinking of that prayer when he wrote the next part of his quotation, *Benedicamus patrem et filium cum sancto spiritu*, or "Let us praise the father and the son and the holy spirit." It's a common liturgical phrase (as well as a part of one particular mass), and you can see how someone with only small Latin might have gotten them confused. After all, they both tell us to praise "the father, the son, and the holy spirit."[8]

Even if they didn't read or speak Latin the way scholars and monks did, Sir Geoffrey and his daughters might have owned prayer books written in Latin. Because they were wealthy aristocrats, the household probably owned a psalter and a book of hours, and possibly a gospel book containing the story of Jesus as it appears in the words of Matthew, Mark, Luke, and John. Entire Bibles were rare—they were huge, cumbersome, and very expensive. Whole herds of cattle gave their lives to provide the parchment for a single Bible. It was far more common for books or sections of the Bible to be bound together as a book, giving us Gospel books only, or psalters (books of Psalms). Even those books were different from what we are accustomed to. Our modern biblical subdivisions into numbered chapter and verse weren't used. Psalms were known by their opening lines, which is why Sir Geoffrey can write *Laudate dominum omnes gentes* and expect his daughters to know what psalm he means.

In the thirteenth and fourteenth centuries, in both France and England, psalters were a popular devotional book. The very wealthy owned beautifully illuminated psalters decorated with gold and intricate miniature paintings, such as the fourteenth-century English Luttrell Psalter, made for Sir Geoffrey Luttrell, a knight whose portrait is included inside the manuscript. In the portrait, his wife and daughter attend him. The further down the social scale you were, the less luxurious the psalter (if you owned one at all, that is). The book-owning social scale stopped abruptly at the middle class, however. Even a psalter with no pictures at all would be too expensive for a peasant to own, and besides, no one in the family would be able to read it.

Sir Geoffrey's family probably owned a psalter, perhaps one with gold initials and delicate floral tracery etched into the blue and red decorations. The family was even more likely to own a book of hours. By the late fourteenth century in France, and through the fifteenth and sixteenth centuries in England, books of hours overtook psalters as the most popular devotional texts, so it's hard to imagine the stylish members of the Tour Landry family not purchasing one. Master Goodwyn, too, would certainly have bought one for Katherine and Elizabeth and his wife Alice, since books of hours, like psalters, could be marks of prestige, not just of piety. And like psalters, many stunning examples of books of hours survive, some with lavish illuminations. Unlike psalters, which were used by both clerical and lay audiences, books of hours were written specifically for the laity. They contained prayers, hymns, psalms, and lessons. Many had pictures on which a person could meditate, most commonly of the Virgin Mary, but also of Christ's suffering and death, of the Trinity, and of saints. The prayers and pictures were arranged according to the liturgical year, that is, the feasts of the church that correspond to events from the lives and deaths of Mary, Jesus, and the saints. A strong penitential aspect pervaded books of hours, and many prayers for the dead were included, the kinds of prayers Jeanne and Anne would have recited before they settled themselves onto the mattress, making room for Dame Agnes, the lady-in-waiting who shared their bed, smothering the candle, and finally pulling the curtains closed around them for the night.[9]

With only firelight and candle flame to light them, medieval nights were longer and darker than ours. And like darkness, death was ever-present in both the lives and minds of medieval writers. As they said their evening orisons, Jeanne and Anne would pray for people they knew who had died, and even for dead people they had never met. Prayers for those who have already died are important both for the immortal souls of the departed and for the protection of the living. Souls expiating their sins by suffering the pains of Purgatory can be helped by the prayers of the living, but damned souls receive no benefit at all. However, except in a few instances of the type we'll see in later chapters, ordinary people had no way of knowing who was in Hell and who was in Purgatory. They could know that saints and martyrs were in Heaven, and therefore they prayed not *for* but *to* them—for the saints' help with the souls of the dear departed who might not yet have experienced the Beatific Vision. As the following two stories demonstrate, prayers for the dead were popularly perceived to benefit the living Christian, even if Church doctrine didn't officially approve this perception.

Of twoo doughters of the Emperoure that one synfull And that other deuoute
(Concerning the two daughters of the Emperor, one sinful and one devout)

According to the history of Constantinople, the Emperor had two daughters. The youngest had good manners, loved God, and always honored and prayed to him when she awoke, saying prayers for the souls of those who had died. She and her sister slept in the same bed, and when the elder awoke and heard her sister praying, she mocked and scorned her and told her that she was keeping her from sleeping.

It happened that they both fell in love with two good, noble knights who were brothers. Each of the sisters told her knight of her love, and both sets of lovers decided on a certain hour one night for a tryst.

When the knight who was coming to the younger sister got just inside the curtains, it seemed to him that he saw over a thousand men standing around the damsel. All of them wore shrouds as if they were dead. The knight was so overcome by fear and horror that he was taken with fever, sick in his bed.

No such thing happened to the second knight, and he got the Emperor's older daughter with child. When the Emperor found this out, he commanded his daughter to be drowned during the night, and the knight to be flayed alive. And thus for their false delight both of them died.

Concerning the younger daughter, in the morning after her knight took ill, she went to see him. He told her about the shrouded men who had surrounded her, and about his dread and terror. When the damsel heard these words, she was filled with joy and humbly thanked God for saving her from dishonor. From that day forward, she honored God whenever she woke up, she prayed devoutly for all the Christian souls, and she kept herself chaste.

Not long afterwards, a great king of Greece asked her father for her hand in marriage. Her father agreed, and she became a good, devout lady of great renown, and all because she prayed to God and for the souls of the dead. And her older sister, who had scorned and mocked her, was drowned and dishonored.

And therefore, my dear daughters, remember this example when you wake up in the morning, and don't sleep again until you have prayed for those who have departed from this world, like the daughter of the Emperor did.

We shouldn't conclude from this story that medieval fathers regularly drowned their erring daughters or flayed the young men who wooed them. The story is given an exotic setting, long-ago, far-away Constantinople where people did things very differently than they do in Sir Geoffrey's time or in Caxton's. Chaucer does the same thing when he gives many of the more fantastic *Canterbury Tales* far-off settings such as Asia, long-ago ones such as ancient Greece, or exotic ones such as Brittany, a land known for its magic. The formula frees the storyteller to roam through imaginary events while still imparting a lesson, just as our formula, "Once upon a time," signals a fantasy story that's often accompanied by a moral.

Katherine and Elizabeth Goodwyn certainly harbored no fear of flaying from their father. In their comfortable house (if somewhat dark and smoky by modern standards) on the fictional Duck Lane in the equally fictional parish of Saint Katherine in the eastern part of London, not far from The Tower, they might be titillated by the story, but they knew their father was hard at work down by the River Thames, arguing with an agent in the Customs House or at the wharf inspecting a shipment of wool. Whatever he was doing, he was increasing the family wealth and thus, the girls' marriage prospects, not preparing gruesome means of punishment for errant daughters.

Sir Geoffrey's moral above, as well as in the following story, isn't just about praying for the dead. The importance of chastity is equally emphasized, as the story's title in the earlier Middle English translation demonstrates: "Concerning the knight who followed a gentlewoman into the bushes." The French title is even more explicit—it tells us the story is about "a damsel whom a knight wished to violate."

How we ought to praye for them that ben dede
(How we ought to pray for those who are dead)

Similarly, there was once a damsel whom a great lord spied upon. He wanted to have her in order to accomplish his foul pleasure and delight, but the damsel hid herself for fear of him and said vigils for dead men. When the lord found her, it seemed to him that he saw more than ten thousand buried prisoners protecting her. He ran in terror and sent her word that he would leave her alone. Afterwards, he asked her who that great company of people was who was with her. She told him she knew nothing about it, except that when he pursued her, she had said the vigil for the dead. Then the lord knew it was the dead who protected her—and this is a good example to always pray for those who have departed from this world.

In the medieval West, death was much more a part of life than it is in developed countries nowadays. The Black Death ravaged Europe in 1348–50, while Sir Geoffrey was a young man, and during his lifetime, recurring epidemics reduced Europe's population by almost a third. Giovanni Boccaccio describes the horrors of the pestilence in Florence in the beginning of his *Decameron*. Attributing the disease to either the stars or God's punishment, Boccaccio tells of the egg-sized swellings in people's armpits and groins and the black spots on their bodies that signaled almost certain death by the third day. Even more terrifying than the pestilence itself was the way people responded to it, abandoning neighbors, spouses, and even their own children to save themselves. No funeral processions accompanied the dead to the churchyard for burial; in fact, people often died on the streets or alone in their houses, their bodies discovered only when they began to stink. There were so many bodies that gravediggers dumped hundreds of them, of all social classes, in huge trenches "like a ship's cargo." Boccaccio says that over a hundred thousand people died in Florence alone, leaving empty the palaces and homes that noble ladies and gentlemen and their servants had formerly filled.[10] Even Laura, the woman who inspired the Florentine poet laureate Francesco Petrarch to write his love sonnets, the *Canzoniere*, fell victim to the Black Death that Boccaccio describes.

Some form of plague struck England and the Low Countries in the late fifteenth century. The Goodwyn family would have left London for their country estate in Essex to protect themselves and sent their servants into London to conduct business. Alice Goodwyn would have worried about her sons, Richard, who was in Calais, and John, at Oxford, and they might have written letters in which they mentioned the disease, such as the one the woolmerchant William Cely wrote to his London family in 1487, in which he said that "almighty God visiteth sore here in Calais and the marches with this great plague of sickness that reigneth."[11]

Katherine and Elizabeth would have worried about their brother, too, but their more immediate concern might have been their friend Mary Rawson, whose family—too poor to own a country estate—had stayed in their London house on Duck Lane. When Joan, the servant, traveled to London to deliver messages for the girls' parents and to make sure the house was in good order, Katherine begged her to stop by the Rawson's house, and to bring news of Mary, her mother, and her brother George. The coin Katherine pressed into Joan's hand would no doubt have been even more convincing than her entreaties.

Although the plague recurred several times in the fourteenth and fifteenth centuries, it was just one of the things that worried medieval Christians. People of all social classes feared dying suddenly without having time to confess their sins. Doing so sent you to judgment with sins weighing heavily on your soul. A fifteenth-century French romance written for courtiers includes a Latin verse that gets translated, "when a rich man dieth, he and his goods shall be parted into three parts: and firstly, his flesh shall be given to the worms; his gold, his silver, and his rings and all that he hath, to his kin; and his soul to all the fiends of Hell, unless God in his grace have mercy of him."[12] You can hear the same fear of certain death and an uncertain afterlife in the rhyme a London grocer named Richard Hill copied into his commonplace book at the very end of the medieval period:

> Whan I thynk on thyngis thre
> Well carefull may I be:
> One is, that I shall henne;
> An other is, I wot not when.
> Offe the thirde is my most care,
> For I shall dwell I wot not wher.[13]

Thinking on three things fills him with anxiety, Hill says. The first is that he will go hence, that is, he'll die. The second? He doesn't know when death will come. The third care is the most significant: where he'll end up after he dies. Heaven? Hell? Purgatory? The poem continues with a moral telling people to remember "whence thou come and where thou shalt" go, and to have mercy on others in the hope that God will have mercy on you.

Having mercy on others might take the form of praying for them after they have died, the way the damsels in the above stories do. But it wasn't just individuals who prayed for the dead long after the funeral masses were over. The rich could pay to have Masses said especially for them in the years after they died, the way Sir Geoffrey did for his first wife, Jeanne de Rougé. Money lubricated the monks' voices so they could lift them in prayer. In fact, some religious communities' finances depended on the rich leaving bequests in their wills for the monks or nuns to pray for their souls.[14]

A few years before she died, Jeanne de Rougé suffered a grievous illness. Thinking her time was up, she prepared a will, naming her mother and her sister Huette as her executors. She also chose a burial spot next to her father's tomb in the church of Notre Dame de Meleray.[15] She wanted to leave nothing to chance, neither her soul nor her body nor the earthly goods she would leave behind her. As she lay ill, her daughters, her sister, and her mother would have knelt on the stone floor of the parish church, praying for God to have mercy on her soul when she died. Although they would mourn her when she died, grieving just as much as we would, they would also believe that sparing her soul was more important than keeping her earthly body alive longer than its allotted time.

When Robert Goodwyn's father died, his son would have left nothing to chance, instead paying a soul-priest an annual salary to sing Masses for his father's soul. This was in addition to the funeral Mass itself, and the Masses at the month-mind and the year-mind, at which money would be given to the church and to the poor. Robert's father might have left a bequest to build an altar in the parish church of Saint Katherine, and Robert himself would have overseen the hiring of the freemasons and marblers to build it.[16] In these ways, long after his body was gone, his soul would be remembered.

After his two stories about the efficacy of praying for the dead, Sir Geoffrey adds a moralizing chapter reviewing and, as is his wont, repeating some of the most important things he knows about when, how, and why his daughters should pray. He tells them that some of his expressions come from "holy scripture," but in truth, they don't. Like so many medieval people, he quotes from memory, perhaps from sermons he's heard or devotional tracts he's read. Since chances are so small that he would have owned a complete Bible, his knowledge of it would have been filtered through other sources, written and oral.

The same is true for the stories of the holy women he mentions: their stories made wonderful sermon-fodder and Sir Geoffrey's daughters would have heard them with all their gruesome details, such as how Saint Margaret was swallowed by a dragon, and how Saint Katherine was first tortured on a wheel and when that didn't kill her, beheaded. The saints were usually pictured holding the implements of their torture—a dragon for Margaret, a wheel for Katherine—in stained-glass windows, in church wall-paintings, and in books of hours, so Jeanne, Anne, and Marie would grow up knowing the "holy virgins and other holy women" their father mentions through images as well as words. The Goodwyn girls, too, knew the saints, and Saint Katherine, for whom the eldest daughter was named, would have been particularly important to them, since their parish church was dedicated to her. It probably included a wall painting, a stained-glass window, or a sculpture of the saint, which Katherine and Elizabeth would have seen during their regular visits to the church. They might have focused their eyes on the image while they prayed in order to keep them from thinking about worldly matters, one of the fears Sir Geoffrey addresses in his next story.

How we ought to saye oure houres and prayers
(How we ought to say our hours and prayers)

Fair daughters, when you rise out of your bed, immediately enter into the service of the high Lord and begin your matins. This ought to be the first thing that you do. And when you pray, pray with a good heart and think on no other thing. You can't go two ways at once, but you have to choose one way or the other. In the book of wisdom the wise man says the one who reads and doesn't understand is like the one who hunts without taking any game. Therefore he who thinks on earthly things while he says his paternoster or prayers, which are about heavenly things, doesn't profit but instead mocks God. That's why the holy scripture says that a short prayer said with a devout heart will pierce heaven, unlike a great long prayer said while you think of other things. But when you pray for a longer time very devoutly, it's worth more and deserves more merit. The holy scripture says that just as the sweet dew of April and May pleases the earth by refreshing it and making it grow and become fruitful, so are your prayers pleasing to God.

In the legends of the holy virgins and other holy women you will discover that they made their beds of hard and rough material in order to sleep less so they would weep often, waking up many times in order to pray. They held themselves to the service of God both day and night, and because of that, they were allowed to be in holy joy with him, as it has been openly shown to the world. God does evident miracles for them. In this way, God rewards the service done to him a hundred-fold, as I have said before.

And so, my fair daughters, say your hours and prayers devoutly and with a good heart, without thinking about anything else, and beware that you don't break your fast until you have said your matins and hours. For a full belly will never be humble nor devout. Also, hear all the Masses that you can, because great good will come of doing so.

Chapter 4

Driving the Devil Out—Fasting and Confessing Your Sins

A Full Belly Will Never Be Devout—Fasting

"A full belly will never be humble or devout," Sir Geoffrey tells his daughters when he admonishes them to pray before breaking their nightly fast. If Jeanne and Anne were being particularly good, they would step out of the warmth of their curtained bed to kneel in prayer before they began chattering with each other. A maidservant would bring them water to wash their faces and hands and then help them dress. On some days, the girls might accompany their mother to the chapel to hear Mass, after which they finally got to quell their hunger with bread and watered ale or wine. But on fast days, they might eat nothing at all before noon.

Katherine and Elizabeth Goodwyn's morning would follow a similar ritual, despite their separation from the Tour Landry girls by a hundred years and the English Channel. They would pray upon waking, kneeling on the uncarpeted wooden floor. Then in the metal basin of water the servant girl Lucy brought them, they would wash their hands and faces, perhaps using the Castile soap London apothecaries sold. Lucy would help Katherine comb her hair while Elizabeth cleaned her teeth with a wooden stick, and then it was Katherine's turn for combing. Finally they dressed and headed down the precariously narrow wooden stairs to the hall. Although they would probably go to the parish church to hear Mass only a few times a week instead of every day, they, like Jeanne and Anne, would regularly fast.

Fasting was an important act of religious devotion. People fasted on certain days prescribed by the Church and during seasons such as Lent. However, fasting didn't necessarily mean the abstention from eating, as Sir Geoffrey's stories will show. You can also see this in a scene in the fourteenth-century English poem *Sir Gawain and the Green Knight*, which shows a veritable feast of fasting on Christmas Eve. Because it's a fast day, Sir Gawain is served only fish, but what sumptuous fish, in one lavish course after another! In his book, the Householder of Paris includes recipes the Duke of Berry's servants have told him about for both meat-days and fish-days. The fish recipes rival those served to Sir Gawain and hardly sound like penitential food.

Fasting took different forms. Sometimes it meant not eating meat, sometimes it meant eating very little food, or even none at all. From the thirteenth century on, some households served fish but no meat three days a week: Wednesdays, Fridays, and Saturdays. By the fourteenth century, many aristocratic English households only served one meal on Fridays, and they waited until later in the day than normal to eat it. Nevertheless, a fast-day meal might include four kinds of fish in addition to butter, eggs, almonds, bread, and ale.[1]

Throughout the year, many, many days were set aside by the Church as holy days of abstinence, confusingly called feast days (the word *feast* comes from a Latin word meaning festive). In fact, fifteenth-century records indicate that a knight's household should ideally have 198 annual meat-days and 167 fish-days, thereby fasting almost forty-five percent of the year.[2] The Virgin Mary alone commands four days of abstinence. Christians fasted on the day before her Purification (February 2, also called Candlemas), the angel's Annunciation to Mary that she is pregnant (Lady Day, March 25), her Assumption into heaven (August 15), and her birth (September 8). Likewise they fasted on the days commemorating saints, such as the Nativity of Saint John the Baptist on June 24, Saint Lawrence on August 9, and Saint Katherine on November 25; and on other holidays, such as Corpus Christi, All Saints, or the Exaltation of the Cross. The forty days of Lent were fast-days, just as they still are for many Christians, and in medieval England the fast was broken on Easter with meat—"a little lamb as Paschal symbol."[3]

Except on Good Friday, not everybody fasted. Laborers expended too much energy in the fields to go without food, and in her *Book of the Three Virtues* Christine de Pizan says that servants aren't required to fast. Many of them, she says, have to eat meager meals whenever they can get them, grabbing a bite between chores. Their long hours and hard work might also keep them from attending Mass regularly, which Christine says God will excuse in a way that he wouldn't for a "lady of leisure."[4] Surprisingly, with all her focus on honoring God, Christine never suggests to highborn women that they make sure their servants have time to attend church and say their prayers. She is as suspicious of servants' morals as Sir Geoffrey is in the following story, when he shows the servants hiding with the lady in the garderobe (which in this case is a small storage room, a wardrobe, although the word can also mean a privy).

How good doughters ought to faste
(How good daughters ought to fast)

There was a knight who had two daughters, one by his first wife and one by his second. The first daughter was very devout. She never ate until she said all her hours and heard all the Masses she might hear. The second daughter was spoiled. As soon as she had heard a little Mass and said two or three paternosters, she had a bad habit of going into the garderobe and eating soup or some tasty thing and said that her head ached from fasting. Also, she treated herself to good food after her parents went to bed.

This went on until she married a wise knight who realized what she was doing. It was bad for both her body and her soul, and although he often talked to her about it honestly and sweetly, she wouldn't listen. One night after he went to bed, he felt beside him in the bed—and she wasn't there. Angrily, he arose, threw on a fur-lined cloak, and went to the garderobe. There she was, with his clerk and two servants, all eating and playing and making an uproar, the men together with the women.

The knight was angry. He took a staff to hit one of the servants who was embracing a chambermaid, and he hit the servant so hard that a splinter from the staff went into his wife's eye, blinding her. And thus her husband hated her and he took his heart from her and gave it to another so that her household went to ruin.

The cause of everything was her dissolute living both in the mornings and the evenings, and it was her fault that she lost her eye and the love of her husband. After this, nobody wanted to be around her anymore. And therefore, it is good to say your hours and to hear all your Masses while fasting, and to eat moderately at about the hour of terce at midday. If you get in the habit of living that way in your youth, you'll do it in your old age, too.

The story goes on to say that the virtuous daughter turned out well, marrying a rich, powerful knight. When her father discovered what had happened to his second daughter, he got angry with his own wife—for spoiling her. However, even the spoiled daughter hears a low Mass and says two or three paternosters before she breaks her fast. Although the story is mainly about fasting, Jeanne and Anne would take other morals from it, too: women should be obedient to their parents and their husbands; and gluttony is a sin that leads to other sins, especially lechery. The husband's violent anger, however, is not part of the lesson—his actions may seem egregious to us, but not to Jeanne and Anne, and certainly not to their father, who would think them justifiable. Nor would they be overly bothered by his taking another lover after blinding his wife. What other options are left to a wise knight when his wife won't listen to him?

Few of Sir Geoffrey's tales have just one lesson. The next one, with its themes of confession and chastity woven into a story about fasting, is no exception.

How good doughters ought to fast till they be maryed
(How good daughters ought to fast until they are married)

Also, my dear daughters, you ought to fast three or four days a week until you're married. It's important to subdue your flesh so it won't become aroused, and this will keep you pure and sound in the service of God, for which you will be doubly rewarded. If you can't fast three days, at least fast on Fridays in honor of Christ's suffering. And if you can't eat just bread and water, at the very least don't eat anything that has to be killed. That is a very good thing, as you can see from the story of a very noble knight who was in a battle of Christians against Saracens. This Christian knight's head was cut off with a sword—but he kept right on talking until a priest came to confess him. When the priest asked him how he could speak without his body, the head answered him, saying there was no good deed done to God that didn't receive grace. The Christian knight had not eaten meat on Wednesdays in honor of the son of God, and on Fridays he didn't eat anything that suffered death. Because of this, God didn't want him to be damned or to die in deadly sin for not having been confessed.

So, my fair daughters, this is a good example to help you remember on Fridays not to eat things that have to die. It's also good to fast on Saturday in honor of Our Lady and her virginity, because she will help keep you chaste, and will help keep evil temptations from mastering you. This is a great victory over the flesh and a very holy thing—and it's not that difficult to get used to. It's as natural as hearing Mass and saying your hours and doing holy works, just as the holy women in the lives of saints have done.

Sir Geoffrey is deeply concerned with his unmarried daughters' chastity, not the least because of the way he's seen his fellow soldiers act, and here he emphasizes another reason for fasting: as a way to subdue the flesh. The Church advocated fasting as a penitential practice because even as abstaining from food weakens "the attractions of the sensible pleasures," it strengthens "the spiritual life."[5]

Ironically, pleasurable stories could lead you to a stronger spiritual life. Preachers spiced their sermons with good tales designed to teach lessons. The talking head in Sir Geoffrey's story wouldn't have shocked his French audience any more it would have Caxton's English readers. Disembodied heads were a standard feature of medieval stories, from saints' lives to romances. Jeanne and Anne would have heard about Saint Denis, the patron saint of France. When villains chopped off the saint's head with an axe, his body reached down, picked up its head, and—led by an angel—carried it two leagues away to his final resting place. This was the least of Denis's woes: he had already been roasted on a gridiron, thrown among ravenous wild beasts, and tossed into a fiery furnace, all of which he survived by the grace of God.

Disembodied heads didn't just get carried about by their bodies—many of them kept on talking. Consider Edmund, the early English king and saint: when he was beheaded by Vikings in the ninth century, his head was not only guarded by a wolf, it kept crying out, "Here, here, here!" as his men searched for it, calling, "Where are you now, friend?" Five hundred years later, in Chaucer's "Prioress's Tale," which has many characteristics of a saint's life, a little Christian boy guides his mother to find his body by continuing to sing after Jews have slit his throat and dumped him in a privy. His head, unlike King Edmund's, is still attached to his body.

In fourteenth- and fifteenth-century France and England, such stories of saints and martyrs were a part of daily life. People heard about them in sermons; they saw images of the holy martyrs on church wall-paintings and in stained-glass windows. Saints interceded with God for more common humans. Because the saints and martyrs themselves were so holy, they had a direct line to God. Pray to a powerful saint, and the saint might take your request to the Lord, especially if you had made a pilgrimage to the saint's shrine or given money to a church honoring your saint.

The stories people heard about saints follow a standard formula beginning with the life of the saint, who even as a child often performed feats that suggested the honor yet to come (such as the infant Saint Rumwald who—despite living only three days—preached a sermon about the Holy Trinity and arranged his own burial). The saint's life, or *vita*, is followed by the passion, the often grisly suffering leading to the saint's death. It frequently includes torture by evil pagans who want the saint to renounce Christianity, and just as frequently there's a scene in which some of the evil pagans are so touched by the saint's faith that they become Christians themselves. Finally, the story relates the miracles the saint performed after death, the very miracles that prove his or her sanctity.

The pagans who torment the saints in these stories are sometimes Jews. Anti-Semitism is a troubling but very real aspect of medieval life. In England, Jews had an uneasy existence from the late eleventh century, when the king invited (or perhaps even commanded) them to move there from Normandy in order to help with commerce through their financial skills. During the Crusades, when Christian sentiment was running high, Jews became scapegoats. They were accused of the ritual murders of Christian children, and by the late twelfth century, English Christians began to massacre English Jews. Jews were also subjected to heavy taxes, even as their moneylending helped the English economy. Finally, two centuries after they had entered the country, the Jews were expelled from England on November 1, 1290, by royal edict. Not for another 400 years did an organized Jewish community settle in England again.[6]

Stories such as the one about young Hugh of Lincoln stimulated hatred of the Jews long after they were gone from the country. Hugh was only nine when his body was found in a well in the year 1255. Nobody knows whether he fell in or was murdered, but a large community of Jews lived in Lincoln, and they were accused of crucifying him. Nineteen Jewish men were executed for his death, and other Lincoln Jews were imprisoned and fined. Almost a century after the expulsion of the Jews from England, at a time when few English people would ever have met a Jewish person, Chaucer tells his pious and mindlessly anti-Semitic "Prioress's Tale," which echoes the story of Hugh of Lincoln. As much as we'd like to believe that Chaucer was more enlightened than the average fourteenth-century English person, he was a man of his times. Like his countrymen, he found Jews a convenient scapegoat. And we can assume that Katherine and Elizabeth, the daughters of the bourgeois Robert Goodwyn, held equally negative opinions of Jews, based on stories they had heard, stories such as young Hugh of Lincoln and *The Prioress's Tale*.

In France, Jewish people had a much longer history than in England. They had lived in parts of southern France since antiquity, but significant numbers of them didn't settle in northern France until the twelfth century. They were known for their legal learning, their biblical exegesis, and their expertise in philosophy, especially those who studied the works of the twelfth-century Spanish philosopher Maimonides. Beautifully illuminated Hebrew manuscripts survive from this period, as well.

Yet in France, as in England, Jews and Christians coexisted uneasily. As in England, Jews were accused of killing Christian children or of poisoning city wells, and stories such as the one about Hugh of Lincoln perpetuated these myths. From the twelfth through the fourteenth centuries, Jews were subjected to increasing regulations about where they could live and what occupations they could hold. Often the only way they were allowed to support themselves was through moneylending, which was necessary for commerce but forbidden to Christians. Despite requiring them to be moneylenders and benefiting from their services, Christians despised Jews for holding such an occupation and for having money in difficult economic times. In different regions of France, Jews faced persecution and even expulsion until finally, in 1394, during the lifetime of Sir Geoffrey and his daughters, they were expelled from all of France and made their way into eastern Europe.[7] The treatment of Jews at Christian hands in the medieval period was shameful and barbaric, but it pales in comparison to the twentieth-century Holocaust.

Sir Geoffrey's attitude toward Jews is hard to discern. He recognizes some biblical figures as Jews, but he gives them no overtly Jewish characteristics, as for example in the story of Susannah and the elders, where he says, "There were two priests of their law saying their hours and matins in a garden where the good lady combed her hair." The elders are "priests of their law," that is, rabbis, but the rituals they perform, "saying their hours and matins," are expressed in Christian terms. Although the elders are evil men, Sir Geoffrey never again brings up their religion. In fact, throughout his book he mentions generic pagans, but he never singles out Jews, either positively or negatively. His gaze isn't broad enough to encompass other religions except when he mentions the Saracens in the story above. Yet again, the story isn't *about* Saracens, it's about the rewards the knight receives for fasting so devoutly—the kind of rewards Sir Geoffrey hopes his daughters will also receive.

Black Spots on a Silver Plate—Confessing Your Sins

One way to ensure that you would receive your Christian rewards was to confess to your parish priest every Easter. In the year 1215, the

Fourth Lateran Council decreed that all Christians must go to confession at least once a year, although members of Sir Geoffrey's and Robert Goodwyn's families probably confessed much more frequently. Dying without having confessed your sins was to be launched upon a grievous path that could lead one to spend countless years in Purgatory, if not eternity in Hell itself. The great gift the Christian knight in the last story received was not to live into old age, but to be allowed just enough time to make a final confession before he died—and all because of his abstemious life, his fasting on both Wednesdays and Fridays.

In his book for his young wife, the Householder of Paris describes confession, reminding her of its three necessities: contrition, confession, and penance. If the sinner isn't truly sorry for the sin, if he's thinking of other things as he prays, then confession doesn't count. To illustrate his point, the Householder tells the story of the man who was promised a horse "if he said a *Paternoster* and kept his thoughts on that alone." However, while he was praying, the man began to wonder if he was also to get a saddle, and so, the Householder says, he "wretchedly lost both."[8] Similarly, the sinner must be truly contrite, thinking only of his sins, his sorrow for having committed them, and his desire for forgiveness. The hot tears of our heart's contrition, the Householder says, drive the devil out of us in the same way that hot water drives "the dog out of the kitchen."[9]

During confession, the sinner tells her sins to her confessor, who prescribes some sort of punishment, or penance. Far better for the sinner to have atoned for her sins here on earth than to face punishment after she dies. In the fourteenth and fifteenth centuries, a priest might require the sinner to fast, to repeat prayers, even to go on a pilgrimage to a holy shrine, depending on the seriousness of the sin. The sinner removes the fault through contrition, which is followed by absolution.

Many of the penances were based on the idea of the mortification of the flesh. The word "penance" comes from *poena*, Latin for punishment, and "mortification" from *mortificare*, to kill. Killing fleshly desires—the ones that led to sin—served the purpose of punishing sins already committed and helping to keep Christians from committing more sins.

Of sins, there were plenty. There were the deadly ones, seven of them—pride, greed, lust, envy, gluttony, anger, and sloth. All of them had to be confessed. It was up to the individual Christian to choose a wise confessor and avoid bad priests. Many medieval writers caution people about going to a priest who gives easy penances, or telling some of your sins to one confessor and others to another to sidestep the shame of having sinned quite so much (as well as to avoid a harsh penance). Christians were warned to confess all their sins at once, leaving nothing out.

Some people might have carried the idea of leaving out nothing to extremes, especially a talkative girl such as Elizabeth Goodwyn. Although it has been three years since she reached what was called the age of discretion, when she could make her first confession (twelve for girls, fourteen for boys), she still tells *all* the details of *every* sin, as if she has had no practice confessing at all. We can see her kneeling before a hooded parish priest in a side chapel—confessional booths not yet having come into vogue—while her older sister Katherine sighs in her impatience to get home, just in case their neighbor Mary Rawson stops by with the latest gossip. Instead of merely confessing that she has engaged in idle chatter or rejoiced in someone else's misfortune, Elizabeth details every single instance of idle chatter. As Elizabeth lists sin after sin, Katherine pulls her cloak around her in the chill air of the church. She begins to recite the first of three paternosters Father John has imposed upon her—a light penance for her venial sins.

Like Katherine and Elizabeth, Jeanne and Anne de la Tour also knew the power of confession. All of the girls would understand the message of the next story—that both confessing and fasting can lead even a sullied soul to light.

Of a comyn woman that wente to see her loue and fylle in a pytte
(Concerning a prostitute who went to see her lover and fell in a pit)
There was a wanton woman in the city of Rome who always fasted on Friday in honor of the passion of Jesus Christ, and on Saturday in honor of the virginity of Our Lady. She always kept this fast. One night when it was dark, she went to see her lover—but suddenly she fell into a pit twenty fathoms deep. As she fell, she cried out in a high voice, "Lady, help!" and when she reached the water, it was as hard as a stone. Then a voice said to her, "In honor of the Virgin Mary and of her son for whom you have fasted, you are saved. And from henceforth, keep your body clean from the sin of the flesh."

In the morning when people came to draw water, they found her in the pit and marveled how she had been saved. She told them what the voice had said, and she made a vow to keep herself chaste and to use her life in the service of God and his church.

Afterwards, she worked in the church lighting torches, tapers and lamps, and keeping the church clean. One night she had a vision that she took a vessel like a plate of silver out of a dunghill, and it was covered with black spots. A voice told her to clean the plate till it shone like it had come from the hands of the master goldsmith. Three times she had this vision, and when she woke she went to confession.

The holy man who heard her confession said that God was telling her to clean herself by confession. The spotted silver vessel in the dunghill signifies the soul in the body, and if her body did not consent to sin, she would be as white as the vessel of silver that comes from the goldsmith. In the same way, the holy man told her, is the soul when it comes from baptism. The body is nothing but dung and filth like the dunghill, because when it sins, the soul is covered with black spots. You should cleanse yourself through baptism, abstain from sinning, and confess and not turn again to sin, which is worse than sinning the first time. When you confess, he told her, say everything, hiding nothing.

Of course, when the priest told the woman to confess *everything*, he didn't mean every tiny detail the way Elizabeth Goodwyn understood it. Within the story, the priest engages in some standard medieval dream interpretation. As his reaction to the woman's confession shows, he believes that neither dreams nor visions should be scoffed at. In fact, medieval physicians, philosophers, and theologians wrote treatises expounding theories of dream interpretation, drawing on the accounts of dreams in the Bible as well as on classical sources. One of the most influential of these treatises throughout the Middle Ages was Macrobius's fourth-century commentary on Cicero's *Dream of Scipio*. It classified five kinds of dreams: the enigmatic, the prophetic, and the oracular, as well as the nightmare and the apparition. The last two have no meaning, so we shouldn't try to interpret them, according to the commentary. Nightmares are caused by anxiety or physical distress, or even overeating, while apparitions come to us in the first moments of sleep when we think we're still awake. The apparition may seem real, but it's not. However, Macrobius says, pay attention to the other three kinds of dreams, because they can reveal the future or tell some kind of truth to the dreamer. In the story above, the woman's first experience, when the voice speaks to her, is a prophetic vision because it comes true. The second, about the spotted silver vessel, is enigmatic because its meaning is hidden and has to be interpreted by the priest.[10]

Sir Geoffrey tells several stories about visions that come to people in dreams, and in each case, the dreamers take their visions seriously, running to a priest for an interpretation. In almost every case, the dream warns the dreamer about a sin that could keep her from entering heaven if she failed to confess it. Being a good Christian in all other ways couldn't help you at your hour of need if you hadn't confessed, as the fate of the woman in the next story shows. You could demonstrate all of the seven virtues—faith, hope, charity, justice, prudence, temperance, and fortitude—you could be as abstemious as possible, but if a secret sin lay heavy on your soul, you were in serious spiritual danger.

Of her that deyde and durst not confesse hir synne
(Concerning the woman who died and didn't dare to confess her sin)

There was a woman of great renown, famed for being blessed and charitable because she fasted three days a week—two days on just bread and water. She gave many alms, visited the sick, nourished orphans, and stayed at Mass until midday. She said many prayers and lived a holy life as a good woman ought to do. When she died, our Lord used her as an example of how a person could be lost for only one deadly sin.

The sepulcher in which she was laid began to fume and smoke, the earth began to burn, and the grave moved about. The people of that region marveled at what it meant, because they knew she had been saved above all other women.

Then a holy man took the cross, the stole, and the holy water and conjured the woman's soul in the name of God. He asked Almighty God, if it pleased him, to show the cause of this stink and torment.

Then a voice said, "I am the poor sinner who is damned to perpetual fire. God makes my wretched body smoke and twitch as an example. I'll tell you how the sin of the flesh befell me. Once I lay with a monk and I never dared to confess it for fear of the shame of the world. I feared the mockery of the world more than the spiritual vengeance for my sin. I fasted, I gave up my property for God's sake, I heard Masses, I said many prayers, and it seemed to me that all my good deeds and abstinence quenched my sins, which I never dared tell to the priest. And therefore I am ruined and lost, for I tell it to all: whoever dies in deadly sin without repenting is perpetually damned. The sin must be confessed as fully as the deed was done."

When she had spoken, everybody was abashed because each one of them had thought she was saved.

Sometimes Sir Geoffrey's examples seem a bit extreme. The good lady in this story has not only never confessed her mortal sin, the sin was having sex outside of marriage—and with a monk! The sixteenth-century commentator Master Fitzherbert thought Sir Geoffrey's book would lead people into sin rather than out of it by teaching them about vices they would never have thought of themselves; perhaps this was one of them.

The woman with the smoking sepulcher is damned to perpetual fire because she died without confessing the mortal sins of pride and lechery. Had she not confessed a venial sin instead of mortal ones, she would have been condemned to Purgatory where she could expiate that sin through punishment. Purgatory also awaited her if she had confessed a sin on her deathbed, when there was no time for her to do acts of penance for it, but her pride kept her from confessing even then, so worried was she about the opinion of the world.

The varieties of sins were legion, and books of virtues and vices consulted by confessors are sometimes as shocking to modern readers as Sir Geoffrey's book was to Master Fitzherbert, since they list sins you would never even have imagined. In addition to the more quotidian transgressions, priests are advised to ask penitents where and with whom they have had sex: In a church? With a nun? With your godmother? Your nephew? Some manuals are much more specific. For example, one book tells priests to ask women whether they have tried to rid themselves of tiresome husbands in the following manner: After smearing honey over their naked bodies, rolling themselves in wheat, and baking bread made from the wheat after it's been ground in a mill that turns widdershins, have they served the bread to their husbands, who sickened and died? If so, forty days of bread and water as penance.[11] One wonders whether the celibacy imposed on the priests who wrote these books could have heightened their imaginations.

CHAPTER 5

HEARING GOD'S
SERVICE — GOING TO MASS

The schedules of Christine de Pizan's princess and Cicely, Duchess of York, show that in the household of a medieval knight, people might attend Mass both in the morning and at midday, while in the late afternoon, they would attend Vespers, or Evensong. Upper-middle-class Londoners such as the Goodwyns would have the leisure to imitate their betters, and besides, going to more than one service in a day gave them a chance to see others and to be seen. However, the Church mandated only that they attend Mass on Sundays and holy days.

The Mass itself was in Latin, which neither Sir Geoffrey's daughters nor Robert Goodwyn's would have understood. Nor would the young wife of the Householder of Paris. That's why he suggests that she find a place in church in front of an altar or an image and remain there, her lips moving in silent prayer, throughout the Mass. Or she might keep her eyes on a book of hours — again, in silent prayer — in no way looking around her at other people.[1] Since the priest is speaking a language she doesn't understand, and since he's facing *away* from her, she needs to do something to keep her mind on prayer, not on her neighbor's striking new headdress or the fine legs of her neighbor's twenty-year-old son. She should be aware of her social standing, however, as a young page is warned in a French romance: "kneel down and look not to either side, save to be sure that you are not before any lord or lady, knight or esquire, that by honourable rank hath precedence of you."[2]

As he writes for his wife, the Householder describes the entire Mass, from the robing of the priest and the *Introit* to the disrobing and last prayers. Perhaps taking his description from a book of hours, he breaks the Mass into parts, telling her its purpose and what she should be doing: "After the Introit, sung or said, is said nine times *Kyrie eleison, Christe eleison*, to signify that there are nine hosts of angels called hierarchies . . . . Then should every man pray to these blessed angels to intercede with our Lord for him, saying: O ye blessed angels who descend from glory to our Lord to minister for Him and serve Him on earth, pray Him to pardon our transgressions and send us His grace."[3]

The Latin Mass wasn't originally designed to keep people in ignorance. In early Christian times, in Rome, people spoke Latin. They understood the priest's words and they responded during the Mass's dialogues. But after the Latin Mass was codified, the language itself faded out of common use as it transformed into such Romance languages as French, Provençal, Spanish, and Italian. As the official language of universities, science, and the Church, Latin remained vibrant throughout the Middle Ages, but lay people in Europe no longer spoke it regularly. Thus, until 1969, most Catholics listened to Mass in a language they didn't speak.

Sermons, however, were often given in the vulgar tongue, that is, the common language. In their sermons, priests had the opportunity to teach their flocks through exempla, the kind of stories Sir Geoffrey heard and repeated to his daughters. Their stories might reinforce lessons about attending Mass, going to confession, and giving alms. They used the opportunity to catechize their parishioners, teaching them prayers, for example. Each of the following stories is the sort that Sir Geoffrey's priests might have included in their Sunday sermons. In fact, they might be the very tales actually told on Sundays, since his priests helped Sir Geoffrey collect his stories. Jeanne and Anne might have looked at each other knowingly as they came across the next story within their father's book—the demons and the descriptions of ladies' headdresses made quite an impression on them when they had heard the priest tell it a year or so ago.

Of them that playe and iape at the masse
(Of those who play and jest at Mass)

I'll tell you about people who talk at Mass when they ought to be listening to the service of God. The stories about Athens mention a hermit, a very holy man of blessed life, who had a chapel dedicated to Saint John in his hermitage. Because he was so holy, many knights and squires, ladies and damsels of that region came there for a religious festival.

The hermit sang the Mass and after the Gospel, when he turned around, he saw that the ladies and damsels, knights and squires were all joking and chattering and whispering. When he looked carefully at their faces, he could see a black and horrible fiend crouching at the ear of each man and woman. The fiends laughed and talked among themselves, springing on the people's fancy clothing like small birds that leap from branch to branch. They wrote down every word the people said during the Mass.

The holy man crossed himself, marveling. When he neared the end of the Mass, he could still hear the people talking and laughing. He struck his book to make them be quiet, but some of them kept talking. Then the hermit said, "Fair Lord God, make them hold their peace and be still, so they may know their folly."

Suddenly, the people who were laughing began to shriek and cry, both men and women, as if they were possessed. It was a pitiful thing to see and hear their suffering.

When the Mass was over, the hermit told the people how he had seen the fiends of Hell laughing at them with evil expressions during the Mass, leaping and springing on the women's foolish finery. The fiends could tell which of them were thinking of God, and which were thinking about pleasing their lovers, because they didn't touch those who were praying devoutly, even the ones wearing fancy clothing. For the devil, said the hermit, cares more about hearts than clothes. Those who find pleasure in their devotions anger and thwart the fiend, our enemy.

After the hermit said these things, the people who were crying and who were so tormented threw away their festive apparel. For nine days, they acted like people out of their wits. But on the tenth day they were once again brought to their right minds by the prayers of the holy hermit. From that day forth, they were chastened and never talked or joked during the service of God.

The people in the story may never have talked or joked during Mass after their comeuppance, but Elizabeth Goodwyn finds it impossible not to whisper to her sister during the services, no matter how much trouble she might be in later. There is just so much to talk about: who is the fine lady standing with the Riche family, and has Katherine ever seen such a beautiful gown?

Like Elizabeth, Anne de la Tour has trouble keeping quiet during the Mass. Her father tells her that the next story is meant especially for her, and that he hopes the devil will have no trouble fitting all her words onto his bit of parchment.

An Ensample that happed at the masse of seynt Martyn
(An example that happened at the Mass of Saint Martin)

I'll tell you what happened at a Mass of Saint Martin of Tours. The holy man sang the Mass with the help of his godson, Saint Bryce, who was afterwards Archbishop of Tours. During the Mass, Saint Bryce began to laugh. When the Mass was finished, Saint Martin demanded to know why he had laughed. Saint Bryce said he had seen the devil writing down everything that men and women said to each other during the Mass—but they said so much that the parchment on which the fiend wrote was too short. He tried to stretch the parchment with his teeth to make it longer, but it escaped from him and he hit his head against the stone wall. "And that," said Saint Bryce, "is why I laughed."

Although they're not a large part of the Bible, in the medieval mind, demons were real and ever-present. Some theologians thought they sprang from unions of the fallen angels and female humans. They took this idea from the Book of Enoch, now consigned by the Roman Catholic Church to the Apocrypha.[4] Some demonic creatures were survivals of folk traditions antedating Christianity. However, most people didn't concern themselves with theological arguments about the origins of devils. They just tried to avoid them.

Devils and demons didn't afflict lay people alone. A fifteenth-century treatise on the divine service warns nuns and monks against taking pride in their voices when they sing the Mass by telling the story of a cleric who had a sweet and fair voice. Everyone loved to hear him sing until the day that a religious man listened to him and said it wasn't a man's voice at all, but a fiend's. The holy man called out the devil, who left the cleric's body, "and went his way." And therefore, the treatise says, the more pleasant your voice is, the meeker your heart needs to be.

Monks and nuns sang the divine service seven times a day, in heat and in cold, at dark midnight and in the weary afternoon, day in and day out. Titivillus was the devil whose special job it was to collect all the syllables they dropped when they were trying to get the Mass over with faster by singing quickly. The same treatise on the divine service mentions a Cistercian abbot who, standing in the choir at Matins, saw a fiend with a large bag hanging around his neck going from monk to monk and stuffing his bag with dropped syllables, words, and errors. The abbot was afraid of him because he was so ugly and misshapen. "What are you?" he asked, and the fiend replied, "I am a poor devil named Titivillus and I do what I'm commanded."

"What is that?" the abbot asked.

"Every day I must bring my master a thousand bags full of errors and negligence in syllables and words, or else I am badly beaten."

And thus you can see, the story continues, that while we may forget our failings, the fiend doesn't forget them and he uses them at judgment day to accuse our souls.[5]

Titivillus was also responsible for collecting the errors monastic scribes made in their scriptoria. Into his bag went the words their eyes skipped over and left out of the manuscript they were copying, the words they misspelled, the whole passages they omitted when their tired eyes, in the dim light of a cloudy day, looked up to their exemplars and started copying the wrong line, one that began with the same word as a line three inches up the page. You can just see Titivillus smacking his lips over such prizes, insuring that for at least one day, he wouldn't be beaten by his master.

Like the demons in the earlier stories, Titivillus hardly seems terrifying, but devils, or *the* devil, could be. A fifteenth-century English mystic, Julian of Norwich, describes the devil who tormented her in her book, *Revelations of Divine Love*. Julian, a well-educated woman, experienced a series of visions as she lay near death. When she recovered, she devoted herself to trying to understand these divine *shewings*, as she called them. She became an anchoress and spent the rest of her life walled into a chamber attached to a church in Norwich, where she could meditate on her visions and pray. Like other anchorholds, hers would have had a small window opening into the church to allow her to participate in the Mass. Her book is a spiritual autobiography in which she describes and discusses each of her visions.

Of the devil who came to her, Julian says he took her by the throat, putting his face near hers. "It was like a young man's face, and long and extraordinarily lean: I never saw the like," she writes.

> The colour was the red of a tilestone newly fired, and there were black spots like freckles, dirtier than the tilestone. His hair was rust red, clipped in front, with sidelocks hanging over his cheeks. He grinned at me with [a] sly grimace, thereby revealing white teeth, which made it, I thought, all the more horrible. There was no proper shape to his body or hands, but with his paws he held me by the throat and would have strangled me if he could.

The Fiend is accompanied by a "great heat and [a] filthy smell," "foul and nauseating." Twice he appears to her, tempting her to despair, yet she never loses her trust in God, who gives her "the grace to wake up" from her vision.[6]

Ultimately demons are like everything else in the world—created by God. In the end, the fiend who tempts Julian to give up her faith, as well as Titivillus and the devils in the stories above, promote God's will by testing Christians and helping errant sheep return to the fold.

Devils and demons were a favorite of medieval artists. They appear on people's shoulders, whispering into their ears, or crouched in corners, ready to spring. Usually winged, some of them have snouts, some horns, and some tails. Equal-opportunity tormenters, demons bedeviled the rich as well as the poor. In the medieval landscape, they were among the few social levelers.

While the lower classes needed only to attend to their own behavior at Mass, the aristocracy also needed to think about how their behavior affected others. The number of medieval stories about members of the upper classes going late to Mass may indicate a real social problem in addition to illustrating the realities of class stratification. Although many members of the highest nobility and certainly royalty would hear Mass in their own private chapels within their castles and manor houses, Sir Geoffrey's family probably attended services in the parish church just down the lane from the château. As lord of the manor, Sir Geoffrey employed the priests, clerks, and other clergymen, such as the ones who helped him compile his book. They deferred to him in all things, so until he, his wife, and his daughters made it to church, Mass couldn't begin. And when Sir Geoffrey was gone, as he so frequently was on military campaigns, Jeanne and Anne accompanied their mother to Mass. Woe to the other parishioners if the girls overslept or spent too much time getting dressed. The next two stories show the problems that could result.

Of a knyght that causid all a towne to lese theyr masse where as he dwellyd

(Of a knight who caused the entire town where he lived to lose their Mass)

I heard about a knight and a lady who from their youths took great pleasure in sleeping till noon. Because of this, they often missed Mass and caused the whole parish to miss it too, for he was the lord and patron of that parish and the parson didn't dare to speak against him.

One Sunday the lord and lady told the parson he should wait for them, but when they finally came, it was past midday. The people of the parish told the priest it was past noon and he dared not sing the Mass, and so they had no Mass that day. They were very angry but they had to suffer.

That night the priest had a vision. It seemed to him that he kept a great flock of sheep in a field where there was no grass. He wanted to bring them to a pasture to feed them, but the only path was blocked: a black swine and a sow lay across it. These hogs had horns! The priest and his sheep were so afraid that they didn't dare enter the pasture. They went back to the field with no grass, and so they had no food.

Then it seemed that someone said to the priest, "Do you neglect to give your sheep pasture for fear of these horned beasts?" And then he woke up.

On the same night, the knight and his lady had a similar vision. It seemed to them that they became a horned boar and sow and they wouldn't allow the sheep into the pasture. Then they saw a great chase of black hunters on great black horses and with them a large number of greyhounds and black dogs. The hunters blew their horns and set the dogs upon the boar and sow. They bit their ears, their arms, and their thighs, while the hunters urged them on. This hunting scene lasted so long that it seemed that they were taken and slain—and then they awoke, aghast and afraid. Twice this vision came to them.

Now it happened that the knight and lady told the priest about their vision, and the priest told them of his, and they all marveled at the similarity. The priest said to the knight, "Sir, there is a holy hermit nearby in the forest who will interpret this for us."

They went to this holy man and told him their visions. The holy man said to the knight and lady, "You are the black swine who block the path so that the sheep may not feed. That is to say, you are the lord of the parish and because of your long rest, you have kept the people from hearing the service of God, which is like good pasture and refreshes the soul. The horns you were wearing are the branches of your sins, especially the great sins you have done in keeping others from the service of God. You can only amend this by great penance and torment. If you don't, you will be tormented and hunted by the fiends of hell and at the end, you will be slain by the devils, like you have seen in your vision."

"I tell you," the hermit continued, "it would have been less sin by a hundred to one if you had simply not heard Mass than to have kept other people and the priest from their devotions. When the priest waited, he got angry and committed the sin of wrath, and the good people also sinned. Some of them went to the tavern; others gave up their Christian behavior. All these sins and evils come from you and your sloth, for which you will give a reckoning perhaps more hastily than you think, for you will be hunted and put to death like you have seen in your vision. That is to say, you are likely to be damned if you don't remedy this."

The knight was very abashed and asked what he might do.

The holy man said that for three Sundays he should kneel before his parishioners and beg their mercy and ask them to pardon him, and to pray to God for himself and his wife. And from then on they would have to be first at the church.

The knight confessed to the hermit, who gave him that penance and others. And from that day forth, he and his wife were the first at church.

And therefore dear daughters, never let your sloth or negligence keep others from Mass. Also, I hope you'll learn from the example of a lady who spent a quarter of every day getting dressed.

Of a lady that dispended the fourthe parte of the day for to araye her
(Of a lady who spent a quarter of the day getting dressed)
There was a lady who lived by a church who always took so long getting dressed and adorning herself that it angered the parson and parishioners. One Sunday she took so long that she had to send a message to the priest telling him to wait for her. It was already late in the day, and the people were vexed. One of them said, "May God send her an evil sight in her mirror for making us wait so long."

Just then, because it pleased God to set an example, the lady looked in her mirror and saw the fiend showing her his hinder parts. So foul and horrible were they that the lady went right out of her wits and stayed that way for a long time.

Later, after God restored her health, she always got dressed quickly and thanked God for allowing her to be chastised. This story should help you remember not to take so long getting dressed that you miss the Mass or make other people miss it.

Recalling how horrifying the face of the devil in Julian of Norwich's description was gives us some idea about how much more "fowle and horryble" the "hynder parte" of a demon might be—certainly enough to send a person out of her wits.

Sir Geoffrey contrasts spiritually slothful aristocrats with ladies who are devoted to hearing Mass. In his next two tales, as much as we might like to think that the ladies were deeply concerned about their ill or injured chaplains, they seem instead to be very anxious about themselves. Perhaps Sir Geoffrey simply left out the part where the ladies tenderly ministered to their priests.

In the first of the two stories, a pair of friars appears. Friars were as common as fleas in medieval Europe, and about as well liked. However, Sir Geoffrey avoids the almost formulaic condemnation of friars practiced by so many medieval writers, instead reserving his contempt for monks—and later for lawyers. When we remember that he and his wife endowed a house of Augustinian friars who said prayers for the Tour Landry family's souls, his stance no longer seems remarkable.

How god sprange in to the mouthe of a hooly lady
(How God sprang into the mouth of a holy lady)
Once there was a lady who lived a holy life and loved God and his service. On the days when she didn't hear Mass, she was very ill at ease

and ate neither meat nor fish. One time her chaplain got sick and couldn't sing Mass, which upset the lady. She walked outside her castle saying, "Oh, good Lord, forget us not, but if it pleases you, provide for us so we can hear the holy service."

As she spoke, she saw two friars walking towards her. Immediately she asked if they had said Mass, and when they said no, she asked them to sing it.

"Gladly, if it pleases God," the friars said.

"Thanks be to God," the lady said.

The younger friar sang first, and when he broke the sacrament into three pieces, the older friar watched as one of the pieces sprang into the lady's mouth like a little bit of bright radiance. The young friar looked all around to find it, and when he didn't see it, he trembled with fear.

The older friar said to him, "Don't be dismayed—the piece you're looking for is in the lady's mouth."

Then the younger friar thanked God for the miracle that happened to this good lady, who loved the service of God so much. Lo, my fair daughters, this is a good reminder that God loves those who love his Mass.

Of a Countesse that euery day herd thre masses
(Concerning a countess who heard Mass three times a day)

I hope you'll pay attention to the example of a good lady, a countess, who heard three Masses every day. One time when she was on a pilgrimage, one of her chaplains fell off his horse and was so badly hurt that he couldn't say Mass. The lady was exceedingly distressed to lose one of her Masses, and she lamented devoutly to God.

Immediately God sent an angel to say the third Mass in the priest's place. After he had sung and was divested of his robes, they couldn't find him anywhere no matter how much they searched. "God sent him to us," the good lady said, and she thanked him humbly.

This is a good example of how God helps the devout, but I believe that there are many ladies these days who get away with fewer than three Masses. They have so little love and devotion for God and his service that a single Mass suffices them. We find God by hearing his service, and those who love and fear him will often see him and hear his holy word. The contrary is also true: the person who hasn't set his heart on God is easily satisfied with a few services. Many people are like that these days. They set their hearts on the world and on the delight of the flesh instead of on God.

Although Church doctrine required no member of the laity to hear Mass three times a day the way the lady in this story does, it wasn't at all peculiar to do so, as we have already seen in the case of Richard III's mother. In a fifteenth-century letter, a merchant-class English woman named Agnes Paston very matter-of-factly mentions some-one she knows attending three Masses in one day,[7] so we know it wasn't just royalty who took the time for such devotion. However, the devil was deft in finding ways to lead a Christian to sin, and being seen in the chapel so often might be related to the sin of pride. Another fifteenth-century Englishwoman, Margery Kempe, was sometimes accused of taking too much pride in her piety, wanting to be certain that not only was she was more pious than anyone else, but also that everyone else knew it. In this way, she's reminiscent of the Wife of Bath, whom Chaucer says "was oute of all charity" if other women of the parish made their church offerings before she did.

When religion is so deeply integrated into your world, it takes constant vigilance to keep it from becoming diminished or diluted. Sometimes Sir Geoffrey's Christianity is pure and above suspicion, as when he teaches his daughters to pay attention at Mass, to begin and end their days with prayer, or to confess their sins. At other times, however, Sir Geoffrey's attachment to this world takes priority over his desire for the next. Sometimes his devotion to God seems tinged with a devotion to earthly reputation and material wealth. He follows his section on honoring God with stories about manners, about finding good husbands and being good wives—and here he sometimes loses sight of his spiritual ideals.

CHAPTER 6

TAMING THE SPARROWHAWK — MANNERS AND MARRIAGE

When Sir Geoffrey's daughter Jeanne turned sixteen, her behavior in social situations would become increasingly important. Her little sister Anne would feel the tension, too, even though the attention would have been on Jeanne. When an unmarried nobleman visited the Tour Landry family, Jeanne would have been fussed over by her maidservants, her ladies-in-waiting, and her mother until they deemed her clothing grand enough, her carriage stately enough, and her smile demure enough to make her marriageable. Anne would likely have looked on enviously, forgetting that envy was a deadly sin. As she watched, she would learn how she herself would be expected to act in a few short years. In her parents' bedchamber, contentedly sucking at the wet nurse's breast, baby Marie would be oblivious to the scene that awaited her when she grew up.

According to a modern myth about the Middle Ages, all girls at the age of twelve either married men three times their age or else were forced to become nuns. The only alternative was to dress as a boy and escape with a band of traveling minstrels. Whereas it's true that girls of the nobility were often betrothed at a younger age than those of the merchant or peasant classes, generally only royalty and the very high nobility, concerned with alliances of land and wealth, married their children at improbable ages, sometimes as young as six or seven. Princess Margaret of Burgundy was eleven when she married the dauphin in 1404. In the following year, Christine de Pizan wrote for her *The Treasure of the City of Ladies*, a companion book to *The Book of the Three Virtues*.[1] Christine herself, a member of the aristocracy who spent much of her time at court, was fifteen when she married. Yet even the daughters of dukes were more likely to marry at twenty or twenty-five than at fifteen, and the idea of the medieval child bride has fortunately faded in the light of recent scholarship.[2]

Similarly, notions about girls disguising themselves as boys are vastly overstated. One thirteenth-century French story, *Silence*, does feature a girl dressed as a boy who joins a band of minstrels, but her parents are the ones who come up with this ruse. They pretend she's a boy so she can inherit their estate after a king declares that girls can't do so. In the Middle Ages, as in Shakespeare's plays, the girl disguised as a boy was a feature of fiction, rarely of fact.

Canon law, the law of the Church, decreed that girls could marry at twelve, boys at fourteen. Sometimes noble girls who married as children lived with their mothers-in-law, not with their husbands, for a few years until they were considered old enough to be wives. Sometimes a very young girl was betrothed to a man but not actually married to him until years later. But this applies mainly to the very highest rungs of the social ladder, those nearest the crown. When we lower our gaze to the merely aristocratic inhabitants of Sir Geoffrey's country castle, we find that the average age of marriage for girls was seventeen.[3] And in England in the following century, Katherine and Elizabeth Goodwyn, the daughters of the prosperous woolmerchant, would have married at nineteen or twenty. Their husbands would have been older, perhaps thirty, because they first needed to finish their apprenticeships and establish themselves as merchants.[4] Other English women of the upper middle classes were at least twenty when they married, including Elizabeth Paston and Margery Kempe, and peasant girls were usually twenty or more, whereas their husbands would be two to four years older.[5]

Yet from the time they became teenagers, both merchant class and aristocratic girls and their families would be thinking about marriage. And in thinking about marriage, they would be considering social deportment. In the first two stories in this chapter, Sir Geoffrey is apparently concerned simply with proper ways to behave in company. He shortly moves toward his real topic—the courtesy of courting. The word *court* appears in "courtesy" for good reason. Courteous behavior is courtly behavior, the manners that are appropriate for the court and that trickle down to provincial castles and manor houses. Etiquette is like fashion—it changes with the time and the place. Nevertheless the manners Sir Geoffrey advocates would have been current a hundred years later in England, when men such as Robert Goodwyn of London, Thomas Lane of Gloucester, and John Goodyere of Monken Hadley were buying William Caxton's edition of *The Book of the Knight of the Tower* to discover ways to make themselves and their daughters welcome—if not at court, then at least in the homes of their social superiors. These men's daughters, like Jeanne, Anne, and later Marie de la Tour, had to remember how deeply their speech, their dress, even their physical movements could affect their reputations, which in turn could have huge implications for their marriage prospects.

Up to now, Sir Geoffrey's stories have sounded as if they came from sermons, packed as they are with didactic admonitions of a general, one-size-fits-all nature. In the following tales, he includes personal anecdotes—tales of people he's known and things he's done—that reveal a little more of his character, a little more about what daily life might have been like for a fourteenth-century French aristocrat and his family.

How good wymmen ought to mayntene them self curtoysly
(How good women ought to comport themselves courteously)

My daughters, be gracious and modest because you will earn both the grace of God and the love of all people this way. Courtesy overcomes wretches, as the sparrowhawk shows. If you call an untamed sparrowhawk courteously, you will make him come freely from the tree to your fist. If you are rough and cruel, he will never come. Since courtesy subdues a wild bird who has no reason, think how much more will it restrain men and women, at least those who don't have fierce, proud hearts. Courtesy is the path to all friendship and all worldly love, and it can vanquish the high spirits and anger of all creatures.

I know a lord in this region who, through his great courtesy, conquered more knights, squires, and other people, getting them to serve and obey him than others were able to with money or in other ways. This is my lord of Craon, who ought to be honored and praised for his courtesy above all other knights I know. I know that by means of his courtesy he has received much love and respect from great ladies, and also from other people, great and small.

Therefore, my fair daughters, show courtesy to the people of lower classes to do them honor, and speak to them fairly and sweetly, and answer them courteously, and they will give you greater reverence, more praise, and more renown than will the great, because the honor and courtesy that's given to the great estates is but their right. But that which is done to small gentlemen and gentlewomen and to others of lesser degree—that honor and courtesy comes of a noble and courteous heart. The low or poor man or woman to whom it is given is happy to receive it and gets great pleasure from it.

Once when I was in a company of knights and ladies, a great lady took off her hood and humbled herself courteously to a tailor. One of the knights said to her, "Madame, why have you taken off your hood to a tailor?" She answered that she had rather take it off to a tailor than fail to honor a gentleman. And everyone else said she had done the right thing, and done it well.

The knight who questions the great lady about her treatment of the tailor implies that being respectful to someone of such low social status is odd. A similar story is told about the great knight Boucicaut the younger, whose father Sir Geoffrey knew. When Boucicaut saluted two prostitutes his fellow knights upbraided him, but he said he preferred to risk such a mistake rather than fail "in his duty toward a lady."[6]

It was not the least self-evident to Western Europeans of either Sir Geoffrey's or William Caxton's day that all people were created equal. The higher you were on the social scale, the better you were, inalienably. Just as the wife is always subordinate to the husband, so people of lower social rank are subordinate to their betters. In her advice to princesses, Christine de Pizan—like Sir Geoffrey—reinforces the social hierarchy: she tells princesses that when they give gifts to the lower classes, the ones Caxton calls "the mene and smal peple," the very act of giving the gift humbles the princess so much and brings such joy to the lower-class person that the gift itself need not be at all substantial—noblesse oblige in action.

Having grown up at court, Christine probably had far less contact with "mene and smal peple" than Sir Geoffrey and his daughters would have. As lords and mistresses of country villages, they would have seen the villagers in the parish church, walked in the fields that were being winnowed, and perhaps even visited the cottages of ill or pregnant peasants. Sir Geoffrey's attitude toward the ordinary people may seem a little condescending to us, but compared to Christine, he seems the very model of modernity.

Katherine and Elizabeth Goodwyn would have seen even more of their social superiors and inferiors than the Tour Landry daughters because London neighborhoods were microcosms of the larger world. Beggars sometimes paid for prime positions outside the door of the parish church, and Katherine and Elizabeth would pass them daily. They might have even known some of the beggars' names. Walking home along the narrow, winding streets, the girls would rub shoulders with high-class servants and laundresses of the lowest social stratum, while lords and knights might pass them on tall horses. Even the neighborhood houses participated in this mingling of classes: the Goodwyn house might have been flanked by a mere tradesman's dwelling on one side and a prosperous goldsmith's on the other. On the opposite side of the narrow street, two doors down, a bawd and several prostitutes might have lived. No wonder the social hierarchy was so strictly maintained.[7]

For Sir Geoffrey that hierarchy is all-important, and his name-dropping indicates the value he places on social position. Knowing "my lord of Craon" personally gives him both an example for his daughters to follow and also a social boost, since the Craon family was well regarded in the region and Sir Geoffrey served with one of them in the military.[8] That's why it's useful, however hard it is to prove, to think of Sir Geoffrey's sons Charles and Arcades serving as pages in the Craon household: families sent their sons to places of higher social standing to help them make good connections. Throughout his book Sir Geoffrey refers to great men and women he knows or has heard of, and in doing so, he increases his own prestige, as well as that of his family—including his marriageable daughters.

In the next story, he turns his attention from behavior toward others to physical comportment, a topic important for all ladies, but one that unmarried daughters should especially heed.

How yonge maydens ought not to torne their heedes lyghtely here ne there

(How young maidens ought not to turn their heads thoughtlessly here and there)

Daughters, don't be like the tortoise or the crane, which turn their faces and their heads above their shoulders, winding their heads here and there like a weathervane. Instead, hold yourselves steadfast like the hare, a beast that always looks in front of him without turning his head all about. Always look directly in front of you and if you must look to the side, turn your face and your body together, holding yourself firm and sure, for those who frivolously cast their eyes about and turn their faces here and there are mocked.

The moral of this story may have given Jeanne de la Tour no cause for alarm, but not her sister Anne. A curious thirteen-year-old, Anne is ever whirling to see who has ridden into the courtyard or tipping her head back to watch a spider in the corner of the room or a magpie flying past. When the grizzled, one-armed soldier responsible for teaching the young pages how to joust calls them to the tilting yard, Anne finds herself leaning out of the window to watch—without being exactly sure how she got there. Jeanne may know how to comport herself, but Anne despairs that she will ever learn.

Yet Anne must hardly have been alone in her impetuous behavior: ladies turning their heads caused great consternation to medieval Amy Vanderbilts. Sir Geoffrey's caution is echoed by the Householder of Paris, who tells his wife not to look wildly around like a runaway horse. The poem "How the Goodwife Taught Her Daughter" offers similar counsel, only without the animal metaphors. In Sir Geoffrey's French, as well as in the anonymous English translation, the animal who holds its head straight in front of it is a bloodhound; in Caxton's version it's been changed to a hare. (The change may not have been Caxton's; it could have occurred in the now-lost manuscript from which he was translating).

If you think all this head turning is a minor matter, think again. The next two tales show that marriage itself may be at stake.

How the doughters of the kyng of denmarke lost their husbonde by cause of theyr maners
(How the daughters of the King of Denmark lost their husbands because of their manners)

I hope you will take seriously the example of the daughters of the King of Denmark. The King of England wanted to marry, and he heard that the King of Denmark had three fair daughters. He sent the most capable knights and ladies of his realm to see these daughters, and the Danes welcomed them with feasts. No one knew which daughter would be chosen.

A very wise and knowledgeable knight and lady watched the three young ladies and spoke to them. It seemed to them that although the oldest was the fairest, she often looked around her, turning her head about, and shifting her gaze like a weathervane. The second daughter spoke too much, often before she understood what had been said to her. The third daughter was hardly the prettiest, but she was the most agreeable. She was sober in manner, and when she spoke, which was rare, she was demure. She held her head firmly instead of looking all around her the way her sister did.

The ambassadors returned to their lord the king and told him what they had found. The wise king said, "Beauty is less important than a steadfast manner. There is nothing in the world as good as having a sure, steadfast wife, and therefore I choose the third daughter—I'll have none of the other two."

When he sent his ambassadors to fetch his bride, the two older daughters were angry and indignant. But so it was that the daughter with the best manners became Queen of England, while the older daughters were refused, one because of her wild looking about and the other for her chattering.

And thus, my fair daughters, take example from the daughters of the King of Denmark, and don't cast your eyes about at others, nor turn your neck here and there, and don't be too full of words, for one who speaks too much isn't thought to be wise. You should understand before you answer, and if you pause a little before you do, you will answer better and more wisely. For the proverb says that he who hears and doesn't understand gains as much as he who hunts but takes no game.

Let me tell you about something that happened to me. Once when my own marriage to a certain noblewoman was being considered, my lord my father took me to see her. I looked at her and talked with her about many things in order to know her behavior better, and we started speaking about prisoners. I said to her, "Damsel, I would rather be your prisoner than anyone else's, and I think that your prison wouldn't be as hard or as cruel as the prison of the Englishmen."

She answered me, saying that recently she had seen someone whom she wished were her prisoner. I asked her if she would give him an evil prison, and she said no, but that she would keep him as lovingly as she kept her own body.

"He would be lucky to have such a pleasant and admirable prison," I said.

I tell you, she loved that prisoner, and her eye was lively, and she was full of words. When we had to leave, she was pert, asking me two or three times not to leave but to come see her. But I was quiet because I had never seen her before this, and she knew well that marriage was spoken of between us.

When we left, my lord my father asked me what I thought of her.

"She's good and fair," I told him, "but I'll never be nearer to her than I am, if it please you." Her pertness and frivolous manner discouraged me so that I didn't marry her, and thus I have thanked God many times, for not a year and a half later she was blamed for something, rightly or wrongly, I don't know. Soon afterwards, she died.

And therefore, my fair daughters, all gentlewomen and noble maidens of good lineage ought to be quiet, modest, mature, steadfast in manner, and of little speech. They should answer courteously, and not move restlessly nor cast their sight around easily. Those who haven't acted the way they should have lost their marriages.

The King of Denmark and his daughters — in fact, the whole episode about them — are pure fiction, but the story from Sir Geoffrey's own courting days rings of truth, and Jeanne and Anne must have listened closely, fascinated by the portrait of their father as a young man.

The tale features the fashionable metaphors of courtly love, which Jeanne and Anne would have known from reading romances or listening to traveling minstrels. Some of those same romances were translated into English, and Katherine and Elizabeth Goodwyn might have read or heard them a hundred years later; they, too, would have been familiar with metaphors of hearts as prisons; lovers, lucky prisoners. Although Sir Geoffrey begins the fashionable bantering, when the lady he's courting plays along, he's displeased by her frivolity. In fact, he implies that her lack of decorum lies behind the accusations people made about her (their veracity matters not a whit once they have been bruited)—and even her untimely death. For an unmarried woman, the value of stylish comportment and clothing always has to be weighed against men's desires for demure, obedient wives. "Those who haven't acted the way they should have lost their marriages," Sir Geoffrey says—but of course, he's really only talking about women.

To emphasize his point, he continues with a romantic tale in which yet another fictional king dresses as a servant in order to spy on two sisters he's thinking of marrying. Despite the older sister's remarkable beauty, her haughtiness loses her a royal union; her modest younger sister is chosen to be queen. The story ends by paraphrasing a passage from Matthew 21: "As God says in the Gospels, he who is most worthy is most humble, just like the youngest daughter, who through her humility and courtesy, took the throne of Spain from her older sister." Yet in the Gospel passage the exaltation the humble look forward to is the kingdom of God, not the throne of Spain. Sir Geoffrey knows this, but he's also realistic, with three daughters he wants to marry well, into good estates that will bring the family important connections and guarantee the material comfort of the girls.

Frivolous behavior and haughtiness weren't the only thing that could cost a family a marriage; foolishly fashionable clothing is the culprit in the next story. However, this time physical beauty is just as important as manners. It could hardly harm a lady's prospects if she could manage to be both the most courteous *and* the most beautiful.

How the doughter of a knyght lost her maryage

(How the daughter of a knight lost her marriage)

I'll tell you about the daughter of a noble knight who lost her marriage because of her fine clothing. Her eldest sister was already married when a knight asked to marry the second daughter, and her father granted it. When the knight, who had never seen her before, was coming to the betrothal, she adorned herself in a close-fitting gown with no fur so she might seem fairer, smaller, and better-shaped. It was very cold that season and when a great wind rose up, her clothing didn't protect her very well. She got so cold that she turned pale. When the knight arrived, her color seemed deadly white to him, unlike her younger sister, who was fresh and pink. The sister, who didn't think she would be married any time soon, was wearing good warm gowns.

The knight looked them both over. After dinner he said to two of his kinsmen, "Fair lords, I know well that I may have for a wife whichever of the daughters I choose, and I want the younger daughter."

"It would be a greater honor to take the older daughter," his kinsmen told him.

"Fair friends," answered the knight, "I see little advantage in that choice. They have a married sister who is older than they are and the firstborn. I think the third daughter is more fresh and beautiful and has a better color than the second. My pleasure is in the third, and my love is set there before any other. I will have her."

His relations told him he should do what he wanted, so he asked for the third daughter to be his wife, and the father granted her to him. Many people marveled at this, especially the second daughter, who was very abashed and sorrowful.

A little while after this, the second daughter dressed herself in the kind of gown she was accustomed to wear in cold weather. Her color came to her again, and she looked much fresher than the sister whom the knight had married. He was astonished and said to her, "Fair sister, when I came to see you and took your sister instead, you weren't nearly as beautiful as you are now. Now your color is fresh and rosy, but then you were all pale and your sister looked better than you did. Now you are more beautiful than she is, and I marvel about it."

His wife told him what had happened, saying, "I thank God that I was warmly dressed and my color was better than hers because that's how I got your love. Blessed be the hour that my sister clothed herself so foolishly, because if she hadn't, you wouldn't have taken me and left her."

And that's how the older daughter lost her marriage. Now you've heard a good example about how one ought not to array her body to make it look smaller or better shaped, especially in the winter, since that was why she lost her beauty and her color. And that's what happened to Sir Foulques de Laval, as he told me after it happened, and I'll tell you what he said.

Sir Geoffrey no doubt knew Sir Foulques de Laval, since they were from the same region and both men served in the army of Charles de Blois,[9] although Sir Foulques was a *grand seigneur*, and thus of a higher social class than Sir Geoffrey, the country knight. We can hear Sir Geoffrey flattering his social better as he tells the story, and hinting to his audience about their close relationship. Sir Foulques's own error in fashion occurs not when he is hunting for a wife, but perhaps after he had already married Jeanne Chabot. In his tale, he's off to see a lover when he—like the daughter who was passed over for her rosy-cheeked sister—puts fashion above comfort, to his misfortune.

How loue wylle be kepte warme
(How love will be kept warm)

Sir Foulques de Laval was an elegant, handsome, polite and good-mannered knight. He told me that he was going to see his paramour one winter season when there was a great frost and the weather was very cold. In the morning he put on an embroidered scarlet surcoat and a hood of unlined scarlet without any fur. He didn't wear anything else except his fine shirt—no cloak, no gloves. The wind was so cold that he turned pale. Neither the pearls nor the precious stones on his thin surcoat could warm him. Along came another knight who was amorous towards the same lady, but he wasn't so gaily adorned, nor so lightly dressed. Instead, he wore a good warm gown, a cloak, and a double hood. He was as red as a rooster and had a good, lively color. The lady welcomed this knight and made him better cheer than she did to Sir Foulques. To the latter, she said, "Sir, stay near the fire. I fear you aren't well because your color is deadly pale."

Although he told her that he was joyous and well at ease in his heart, the other knight was fairer in the lady's sight.

But on a later occasion, when Sir Foulques saw that knight going towards his paramour's house, he dressed himself warmly and hurried to see her. This time, his lady thought he was the most handsome and the best colored. And so he told me that love will be kept warm, and he proved it. Therefore it's a great folly to wear thin clothes to make your body look better.

Sir Foulques de Laval can flirt with ladies and still be well regarded, but let a woman banter coquettishly with a man the way the lady whom Sir Geoffrey courted in his youth did, and she will call down upon herself only opprobrium and shame. Yet instead of fighting this double standard, Jeanne and Anne may not have even noticed it. In fact, Jeanne, for whom marriage loomed much nearer than it did for Anne, might have worried about what to wear if she is courted during the wintertime, or how to know whether she has said too much or too little when a suitor speaks to her. In fact, she concentrates so hard on how to win a husband that she spares little thought for its consequence: being a wife.

CHAPTER 7

OBEY WITHOUT COMPLAINT—BEING A WIFE

Medieval attitudes are as contradictory as modern ones, including ideas about marriage. Sir Geoffrey depicts his own marriage as ideal. His wife is good and kind and he defers to her wise judgments, yet his stories about marriage in general make it sound like nothing a woman ought to get involved in. These contradictions are found everywhere you look in medieval literature. Christine de Pizan gives a felicitous description of her own marriage, undertaken when she was fifteen and her husband twenty-four. They loved and respected each other, as Sir Geoffrey and Jeanne de Rougé seem to have, yet in her advice for married women, Christine stresses the importance of a wife's subservience to her husband, no matter how badly he treats her. And look at the portraits of matrimony Chaucer's pilgrims put forward. From "The Clerk's Tale," detailed below, you'd think husbands were the very devil, but the Wife of Bath, the Miller, and the Reeve all imply that wives are the culprits in bad marriages because of their lechery and dishonesty. Then comes "The Franklin's Tale," with the ideal marriage of the lady Dorigen and her husband Arveragus. They love with a patient love, they respect each other, and neither has *maistrye*, or superiority, over the other.

Despite these contradictions, the Middle Ages were still no time to be a woman. Although Jeanne and Anne may have watched their parents treating each other with the same sort of love and respect Dorigen and Arveragus shared, their father's book reinforces ideas about marriage they would have heard from childhood—in Sunday sermons, in moral stories told after meals, even in daily gossip. When Sir Geoffrey teaches the girls how to be good wives, he stresses obedience to their husbands. No matter how cruel and wicked her husband, the good wife will support him. She'll curb her jealousy, and she'll do everything she can to make her husband look good. This is only fair because after all, women are the cause of all the evil in the world. Why? Because Eve disobeyed God.

Sir Geoffrey echoes common sentiments of his day; sentiments agreed on by both sexes, who took as two of their texts the Bible (especially Genesis and Ephesians) and the writings of the bitterly antifeminist St. Jerome, one of the four fathers of the Church (Saints Augustine, Ambrose, and Gregory the Great are the others). Jerome may have done a lovely job of translating the Bible into the Latin that was used from the fifth century until Vatican II in 1969, but his views about women helped to brutally define their place, or lack of it, within the Church for over a millennium. Yet Jerome was hardly singular; he was one in a long line of antifeminist writers, early Christian and medieval, whom husbands could quote to their recalcitrant wives.

Although there's a modern tendency to want medieval women to have seen things differently from their husbands, even Christine de Pizan emphasizes a wife's obedience and subordination to her husband. "She will humble herself towards him, in deed and word and by curtsying; she will obey without complaint; and she will hold her peace to the best of her ability," she writes.[1] If a wife knows her husband is sinning in some way but she fears confronting him, Christine says the wife can mention the sin to her confessor and have the priest talk to her husband. If he has an affair with another woman and she can't do anything about it, she should pretend not to notice. If she challenges him, he might leave her, and then she would gain nothing but mockery, shame, and dishonor. "You must live and die with him whatever he is like," Christine says, and she reminds ladies that it's in their best interest to do everything they can to keep their husbands' favor.

At least Christine doesn't use dog metaphors. The Householder of Paris compares loyal wives to mastiffs who stay with their masters for life. Both he and Christine (in *The Treasure of the City of Ladies*) tell the popular medieval story of Patient Griselda. Boccaccio wrote an Italian version, Petrarch wrote one in Latin, and Chaucer included it in *The Canterbury Tales* as "The Clerk's Tale." In five different manuscripts, the story of Griselda has been bound with *The Book of the Knight of the Tower*.[2] It's a difficult story for modern readers, an outrageous offense against our sensibilities, but one Jeanne and Anne, and in the next century, Katherine and Elizabeth, would have listened to with great interest as they sat at their embroidery.

In the tale, Walter the Marquis marries a poor, virtuous young woman whose beauty he admires. Then he decides to test her. First, he takes away their baby daughter, telling Griselda he has had her killed. She accepts this uncomplainingly. Next, it's their son. Again, not a peep from Griselda. Finally, Walter tells her that the people no longer want her as their ruler so she must return home to her hovel wearing nothing but her shift. But first she must prepare the bedchamber for his new young bride since, after all, she knows how he likes things. This is the only time Griselda responds at all to her husband. She tells him to be careful with his new wife. Because the girl has been raised as a noble, Griselda says, she won't be able to endure what Griselda has suffered. It's Griselda's only criticism of Walter, and it's veiled in her concern for his bride. In the end, Walter breaks down, overwhelmed at Griselda's goodness. The bride turns out to be Griselda's own daughter, now returned to her, as is her son. Walter takes Griselda to his bosom as she weeps over her children.

The Householder says the story doesn't really apply to his wife since he would never test her that way, and besides, he's not a marquis. He hopes it wasn't too brutal a story and blames Petrarch if it was. Nevertheless, he says, obedience is the way to a good marriage. Eve was disobedient to God, and look what happened—all women after her are cursed by God. Lot's wife disobeyed her husband and look what happened—she was turned to a pillar of salt.

On the other hand, the Householder says, Mary is the image of obedience. When the angel Gabriel told her she was pregnant, did she tell him he was being unreasonable, since she was a virgin? No, she obediently believed him, just as Griselda obeyed Walter. A husband, no matter what his station before marriage, is his wife's lord and master, so marry him for his character, not for his money, the Householder says.

Jeanne and Anne, with the help of a priest, might have interpreted the story of Patient Griselda allegorically, with Walter standing for God and Griselda, for the good Christian. Like other medieval people, Jeanne and Anne would have been accustomed to allegory, and the priest might have helped them to understand the parallels between Abraham's obedience when God tells him to sacrifice his son Isaac and Griselda's obedience to Walter in letting her own children be killed. But at end of his version of the story, Chaucer's Clerk mourns the lack of obedient wives these days, perhaps in an attempt to undercut an allegorical interpretation. Then again, Chaucer is so sly in his use of irony that he seems to both invite and discourage several different interpretations, all at the same time.

Irony rarely appears in Sir Geoffrey's tales. He's utterly straightforward in his tales emphasizing the importance of wifely obedience, even in comic stories such as this one about a troublesome pet bird.

Of her that ete the Eele and plumed her pye
(Of her who ate the eel and plucked her magpie)

I'll tell you the fate of women who eat choice dishes behind their husbands' backs. Once there was a damsel who had a magpie in a cage. The bird could talk, and it told everything it saw. The lord of the house kept a great eel in a floating box in a pond so he could give it as a gift if some lord or friend came to see him. The lady told the housekeeper it would be good to eat the eel, and they would tell the lord that thieves had eaten it. But when the lord came home, the magpie said to him, "My lady ate the eel." When the lord heard this, he went to his pond and couldn't find his eel. He came home and asked his wife what had happened. She made some excuses, but he said he knew the truth because the magpie had told him.

Everyone in the household was upset. When the lord left, the lady and the housekeeper plucked all the magpie's feathers from its head saying, "You told my lord about the eel." Thus the poor pie lost its plumage.

And from that day forward, whenever a bald or tonsured man, or someone with a high forehead came to the house, the magpie would say, "You told my lord about the eel."

This is a good story to show that for the sake of greed, a woman shouldn't eat delicacies without her husband's knowledge. This damsel was scorned and mocked about the eel because the magpie reminded everyone whenever it saw a bald head.

Beast fables, or animal stories with morals, were a popular medieval genre, and Sir Geoffrey may have borrowed the talking bird from them. With their short texts and clearly stated morals, they were attractive to preachers, who incorporated them into sermons in order to illustrate proper behavior, so Jeanne and Anne were likely to have heard beast fables before, especially those about Reynard the Fox. A cycle of French stories about this sly trickster was so well known that "Reynard" became the standard name for a fox. Katherine and Elizabeth Goodwyn might have known such stories, too, because they were popular in both fourteenth- and fifteenth-century England. Chaucer's "Nun's Priest's Tale," about the rooster Chauntecleer, his wife Pertelote, and the crafty fox is his masterful retelling of a story known throughout the medieval period, and William Caxton translated and printed a version in his *History of Reynard the Fox*. He also translated a collection of Aesop's fables, as Marie de France had done in the twelfth century.

The magpie story might bring Marie's fables to mind, whereas the next tale may make us think of her *Bisclavret*, about an unfortunate werewolf and his unfaithful wife, who has her nose bitten off. A straight nose is a particularly important part of a woman's beauty, since (as

Sir Geoffrey points out below) the nose is central to the face. In Marie's story, the faithless wife's punishment is so harsh that not only does she lose her own nose, all her daughters are born without noses, too. And remember, this is a woman writing.

From chapter 6 we know that in Sir Geoffrey's view, men should choose character or manners over beauty when they decide whom to marry. However, we've also seen the importance he places on pulchritude, and in the following stories both inner and outer beauty come into play in the relationships between husbands and wives. Often, he equates a woman's physical attractiveness—including that straight nose—with both her moral goodness and her capacity to be loved by others. The standard is, of course, double. In a later story we will see that although a man may be ugly as a demon, a good wife will cleave to him. Only women must maintain their physical beauty, curb their jealousy, and be humbly obedient. Neither Jeanne and Anne nor Katherine and Elizabeth would find anything to question about this inequity, nor would their mothers.

How wymmen ought not to be Ielous
(How women ought not to be jealous)

I'll tell you a story about that evil thing, jealousy. A damsel who was married to a squire loved her husband so much that she was always jealous of everyone he spoke to. Her husband rebuked her but it didn't help. Above all, she was jealous of a proud woman who lived in that region.

One time the wife chided this woman and reviled her concerning her husband. The second damsel said, "By my faith, what you say isn't true."

"You lie," the first damsel replied, and thus they began to fight and to hit each other fiercely. And she who was accused took a staff and smote the other on the nose with such a stroke that she broke the bone.

After that, the first damsel had a crooked nose—which is the most prominent feature a man or woman can have, since it's right in the middle of the face. And thus this woman was blemished and her husband reproached and reviled her. It would have been better for her not to have been jealous, but to have kept her face undamaged.

Because of the disfiguring of her nose and her ill fortune, her husband didn't love her as much as he had before, and from time to time he took other women. And so, because of her jealousy, she lost her husband's love and esteem. This is a good example for all good ladies and gentlewomen about how they ought to bear things graciously, and, if they have any affliction, to bear it graciously.

My aunt was like this, as I've been told many times. This good woman, the Lady of Anguillier, was married to a rich lord who had fifteen hundred pounds a year.

But her husband was so lecherous that he always had a woman or two in his house. Often at night he rose from his wife's bed and went to his concubines. When he returned from his lechery he would find a lit candle, water, and a towel to wash his hands. She would say nothing except to ask him to wash his hands.

"I've just come from the privy chamber," he would say.

"Since that's where you've come from, you have even more need to wash yourself," she said, but she didn't reprove him in any other way.

However, one time she spoke to him secretly, just between the two of them, saying, "My lord, I know well what you do with so and so and with so and so, but never with me by God's grace, since that's your pleasure. I know I can't remedy it so I won't make worse cheer to you, nor show my emotions to them, either. I would be a fool to break my head disputing about your merchandise. But I ask that at least you don't treat me ungraciously, nor that I lose your love nor your good favor, because I will endure all that it pleases you to bid me."

And truly, the soft and sweet words she said to him melted his heart, filling it with pity, and he reformed himself for a good while. During her life she vanquished him by great courtesy and humble obedience. If she had acted differently, it wouldn't have turned out this way, that in the end he repented and kept himself only to her.

This is a good example of how by graciousness and obedience a woman may keep her lord and husband from doing such things, and this works better than coarseness. A man has such spirit that when you come at him with fierceness and roughness, he will be worse. Of course, a husband ought not to feel resentful towards his wife if she is a little bit jealous of him, because the wise man says that jealousy is part of love, and I believe he speaks truly. I wouldn't much care about somebody who I didn't set any store by, but I would be heavy at heart if my friend or neighbor had any misfortune. There is never jealousy without great love, but it exists in two kinds, one worse because it exists without reason. A man shouldn't feel resentful if his wife is a little jealous over him, because this shows that she fears another may have the love she ought to have by right, according to God and the Church. But the wise woman makes no signs of jealousy. She restrains herself and bears her misfortune secretly. And a man should make as little outward show as he can, and keep himself from undue jealousy. The good wife who suspects a little riot or grief from her husband ought not to love him less, and the same with him.

Perhaps Sir Geoffrey wasn't given to irony, but modern readers might be tempted to give an ironic interpretation to his aunt's calm acceptance of her husband's lie about having just come from the privy chamber. We may read her response metaphorically when she says,

"Since that's where you've come from, you have even more need to wash yourself." After all, he has soiled himself both physically and spiritually by having sex with another woman, and cleansing he certainly needs. We may think she's a fool for not leaving her cheating spouse, but that wasn't something a medieval woman—or man—could easily do. Although Jeanne might have pitied her great-aunt for having to put up with such churlish behavior, when she and her sister discussed the story her comments would probably have focused on how beautifully the lady handled a difficult situation. Anne, however, might be more interested in knowing exactly who the lady was: "Was she the mother of our cousin Huette?" she asks. But her sister doesn't know.

Their aunt's comment to her husband does give the lie to another myth about the Middle Ages, the one that says people never washed. Bathing may have been less convenient than it is now, but people certainly cleaned themselves. Aristocrats washed their hands several times a day and their faces and teeth when they got up in the morning. Washing part of your body, as Sir Geoffrey's uncle does, was more frequent than taking complete baths, but baths were also a regular part of life, especially for the rich. The wealthy used wooden tubs and servants to pour the water whereas some bourgeois towndwellers visited bathhouses. Peasants were the great unwashed; they probably bathed as infrequently as early-twentieth-century bachelor farmers in the American Midwest, especially in winter. Nevertheless, medieval standards of cleanliness were very different from modern ones and the odor of Jeanne and Anne's bedroom—a mixture of unwashed hair and bed linens, smoke and sweat, lavender and herbs sprinkled on the sheets to sweeten them—might have us covering our noses with our hands. But to Jeanne and Anne, those would be the comforting smells of home.

At the end of his story, Sir Geoffrey equates the behavior expected of men and women who suspect their spouses of "a little riot or grief," but his later examples don't bear this out. Instead, he implies (or states outright) that wives who cause their husbands to be jealous are punished by both God and man, but husbands should be allowed to go astray without causing ill feelings in their wives since, after all, they're imbued with "such spirit." Alas that his book for his sons Charles and Arcades has been lost—did the examples Sir Geoffrey include in it urge husbands to be faithful, to quell their high spirits, and to avoid causing jealousy in their wives?

Just as jealousy can bring grief to a marriage, so can arguing. Chaucer, the Householder of Paris, and Christine de Pizan all agree with Sir Geoffrey when he says that a wife shouldn't chide or spar with her husband. Each of them quotes a version of the same medieval proverb—three things drive a man from his home: a leaky roof, a smoky chimney, and a quarrelling wife.[3] However, they don't mention noses, as Sir Geoffrey does once again; you get the feeling that Jeanne de Rougé must have had an exceptionally lovely nose to have been chosen in marriage by Sir Geoffrey.

How a good woman ought not to stryue with her husbond
(How a good woman ought not to argue with her husband)

A woman should never argue with her husband nor answer him in a way that gives him displeasure, like the wife of a burgess did. She spoke back to her husband so shamefully in front of all the people that he became enraged. He was ashamed and told her once or twice to be quiet and leave. When she wouldn't, her husband angrily hit her with his fist, knocking her to the ground, and kicked her in the face, breaking her nose. After that she was disfigured. And because she was quarrelsome and troublesome she got herself a crooked nose and much harm. It would have been much better for her if she had been quiet, and it was only reasonable and right that the husband have the high words. It is honorable for a woman to hold her peace and leave the proud language to her husband and lord. Also, it is wrong for a woman to argue against her husband, whether she is right or wrong, especially in front of other people. When she finds him alone then it's all right for her to reprehend him and advise him and show him courteously what was right and wrong in what he did. If he is a reasonable man, he will thank her. If he isn't, she has still done what she should have, for it's what a wise woman should do. And by this example, see that headstrong women who argue are not the way they should be—like the wife of a merchant, of whom I will tell you.

The wife of the merchant in the following story, like the wife of the burgess above, are given as examples for Sir Geoffrey's daughters despite their lowly social rank. In one way at least, social status is insignificant: all women, from princesses to peasants, were equally subordinate to their husbands. This is why Sir Geoffrey thinks the next story is an appropriate one for his aristocratic daughters. It's not as much about lower-class merchants, as it is about the obedience wives owe their husbands. Only in the very end does he distinguish among the classes when he advises the proper way for gentlewomen to be chastised: not by beatings but through fair words. However, both the way he states this idea and the surviving legal records indicate that not all medieval gentlemen agreed with him about the best way to deal with wives.

How a woman sprange vpon the table
(How a woman sprang upon the table)

One time some French merchants came home from the fairs, where they had been looking for cloth. As they came from Rouen with their merchandise, one of them said, "It's good for a wife to be obedient to her husband in all ways. Truly," he said, "my wife obeys me well."

And the second said, "I believe my wife obeys me better."

The third merchant said, "Let's have a wager—he wins whose wife obeys her husband best and does his bidding quickest." They agreed, waging a jewel and swearing that none of them would tell their wives about the bargain, except only to say to her, do what I tell you, whatever it might be.

When they came to the first man's house he said to his wife, "Jump into this basin."

"Why?" she asked.

"Because it pleases me, and I want you to," he said.

"First tell me why," she said. When he didn't tell her, she wouldn't jump into the basin, and her husband got angry and hit her.

After this they came to the second merchant's house, and he spoke to his wife just like the first merchant did, telling her to do what he said. When he told her to jump into the basin, she asked him why. In the end, she wouldn't do it, so she was beaten like the first wife was.

Finally, they came to the third man's house, where the table was covered and the food set upon it. The merchant whispered to the other merchants that after dinner he would order his wife to jump into the basin. Then he told his wife that she should do whatever he said. His wife, who loved and feared her husband, listened carefully.

When they began to eat the eggs and there was no salt on the table, the good man said to his wife, "Sail sur table," which in the French means "Jump on the table."

Fearing to disobey him, she sprang onto the table throwing board, food, wine, and platters to the ground.

"What?" said the good man. "Don't you know any other way to act than this? Are you out of your wits?"

"Sir," she said, "I have done your bidding. Didn't you say I should do whatever you told me? I have done it as well as I could, to your harm as much as to mine. For you told me to jump on the table."

"I said there was no salt on the table," he said.

"In good faith, I thought you said to spring onto the table," she said.

Then everybody laughed and all was taken for a jest. The other two merchants said there was no need to have her jump into the basin, for she had done enough, and her husband had won the wager. And she was more praised than the other two who wouldn't do the commandment of their husbands.

Many people chasten their wives with buffets and blows, but gentlewomen ought to be chastised by fair talk and by courtesy. Women ought to fear and obey their lords and husbands and do their commandment whether it is right or wrong, as long as it's not outrageous.

Caxton's version of Sir Geoffrey's story might have left Katherine and Elizabeth Goodwyn puzzled, since the punchline is based on a pun that's lost in translation. In medieval French, the word *sal* can mean both *salt* and *jump* (from Old French *saillir*; a *sailleur* is someone who leaps or jumps). Thus, when the husband asks for salt, he says it in such a way that his wife hears "Jump on the table," and jump she does. Nevertheless, the Goodwyns and other fifteenth-century English readers would have been familiar with the story of the wager about wifely obedience, a common medieval theme, and small is the chance that they would have objected to its moral. In fact, once their brother Richard—home from Calais with his new and improved French—has explained the pun to them, Katherine and Elizabeth would probably have laughed along with him.

The story was popular in Paris, too—so much so that the Householder of Paris isn't content to tell one such tale; his book includes five versions of it. For the Householder, this type of story is a warning that no matter how odd your husband's commands may seem to you, whether they're in earnest or in jest, you must obey them. In a story of his that's similar to Sir Geoffrey's, men wager about their wives' obedience by seeing which ones will unquestioningly jump over a stick when commanded to. The man whose wife does best wins a dinner from his fellows. Although the larger point is obedience, in the Householder's wager stories a wife often wins something for her husband—money or at least a free meal.

In another of these tales, an abbot and a husband bet on whether monks are more obedient to their abbots than wives to their husbands. The monks win and the Householder remarks that it's only natural for them to be more obedient, since they're men. It's equally natural for wives, being women, to be disobedient, he says.

Presumably, the husband in the next story first chastised his wife with "fair talk and courtesy," as Sir Geoffrey advises at the end of the previous tale. Surely, only then would he resort to the mockery we see here.

How a woman ought to obeye her husbond in alle thynge honest
(How a woman ought to obey her lord in all honest things)

I want you to know the tale of the lady who wouldn't come to dinner no matter what her lord said. He sent for her many times, but it didn't matter. Finally he ordered his swineherd, a foul, hideous man, to fetch the kitchen cloth, the one men use to wipe the dishes and platters. He ordered the board to be set before his wife, had it covered with this cloth, and commanded his swineherd to sit beside her. And then he said to her, "Lady, if you will not eat with me, nor come at my command, you shall have the keeper of my swine to keep you company and this cloth to wipe your hands with." She was ashamed and angry, knowing that her lord mocked her, but she recognized her pride and folly. Therefore a woman ought never to refuse to come at the command of her lord if she will have his love and peace. And for good reason humility ought to come first to the woman, who ought to be meek and humble towards her lord.

When Katherine Goodwyn reads this story aloud in her brother Richard's presence, he laughs and says, "I'll remember that when I marry. If my wife doesn't come when I call, I'll make her sit beside the foulest dong-farmer I can find."

"If she isn't obedient, you shouldn't marry her to begin with," Elizabeth says, but Richard tells her he has no choice—all women are as disobedient as they are proud. The next story suggests that Sir Geoffrey agrees. And even Gertrude Rawlings, the 1901 editor of *The Book of the Knight of the Tower*, said that women can't keep secrets, which is portrayed as a form of disobedience in the next story.

How a woman ought in no wyse discouere ne telle the secrete of her husbond. For ouer many euyls come thereof
(How a woman ought never to tell the secrets of her husband because many evils come of it)

I want you to know the story of the squire who tested his young wife. He said, "My friend and love, I'll tell you a great secret if you will keep it secret. The truth is that I have laid two eggs, but for God's love, don't tell anyone."

"By my faith, I won't tell," she said. But the night seemed very long before she could go tell her friend about it. In the morning when she found her gossip, she said to her, "Ha, my sweet friend and gossip, I'll tell you a great marvel if you won't tell anybody." When her friend promised not to tell, she said, "So help me God, my sweet friend, a great marvel has befallen my lord my husband. It's true: he has laid three eggs."

"Sweet Mary," said her gossip, "How can this be? It's a great marvel."

Her gossip didn't keep this secret long, but went to another friend and told her how the squire had laid four eggs. Immediately that gossip went to yet another friend and said the squire had laid five eggs. And at last this story was known so far that people spoke of nothing else but the squire and how he had laid five eggs.

Then the squire called his wife to him and her family, too, and said, "Lady, you have exaggerated the secret I told you, that I laid two eggs. But now, blessed be God, the number is well-grown, for throughout the town men say I have laid five eggs." Then she was ashamed and considered herself a fool and didn't know what to say.

And therefore by this example all good women ought to keep the counsels of their lords and not tell his secrets for anything.

The squire ought to consider himself lucky he was only rumored to have laid five eggs—in the seventeenth-century writer Jean de La Fontaine's version of this story the number has risen to more than a hundred. Egg-laying wasn't necessarily a trait one looked for in a man, but it was widely known in the Middle Ages that women simply couldn't keep secrets. Chaucer's Wife of Bath not only admits telling her husbands' secrets, she takes great pride in her skill. And although the Householder of Paris knows that women can't keep confidences, he begs his wife not to divulge any of his. Both Sir Geoffrey and the Householder accept that women aren't to be trusted with private information, yet they still want their wives and daughters to go against nature by not whispering their husbands' secrets to their friends and neighbors. Like Sir Geoffrey, the Householder gives examples of gossipy women, one of them closely resembling Sir Geoffrey's story—with a twist. In the Householder's version, a woman, not a man, is said to have laid eggs: embarrassed at having dallied in bed with her husband one morning, the woman tells her friend she is ill. In fact, she says—after she extracts the friend's promise of silence—she has laid an egg. By the end of the day, the gossip about town says that she's laid a whole basketful.

The word *gossip* now means someone who revels in revealing intimate information, or the rumors and indiscretions themselves, but in Caxton's day it could mean a close friend. It comes from *god-sib*, which in Anglo-Saxon times meant your sponsor at baptism. You can see the connection between the baptismal sponsor and the close friend, and from there it's an easy step to someone you share secrets with. For Caxton, both men and women are gossips, in the sense of close friends, but today the word has taken on a feminine connotation (and a negative one), perhaps because of the idea, true or false, that women can't keep secrets.

However, not all women are bad. The next story contains not one but two admirable women, one from the Bible, and one from a classical story. After all the negative stories about women, Katherine and Elizabeth would have been relieved to share with Richard a story not only about wise and strong women, but men who are jealous and cowardly. You can picture their brown-haired brother scowling good-naturedly; these biblical and classical women might make good role models for his sisters, but they're nothing like the women he knows.[4]

How euery good woman ought to answere for her lord
(How every good woman ought to answer for her lord)

A good lady who ought to be praised is Abigail, whose lord was full of anger, and cruel and quarrelsome towards his neighbors. When he offended King David, the king intended to have him put to death. But the wise Abigail so humbled herself to the king that by her pleasant, seemly words she made peace for her lord. She also saved him from many other perils that he fell in through his sharp tongue. This good lady ought to be praised for amending his folly. Likewise, every good woman must be patient with her lord and answer for him, no matter how angry and cruel he is to her, and she ought to keep him from all perils.

There was another good lady, the wife of a Roman senator, who is mentioned in the chronicles of the Romans. This senator was jealous of his wife for no cause, and was cruel to her. One time he accused somebody of treason, and that person challenged him to battle. On the day of the joust the senator was afraid and dared not come. He sent word to the senate that he was sick and that he would send somebody to joust for him—but he couldn't find anybody to do so. When his valiant wife saw her lord's cowardice and the shame coming to him, she armed herself and came to the field. And because God saw her generosity and that she did her duty, he gave her so much force and strength that she won the victory.

When the jousting was finished, the emperor wanted to know who the senator's champion was, so the lady's helmet was unlocked and she was known. From that day forward, the emperor and all the town gave her even greater honor than they had before.

You can see from this story that every good woman must humbly tolerate that in her lord which she may not amend. She who tolerates a great deal from her lord without showing any emotion receives ten times more honor than she who has no cause to be patient or who is not patient, as Solomon says.

As Katherine finishes reading the story, she and Elizabeth give Richard smug, self-satisfied looks. Not to be outdone, however, he reminds them of Jeanne D'Arc, who was hardly regarded as a hero by the English. "Dressing in armor, trying to lead armies," he scoffs, "and where did she end up? Burned for heresy."

Round Two to Richard.

He would have thoroughly agreed with the Householder of Paris, with his stolid merchant's sensibility. Good wives are those whose husbands look forward to coming home to them after their business out in the world, the Householder says. They have suffered cold, rain, snow, and poor lodgings, and they rely on their wives to keep them in clean linen, he says, revealing his middle-class background. Some of the demands he makes of his wife would have been undertaken by several male servants in an aristocratic household such as Sir Geoffrey's. For example, the Householder says that when a man returns home, his wife makes sure his shoes are taken off in front of the fire, that his feet are washed, and he has clean hose and shoes, good food and drink, and good tending. Then she sees to it that he is "well bedded in white sheets and nightcaps, well covered with good furs, and assuaged with other joys and desports, privities, loves and secrets whereof I am silent. And the next day fresh shirts and garments."[5] Except for the private matters about which the Householder is silent, the rest of these matters would be seen to by servants in Sir Geoffrey's castle.

Nor would Jeanne and Anne have to learn how to keep their husbands' room free of fleas and flies, the way the Householder's wife does. Although she, like the Goodwyn sisters, would have several servants to do the actual work, she would have to give those servants instructions. To this end, her husband gives her several remedies, such as this one: place chunks of bread spread with glue or turpentine in a room and set lighted candles in the center of each bread chunk to draw the fleas, who will then be stuck to the glue.[6] Part of the reason the Householder's wife should go to this trouble is to make sure her husband is so comfortable that he will never seek out the company of other women. If he does, the Householder seems to imply, she has only herself to blame.

On this point, Sir Geoffrey would probably agree with the Householder, despite the latter's thoroughly bourgeois notions about housekeeping. Furthermore, aristocratic though Sir Geoffrey is, he is equally concerned with possessions as the Householder. The following story, again biblical, illustrates the connection between manners and physical wealth. Had she not been so courteous to her husband's family, Ruth would have been left destitute after his death.

Thexample of the noble lady Ruth
(The example of the noble lady Ruth)

I'll tell you about a good lady named Ruth, from whom issued King David. The holy scripture greatly praises this good lady, who marvelously loved God and honored and obeyed her lord. And for the love of him she honored and loved his friends and made better cheer to them than to her own friends. After her lord died, his son by another wife intended to leave her nothing, neither land nor property. Thinking that she was from a distant country and far from her friends, he intended to take it all for himself. But her lord's friends and relatives, who loved her for her great generosity and the service she had done them while her lord was alive, helped her against their friends and relatives, so that she got everything that was rightfully hers. Thus, because of the way she treated her lord's friends and relatives, she saved her property. This is a good example of how all good women ought to serve and honor their lords' friends and kin, for a greater token of love they may not show to them and good may come of it.

Christine de Pizan gives similar advice to princesses and "every sensible woman" about the importance of good relations with your in-laws and your husband's companions. Like Sir Geoffrey, Christine suggests that treating them well is not an end in itself so much as insurance for the future. Not only will this kind of behavior please your husband, it will cause those close to him to take care of you both before and after his death. Getting their favor is important, Christine says, "for one has very often seen women greatly harmed by their husband's relatives."[7] She speaks from experience; for years after her husband's death, Christine found herself the unwilling defendant in lawsuits about who owned the rights to his property.

Both Christine and Sir Geoffrey use the example of the biblical Queen Esther to caution women against speaking back to their husbands. Sir Geoffrey liked the story so much that he used it twice, including in a tale called, "How no good woman should argue with her husband when he is angry."[8] Queen Esther loved and feared her husband, who was, in Sir Geoffrey's words,

a wicked and cruel man who said many insulting things to her. Despite his behavior, when they were before other people she never said anything that might anger him. But afterwards, when they were alone and she saw that the time and place were convenient, she courteously showed him his faults. And therefore the king loved her greatly and said that he couldn't be angry with his wife because she reproved him with such fair and sweet words.

Sir Geoffrey goes on to say that one of the best qualities a woman can have is to keep herself from speaking back to her husband's angry words. He and Christine are in agreement: a wife's duty is to humble herself toward her husband and to do all she can to keep him happy.

The stories in this chapter make it clear that medieval husbands and wives were far from equal. Much more important than love to a marriage is obedience—a wife's to her husband. Children were to be as subordinate to their fathers as wives to their spouses; yet, in chapter 8, Sir Geoffrey's stories about children rarely touch on obedience. Perhaps Jeanne and Anne never disobeyed him. Or perhaps he worried more about their behavior in the future, after they were married and beyond his reach—and having children of their own.

CHAPTER 8

BEAT THEM WHEN THEY DESERVE IT — RAISING CHILDREN

For many years, people believed the contention set forth by scholar Phillipe Ariès in his influential 1960 book, *Centuries of Childhood*: that no concept of childhood existed in the Middle Ages.[1] Not until the seventeenth century, Ariès said, did the idea of childhood as a stage of life develop, and Lawrence Stone, another influential scholar, said it didn't happen until the mid-eighteenth century.[2] Other historians built on Ariès's views, telling us that medieval parents didn't love their young children because with such a high infant mortality rate, they couldn't invest themselves emotionally in such a low-risk proposition as a child, that child abandonment was widespread, that parents didn't work very hard to keep their children alive, and that they didn't mourn them if they died. No wonder people call them the Dark Ages! Fortunately, scholars such as Barbara Hanawalt, author of *Growing Up in Medieval London: The Experience of Childhood in History*, and Shulamith Shahar, who wrote *Childhood in the Middle Ages*, came along. By examining a wide variety of medieval sources, including court records and coroners' reports with their fascinating details, they've given us a much more accurate picture of medieval family life. They have restored both childhood and love to medieval families.

It's surprising that the views of Ariès and his followers were so widely accepted when so much well-known medieval literature belies them. For example, in *Pearl*, a widely anthologized fourteenth-century English poem, the poet mourns the death of his young daughter, his Pearl without price. A Middle High German poem, *Parzival*, gives delightful details of Parzival's childhood and his mother's attachment to him. When Parzival is out in the forest with his toy bow and arrows, he sees knights in shining armor riding through the forest and, from his childish perspective, thinks they are angels. His mother has tried to shelter him from the knowledge of chivalry because she fears he will leave her to become a knight. She knows she can't bear losing her beloved son. And the story of Patient Griselda, discussed in chapter 7, makes no secret of the pain Griselda suffers at the supposed death of her two children. In the scenes where she has to give them up to her lord and master's henchmen, the audience clearly sees how strong her love for her children is.

These poems and others imply the existence of both parental love and the concept of childhood; other kinds of medieval texts discuss theories about children more forthrightly. Authorities such as Gregory the Great and Isidore of Seville, whose works influenced later medieval scholars, wrote about the three stages of childhood, *infantia* (birth to age seven), *pueritia* (seven to twelve for girls and seven to fourteen for boys), and finally *adolescentia* ("twelve or fourteen to adulthood"). These ideas, taken from Greek and Roman writers, were well known and echoed in sermons, in treatises about education, even in poems about the ages of man.[3] One thirteenth-century Italian writer added yet another stage to early childhood: from birth to "the appearance of teeth." His second stage stopped at age seven. Other writers found different subdivisions, one seeing new stages at ages four and twelve.[4]

So, contrary to Ariès's views, medieval people did think of childhood as a separate stage of life, and they did love and value their children, even if childbirth was dangerous and the infant mortality rate was high.

However, the higher you were on the social scale, the less time you spent with your child (a practice that still prevails—think of nannies and boarding schools favored by the wealthy). When Christine de Pizan tells princesses to visit their children and to supervise their discipline and their teachers, we realize how distanced royalty could be from their own offspring. Not only were wet nurses employed, governesses and tutors helped raise royal children. Members of the aristocracy, especially on country estates, would see much more of their children, although they, too, would employ wet nurses and tutors. Peasant mothers, however, breastfed their own children, raised them, disciplined them, and taught them.

Their mother would have been a daily presence in the lives of the Tour Landry girls. Servants would have helped them wash and dress when they emerged from the bed they shared in the mornings, but since few medieval buildings had hallways connecting rooms, their mother probably made her way through their chamber on her way out of her own, as she headed for the stairs. We can picture her stopping to look down at her still-sleeping daughters, perhaps smoothing a tendril of brown hair out of Anne's face, before assuming her duties of running the household. The girls probably went with her to morning Mass and saw her at meals. On most days, they would have joined her when the ladies gathered for needlework and entertainment. When Jeanne, Anne, and Marie each turned five or six, their mother would have listened to them reciting the prayers a nurse had taught them—*Ave Maria* and *Paternoster*—and she might have helped them memorize a favorite prayer of hers, or shown them a miniature she liked to meditate on in her book of hours.

The girls would have seen their father much less frequently since he was often away at war. Even when he was home, he would have been busy with the business of being a wealthy landowner: talking to his estate managers, entertaining visiting noblemen, making sure his sergeants were keeping his men-at-arms in fighting trim. But at meals he might see his daughters, and during times of recreation, such as the garden encounter he mentions in his prologue, when his daughters came walking toward him.

Sir Geoffrey doesn't mention young children often, but even his short treatment of the subject gives the lie to Ariès and his followers by indicating that he thinks of childhood as a separate stage of life. As is often the case, the focus of his stories about children is appropriate Christian behavior. For example, within a chapter about "the Valyaunt lady Rebecca the wyf of ysaac,"[5] the Knight includes a story about an unnamed couple who, like Rebecca and Isaac, were long unable to have children.

> Because they prayed for it, God sent them a handsome boy, and shortly after that, another son who was ugly and lame. Truly, they should have given their first child to the Church; but when they saw how deformed their second son was, they decided to send him instead, keeping the first son to be their heir. This angered God so much that he took both sons from them, and they lived in sorrow, never having any other children.
>
> You should never make God any promises you can't keep, and never mock God the way this couple did. Nor should people take their children away from the monastery once they have been given to it, which I have seen happen many times.
>
> I have also seen with my own eyes people being taken from abbeys for the sake of the lands and possessions they would inherit when their relatives died. None of those who were removed from the monasteries ever lived peaceably—in the end they all came to naught. This is true

of women as well: I didn't know a single one who was taken from a monastery who didn't have an evil end. They were defamed and dishonored and died in childbirth, or else had some other bad end to their lives. You can see from this that men shouldn't take from God that which is his.

Both younger boys who wouldn't inherit and girls who weren't to be married might be promised to the church for life, whether or not they were particularly religiously inclined. But you had to be wealthy to place your child in a monastery or convent, so only the nobility, perhaps one percent of the population, usually gave any of their children to the church. It was a convenient place to leave weak, handicapped, or illegitimate children, and church officials sometimes complained about the custom[6] even as they benefited from the wealth that accompanied the child. A girl was required to bring a dowry to the convent, one not quite as large as she would have brought with her to a marriage, whereas boys' families usually gave some kind of gift to the monastery. This meant that generally only noble girls entered convents, but a few boys might also come from lower classes (particularly the boys who joined less prestigious orders). Some noble girls who would eventually marry were sent to convents to be educated instead of being brought up by tutors and governesses at home.

In the next story we see that sparing the rod was hardly considered a proper way to raise a child. Although the story's purpose is to warn parents against cursing their children to the devil, Sir Geoffrey compares cursing to beating and advocates the latter. Boys were routinely whipped and beaten when they were bad or when they didn't learn their lessons at school. Some writers, such as Anselm of Canterbury, spoke out against corporal punishment, and in doing so, they indicate how common the practice was. Girls were also beaten, although probably less often; after all, the writers who mention whippings are usually discussing them in the context of formal education, and girls received far less formal education than boys. Christine de Pizan tells princesses that they should supervise their children's discipline, but she doesn't specify what kinds of punishments they should receive. The wise lady will correct her children "severely herself if they misbehave," she writes,[7] but she goes into no further details, the way Sir Geoffrey does below.

He begins with Jacob and Leah who—he says—never cursed their sons when they were bad, instead finding other ways to punish them, including beating them. For, Sir Geoffrey writes, it's better to beat your children a hundred times than to curse them once—as the next part of his story shows.

How the faders and moders ought to praye for theyr children
(How fathers and mothers ought to pray for their children)
Cursing your children brings about perils, like it did to a woman and her husband who were both easily angered and always brawling with each other. Once their son did something wrong, and both his mother and father cursed him bitterly. Angrily, the child answered them foolishly. This filled the parents with wrath, and they cursed him to the devil. The Fiend came and, seizing the boy by one hand, lifted him from the ground. Wherever he touched the child, fire sprang out—and thus his hand was destroyed. Because of this, he was in peril all his life. Keep this example in your memory and see by it that there is great danger in cursing your children and wishing them any evil, and even greater peril in giving them to the devil out of anger.

The devil is all too ready to take that which is offered to him. Indeed, in a story the fourteenth-century English preacher Robert Manning of Brunne tells, when a mother curses her daughter for not being ready with her clothing after she bathes, the devil snatches the daughter away to his infernal regions.[8]

Parents had to be careful in other ways as well. The excessive celebration over the birth of a son in the next story turns into tragedy for the parents and reminds readers to be moderate, even in their joy. It would have been far better had the parents in this story celebrated through prayers and Masses rather than with feasts and jousts.

How men ought to sette and put theyr children in the wylle of god
(How men ought to entrust their children to the will of God)
I want you to know about a queen of Cyprus who was too old to have children. Nevertheless, because her husband was so good, at his prayer God gave them a son. To celebrate their immense joy, they put on a feast and a joust, and sent for all the great lords and ladies of the land. The feast was nobly and richly held, and nothing was lacking: there was plenty of silk and cloth of gold, and the palace resounded with music. The jousting and the tourneying was fair to see, the knights running at each other like they were in a battle. What pleasure and joy there were. But all this displeased God, and by his providence and will, the child died. When his death was known throughout the court, the joy and mirth turned into great sadness and sorrow. Everyone left, going sorrowfully to their own homes. And thus men ought not to

rejoice too much when God sends them children, for often it displeases God, who immediately takes his gift away again.

The baby's death, like the deaths of many a modern child, is seen as the will of God. But for a medieval audience, God's actions were often considered a direct reaction to human behavior—in this case too much worldly rejoicing instead of quiet, prayerful thanksgiving. Similarly, the case of the parents who reneged on their promise to dedicate their first-born to a monastery and thus lost both sons, along with many other stories in Sir Geoffrey's book, illustrates a common medieval perception—the causal relationship between earthly action and divine reaction. When your own behavior can lead to such dire consequences for others, the necessity of confessing and expiating your sins becomes apparent, as does the importance of educating your children about their duty to God and Church.

Sir Geoffrey's views about girls' education are striking, as we see in the following story. Like the Householder of Paris, who writes in French for his wife (and who offers her religious works such as saints' lives from his library), Sir Geoffrey expects his daughters to be able to read. He knows his ideas about female education are slightly unusual, as the last paragraph of his story indicates. He's aware that other people will disagree with him when he says that girls should know how to read, but he is in agreement with Christine de Pizan about the purpose of education. She stresses first of all that they learn "to serve God," and then to "read and write," and after that, she tells princesses that their children's teachers should make sure they learn their prayers well.

Christine's own education was most unusual for her day. Her father, a court astronomer, taught her to read Latin, and she believes that other children should be taught the same: "The wise lady will try to get the children's father to agree that they be introduced to Latin and that they understand some of the sciences," she writes.[9] Perhaps she means only sons here, since she goes on to talk specifically about daughters, for whom she advocates literacy so they can read "religious offices and the Mass" as well as "books of devotion and contemplation or ones dealing with good behaviour." However, she writes, "the princess will not tolerate books containing any vain things, follies or dissipation to be brought before her daughter."[10] One wonders what Christine would have thought of the Knight's book, which, although it teaches good behavior, is also filled with stories about wicked women. Like the Knight, Christine is deeply concerned with manners and reputation, and she charges the princess with finding governesses known for their wisdom, their respectability, and their high rank.

Aristocratic girls such as Jeanne and Anne also needed to be educated in how to become good wives. Doing so encompassed learning the rules of etiquette, as well as how to ride horses and hunt with falcons, how to sing and play a stringed instrument, how to play games such as chess and backgammon, and how to tell stories or riddles to entertain guests at a manor or castle. They probably didn't learn a foreign language, but their mother might teach them a little practical medicine (such as how to make licorice tea or milk of almonds for the sick), and how to manage the household when their husbands were away.[11] They would certainly have spent long hours sitting quietly with their needles or spindles while their mother or her ladies-in-waiting, or perhaps the girls' aunts and older cousins, taught them and examined their work. Like their brothers, they learned to read and possibly to write a little from a tutor, perhaps one of the priests or clerics who helped compile the stories for Sir Geoffrey's book. Their texts would include the Psalms and other Latin prayers, although they would have learned the Latin phonetically, not actually reading it as much as reciting it with little comprehension. The family might also have owned or borrowed a few manuscripts with French romances in them, texts that gave a very different view of feminine behavior than Sir Geoffrey's stories.[12]

Jeanne and Anne probably didn't spend much time taking care of their baby sister, since aristocrats hired nurses to care for babies and the very young. However, when they were little girls, they might have practiced the art of mothering by caring for their dolls.

Nor would they have learned to set a table or serve a meal. That was considered boys' knowledge (and most cooks in nobles' kitchens were men). While Jeanne and Anne stayed at home, their brothers Charles and Arcades were sent off to become pages in another aristocratic household, that of Pierre, the lord of Craon, whose estate was nearby. Other boys went further from home. Christine de Pizan sent her son Jean to England to become a page to John Montagu, the Earl of Salisbury.[13] From the age of eight or ten (and sometimes even younger), boys learned to become gentlemen and made social connections by serving first as pages and later as squires in a noble household not their own. In addition to learning to dance, sing, and play an instrument, they were taught a little reading, games such as chess, and the rudiments of knighthood: riding and fighting. Some of this they had already learned as little boys, when they staged miniature jousts with their toy knights. Noble boys owned expensive toys such as metal knights, castles, and even siege engines, and they and less wealthy boys also played games with balls, cards, and dice.[14] They continued some of this play when they became pages, but now they also had to work, serving the adults at the table and in the household, and learning the intricate rules about placing food and utensils on the table and serving people in order of their social rank. When the boys were about fifteen, they became squires and began their serious military training. Once they left home, Charles and Arcades rarely saw their sisters or the rest of their family.

Whereas Sir Geoffrey's daughters lived in country castles and would have been taught by the priests and clerks in Sir Geoffrey's employ, as well as by tutors and governesses, Katherine and Elizabeth Goodwyn probably would have been taught to read English by their mother, perhaps with some help from their brother.[15] Their brothers, on the other hand, might have attended a grammar school run by the parish, where they learned Latin as well as French and English. Neither of the sisters may have learned to write, although the evidence about late medieval girls' education is contradictory. A middle-class girl's literacy could be a valuable asset when she was ready to marry, since if she married a wealthy guild member—as Katherine and Elizabeth could expect to do—she could help her husband with his business, and even take charge of it were he to become ill or die,[16] so it's possible that they would have indeed learned to write, and perhaps even spent some time at a grammar school.[17]

Boys and girls attended separate schools in some cities, but in many German, French, and English schools, they learned side by side. Jean Froissart, author of the famous *Chronicles*, grew up in fourteenth-century Valenciennes, a lace-making town in northern France, where he says he and the little girls at his school "exchanged nuts, apples, and pears."[18] When they weren't giving each other gifts, they learned to read French and sometimes to write it, to do some arithmetic, to be pious and well behaved, and to know their prayers. Like Froissart's female playmates, who left school by about thirteen, Katherine and Elizabeth would also spend much of their time being educated by their mother in how to manage a household, how to weave and sew, and like aristocratic girls, how to spin and embroider.[19] Unlike their aristocratic counterparts, however, they would also have learned recipes for cleaning, cooking, and washing clothes, although in a wealthy merchant household like the Goodwyn's, they might have overseen the servants who performed the actual labor rather than soiling their own hands.

As Katherine and Elizabeth's brother Richard got older, he would begin his education in the wool trade by accompanying his father on buying and selling trips. His ability to read and write was as important as his facility in bargaining, especially since in the fifteenth century, many guilds began requiring literacy of their members. Eventually, at about twenty, Richard would become his father's agent in Calais, traveling there with a trusted servant or two to see to his father's business affairs, and regularly writing letters to his family. During his visits home, he would teach his sisters new songs he'd learned, and new dances, as well. Richard's younger brother John, however, excelled in his Latin lessons, so impressing the parish priest that John found himself studying at Oxford to become a clergyman instead of following his father and brother into the wool trade.

The children of merchants and craftsmen less wealthy than the Goodwyns might have spent a year or two in a grammar school, or they might have become apprentices. Both boys and girls were apprenticed, girls most often to silkworkers, weavers, embroiderers, and makers of thread and of dresses. Not until they were between fourteen and eighteen were young people apprenticed in fifteenth-century London, and boys remained apprentices for seven to ten years.[20] Girls, on the other hand, might leave their apprenticeships to marry, but they often continued earning money through their craft as married women. Peasants, however, who made up over ninety percent of the medieval population, received no formal schooling at all. Instead, they watched their parents and learned by doing, starting with simple tasks such as feeding the chickens and chasing behind the furrow to scare away seed-hungry birds. How to say the Paternoster, the Creed, the Ave Maria, taught to them by their mothers; how to plow, sow, reap, thatch roofs, tend herds and slaughter them; how to bake, clean, spin, weave, sew, milk cows, grow a kitchen garden, raise children, and go to confession once a year—this was the schooling of the peasantry.

Despite the vast social gulf between peasants and princesses, in one way women of all classes shared an experience: needlework. They would have been taught to spin, a skill so necessary for the production of cloth, by their mothers, their sisters, their governesses, and other ladies in the household. In manuscript images, medieval women are frequently pictured with distaff in hand. In the records of

Joan of Arc's trial (and the later hearing to dismiss the charges of heresy against her) she and her peasant neighbors mention spinning as a daily activity, one that could be undertaken while watching sheep or babies. Aristocratic women sat together each day to spin, hem, or embroider, as did women of the merchant classes. All women spun, and none of them needed formal schooling to learn how.

In the next story, a little boy's formal education—not to mention his life—is cut short, but not before it assures him a place in heaven. He attends a grammar school such as the one Froissart went to, and like the school in Chaucer's *Prioress's Tale*, where a little boy hears the older students learning a hymn to the Virgin. In that tale, like the one that follows, the little boy is killed by non-Christians (in Chaucer's version, Jews instead of the more generic "pagans"), and in both, a miracle is performed. Both stories present the kind of negative stereotype of non-Christians so common in the medieval West.

How men oughte to sette and put theyr children to scole
(How men ought to send their children to school)

I'll tell you about a nine-year-old child who had been at school four years. Through the grace of God he was able to argue questions of faith with the pagans and master them all. They were very angry with him and spied on him secretly and hurled stones at him. When they thought they held him in their power, they told him that if he would not forsake his god, they would slay him. But no matter how much they tormented him, he held his faith in God.

"Where is your god?" they asked.

"In heaven and in my heart," he said.

In anger, they slew him, and then they opened his side to see if he told the truth. When they cut his heart in two pieces, a white dove flew out of it. From this example, some were converted to the faith of God.

And therefore, as you can see from this story, it is good to put children to school when they are young, to make them learn the books of wisdom, that is to say the books of good knowledge where men will find out about the salvation of both the body and the soul. And don't have them learn from books of fallacies or vanities of the world, for it is better to hear good teachings spoken of that may profit both the body and the soul than to read and study the fables and lies of which no good will come.

This story might not inspire modern readers to take their studies seriously, if a grisly death and a miraculous transformation are all you get for your troubles. But perhaps we're simply too accustomed to metaphors staying metaphorical, not springing to life. That's no common pigeon flying out of the little boy's heart; that white dove is the Holy Ghost itself. Medieval readers would consider the little boy lucky to have been so honored by God—theoretically, at least. Most of them, like most of us, would prefer such an honor be given to someone else.

Sir Geoffrey ends this passage by commenting specifically on women's education.

> Some people say they don't want their wives and daughters to have any learning or to know how to write. I answer them that as for writing, it doesn't matter if a woman knows anything of it, but reading is good and profitable for all women. For a woman who can read may better know the perils of the soul and of her salvation than she who can't, and that's been proven.

We lump reading and writing under one term, *literacy*, but medieval people distinguished between the two. It can be very difficult to know what a medieval record means when it says a person is illiterate. Particularly before the thirteenth century when the vernacular became the language lay people were educated in, the word "illiterate" might mean someone can only read and write in English and French, but not in Latin. It might mean someone can read Latin, but not write it. Or it might mean that someone can read in no language at all, nor write in any, either.

We have to be careful with other kinds of evidence, as well. In the fifteenth century, Margaret Paston sent letters to her husband, letters physically penned by someone else. Does this mean she doesn't know how to write? Not necessarily. Compare modern businesspeople who often dictate their letters to secretaries. For Margaret Paston, as for these businesspeople, not writing your own letters is also bound up with time and prestige. The ability to pay someone else to perform tasks you consider time-consuming or menial raises your social status—both now and in the Middle Ages.

But for the Householder of Paris, it was important that his fifteen-year-old wife know how to write her own letters; he was a merchant who traveled, and he wanted her to be able to write him when he was away from home, letting him know how the household was managing—or not—without him. And, like Sir Geoffrey's daughters, she could read; in fact, her husband owned a number of books he hoped she would avail herself of, since they would aid her soul in its quest for salvation.

The final story in this section tells us a little about the composition of medieval families. Divorce makes for blended families these days; death was the cause in the medieval period. Both widows and widowers often remarried, bringing their children with them into the new marriage. Sir Geoffrey himself had stepchildren, the sons he inherited when he married a wealthy widow after his first wife, Jeanne de Rougé, died. His youngest daughter, Marie, married her brother Charles's stepson. In the following story, ostensibly about how a wife should react to her husband's anger, Sir Geoffrey shifts his focus to very practical advice about the treatment of stepchildren, using as his example a blended biblical family.

> **How the good woman ought to pease the yre of her husbond whanne she seeth hym wrothe**
> (How the good woman ought to appease her husband's ire when she sees him angry)
> I'll tell you about how one of the wives of King David appeased her lord's anger. You have heard how Amon took his sister's virginity, and how Absolon avenged this shame and had him put to death, and then fled from the region because King David intended to have him slain. But this good lady obtained a pardon for him by giving King David many good reasons. Yet she wasn't Absolon's mother, only his father's wife. Nevertheless, she was such a good lady that she loved not only her lord, but also his children.
> Every good woman ought to act this way. She can't show her lord any greater love than to love his children from other women. By doing so, she brings honor to herself, and at the end nothing but good may come to her, as it did to this good lady. For when the king was dead, some would have taken her rights from her, but Absolon wouldn't allow it. He said before them all, "Although she isn't my mother, she always loved me, and many times she obtained pardon for me from the king my father. Therefore I will not allow her to forfeit anything due to her." And therefore, here is a good example about how every good woman ought to honor and love her lord's children and his relatives.

The story itself, although biblical in origin, doesn't follow the Bible closely. It's doubtful that Sir Geoffrey would have owned a copy of the Old Testament in which to look it up. Besides, his immediate source for it was *The Mirror for Good Women*, in which biblical stories had already been reshaped in order to reinforce a particular moral. Details were often added and plots shifted to fit the teller's purpose. Here, it's important to the teller that Absolon dies after David does so he can repay his stepmother's kindness. In the Bible, however, David outlives his son. Furthermore, the woman who pleads Absolon's case in 2 Samuel 14 is not even David's wife.

But Jeanne and Anne wouldn't have known that. They would have heard of the principal players in the story, and they would have understood their father's message. To honor their husbands, women should love their children from previous marriages. Doing so brings them not just honor, but the strong possibility of financial security after their husbands die. The same reasoning applied in the story about Ruth, in chapter 7, who honored her husband's kin. Although bringing honor to your husband this way is important, practical matters are even more urgent: the benefits your husband's friends and relatives offer you after his death might mean the difference between wealth and penury.

In chapter 9, we'll see some of the things a medieval woman might want to spend her money on, if she had plenty of it: clothing and fashion accessories.

CHAPTER 9

I TELL YOU, I MUST HAVE IT—MEDIEVAL FASHION

The ideal body for a medieval woman—small breasts, round bellies—differs enormously from today's standard, yet blonde hair is prized in both eras.[1] However, medieval women's hair was often hidden under veils, wimples, and more elaborate headdresses. In fact, in the popular view of the Middle Ages, all ladies wear tall, pointed hats fluttering with gauzy fabric. By the time Katherine and Elizabeth Goodwyn were reading *The Book of the Knight of the Tower* in the late fifteenth century, the *atour* had come into fashion in England and the most spectacular ones were almost three feet high.[2] If you examine manuscript paintings of women wearing them, you'll see they've plucked the hair away from their temples and foreheads for a more stylish look. To us, their bald, white, oval foreheads may look like chicken eggs, but egg-like, bald foreheads were the height of fifteenth-century fashion. A little loop of velvet hung from the hat onto your forehead on almost every type of *atour*, accentuating your baldness.

The *atour* itself took many different forms, from the tall, veiled cone to a shorter fez-like hat, with or without a veil. Like early-twentieth-century ladies' hats, they were "ephemeral confections," in the words of one historian, since fashion changed rapidly.[3] Ladies might take apart one they had already worn to a joust, using elements of it to construct a new headdress to wear to a feast the following week. At the end of the reign of the *atour*, gentlewomen began to wear them with velvet frontpieces that surrounded their faces, and later still, the frontlets stayed whereas the pointed hats departed.

In thirteenth-century France, the headdresses with two horns that figure in some of Sir Geoffrey's stories were popular. In *The Romance of the Rose*, Jean de Meun describes them as "such towering horns . . . as never buck nor stag nor unicorn could boast."[4] Double horns seem to have made a resurgence at the beginning of the fifteenth century. In both periods, preachers exhorted women not to wear them because they imitated the devil. They were certainly the devil to construct, requiring numerous straight pins and a great deal of starch. In 1391, Charles VII's queen bought "9,800 English pins of various sizes" for her headdresses, as well as starch and gum to stiffen her veils to give them an airy appearance.[5]

In the fourteenth century, horned headdresses competed with other fashions, including hoods and a round headdress called a *bourrelet*, which was still fashionable a century later. The earliest French manuscript of Sir Geoffrey's book, from the century after his death, shows Jeanne and her mother wearing *bourrelets*, embroidered gowns, furred and lined sleeves—the very finery their father fulminates against. The same painting shows Sir Geoffrey just as fashionably dressed, wearing "a stylish blue *houppelande* [a short, showy cloak], with dagged sleeves, scarlet hose, and an extravagant lavender headdress."[6] His younger daughter, Anne, is the only one whose clothing would pass her father's test—she wears that simple gray dress and no headdress at all.[7]

Certainly the Householder of Paris would have approved of Anne's clothing. For his own wife, he cautions neatness and simplicity, asking that the collars of her shift and each of her overgarments be laid tidily over each other, that no hair escape from her wimple, and that her kerchief and hood be as well-arrayed as, in descending order, her short surcoat, her robe, and the flannel dress she wears over her chemise.[8] In a manuscript painting of the Householder and his wife, she indeed wears simple but refined clothing, nothing to call attention to herself, while her husband is much more fashionably attired. Like Sir Geoffrey, he wears a *houppelande* that shows off his legs and his stylishly long, pointed shoes.[9] Her gown is deep blue and trimmed with white fur at the collar, the sleeves, and the bottom edge, and her headdress is simply constructed of white fabric. But her husband wears an elaborately large red turban that matches his red *houppelande*, which itself is trimmed with brown fur. His collar is a different shade of red, and his hose and shoes are black.

In the Late Middle Ages, men's fashions changed much more quickly than women's because, whereas women always wore floor-length gowns, men's gowns could go from the floor on up. And up they went, so much so that by the late fifteenth century, young English and French courtiers were shocking their elders by wearing tunics short enough to reveal their buttocks and genitals "in the same way as people usually dress monkeys," according to a Burgundian chronicler writing in 1467. The same chronicler derides young men's long hair and bangs, the slits in their tunic sleeves that showed off their white shirts below their tunics, their stuffed gowns and shoulder pads, and worst of all, their piked shoes, the pointed toes stretching twelve inches or longer. An English writer of this period complaining about the same fashions includes tight hose in his list of wrongs.[10] In its 1462 ordinances, the guild of London Mercers forbade its members from wearing such fashions, particularly stuffed gowns and shoes with pikes.[11] As an aspirant to the guild, Katherine and Elizabeth Goodwyn's brother Richard would have had to follow its rules instead of dressing as he might have wished, "like a gallant or man of court," wearing long hair and bright-colored clothing.[12] Nor could he have shown off his slender, shapely legs—in the Middle Ages, men's legs, not women's, were associated with sex appeal.

And men's fashionable headdresses certainly rivaled women's. In fourteenth-century France, men twisted their long hoods around their heads so they looked like turbans. Or they might have worn riding hats, like the beaver hats with ostrich plumes Froissart mentions.[13] The varieties of men's headdresses certainly kept pace with women's fashions.

According to one scholar, fashion, that is, dress designed to get attention (as opposed to strictly utilitarian clothing), became important in mid-fourteenth-century Europe. Both men and women had previously worn long rectangular tunics that could be belted to create drapery, but now men began to favor short doublets that showed off their legs, their brightly colored hose, and sometimes their buttocks. Women's gowns became much more tight fitting and low cut.[14] Men and women both wore "dagged" material, cloth with small, decorative holes cut in it. These styles were far less economical than their predecessors. Dagging wasted fabric, and because of the way these gowns and doublets hugged the body, they couldn't as easily be given to others, an important point at a time when rich clothing was made to last for many years and was often a legacy.

For Christine de Pizan, as for the Burgundian chronicler, fashion is important in the way it defines social class. Both of them mourn the days when people wore the styles befitting their rank. Nowadays, Christine says, nobles dress like royals, aristocrats wear the clothes of the nobility, and worst of all, the bourgeoisie dress like their betters.[15] Not only was this a sign of the breakdown of the social order, some of these miscreants were breaking sumptuary laws, the locally determined civil decrees that regulated who could wear gray squirrel fur on their sleeves, how many dresses a bourgeois woman could own, or who was allowed precious stones on their clothing. Chaucer's middle-class guildsmen flout the sumptuary laws that forbid them from carrying tableknives made of silver (only the nobility could do that). Their wives are just as proud, demanding to be called "Madame," even though their social class didn't warrant the title, "My Lady." Monastic rules also defined appropriate clothing, and Chaucer satirizes his Monk in part by trimming his sleeves with *grys*, or gray squirrel fur—which was explicitly forbidden to monks.

In Caxton's England and Sir Geoffrey's France, moralists connected men's and women's excessive fashions with moral decay, as they would half a millennium later, in the case of 1960s Haight-Ashbury styles. In England, such excess was said to bring about great evil, and in France, some moralists found these fashions responsible for the English invasions. When you discover that Charles VII's queen owned "a belt made entirely of gold . . . set with rubies and sapphires," and that in 1392 she bought 111 pairs of shoes, you can see the moralists' point.[16] (In fairness to the queen, however, it's not clear how many of these shoes were intended for her ladies.)

Sir Geoffrey is less concerned with his daughters' effect on national security than with the safety of their souls. He wavers in the extremity of his condemnation of finery, often acknowledging the importance of fashionable clothing even as he derides it. It's been argued that Sir Geoffrey advertises the very styles he decries by describing them in such detail, for example, in the following story where he mentions embroidered edges and hoods among the new *gyses*, or fashions.[17] His depictions of the latest trends in headdresses, gowns, and accessories, the ones he wants his daughters to eschew, would have made these clothes desirable—both to his daughters and to other readers of his book, including girls such as Katherine and Elizabeth Goodwyn. For the Goodwyns, as for Jeanne and Anne, these conflicting values and admonitions may have been as confusing as the mixed messages about innocence, abstinence, and sexuality that bombard today's teenaged girls.

In the following story we see a fashion that was becoming trendy in the fourteenth century—women's skirts with slits in the sides that allow the colors of the *cotte*, or undergarment, to show through. Preachers warned against this style, calling the shocking slits "the devil's windows."[18] The modern era has no monopoly on clothing that titillates by hinting at what's underneath.

Of them that take first newe gyses
(Of those who are the first to take new fashions)

Fair daughters, I beg you not to be the first to try new fashions. Instead, be the last and wait the longest, especially when it comes to new fashions of women from foreign regions. I'll tell you about a debate between a baroness who lived in Guyenne and the lord of Beaumont, a wise and subtle knight, the father of the present lord. This lady reproached him about his wife saying, "Fair cousin, I've come from Brittany and have seen my fair cousin, your wife, who isn't dressed like the ladies of Guyenne or other places. The embroidered edges of her garments and hoods aren't as big as is fashionable."

The knight answered her, "Madame, if she's not wearing your fashion, and if her edges seem small, why do you blame me? Be certain that you won't blame me any more because I shall cause her to be adorned as elegantly and as nobly as you or anyone else—and even more so. For only half your clothes are edged with squirrel fur and ermine, but I'll make her better. I'll make her skirts and hoods all furred on the outside, and she'll have better trimmings and embroidery than you or anybody else."

"Do you think I don't want her to be dressed like the good ladies of the region?" he said. "I do. But I don't want her to stop wearing the clothing that good women wear, like the honorable ladies of France and of this region. They don't dress like the concubines of Englishmen, or the prostitutes who follow armies. *They* were the ones who first started wearing embroidered edges and slits in their skirts—I was there, and I saw what they wore. I think women who dress like this have been poorly advised. Maybe the princesses and noble ladies of England have adopted these fashions after they were around for a long time, and they are entitled to do so, but I have heard sages say that good women ought to wear the clothes of ladies of their own region and kingdom. The wisest are those who are the last to wear novelties and new fashions, which is why the ladies of France have been renowned as the least open to blame."

These words were spoken in front of many people, and the lady felt foolish and didn't know what to say. Many people began to whisper among themselves that it would have been better if she hadn't said anything at all.

And therefore, my fair daughters, you should dress moderately according to the way good women dress in this region. Don't be the first to wear the fashions of foreign women because you'll be mocked and scorned.

But God have mercy on us this day because some will never rest until they have a copy of the new fashion or new kind of gown, and will say to their husband daily, "Such and such a thing would look good on me, and it's very beautiful, and I tell you I must have it."

And her husband says to her, "My love, such a one may have it, but others who are wiser than she is don't."

"What do I care how they dress?" the woman says, and she keeps giving reasons why she must have it. But these women who have their hearts most set on worldly pleasures aren't very wise.

There's currently a habit among serving women of lower classes to wear fur on their collars that hangs down to the middle of their backs, and they also wear fur on their heels, which get all daubed with dirt. I don't recommend this for either winter or summer. It would be better in the winter for them to take the fur that hangs around their heels and put it on their stomachs, because that has more need of heat than their heels, and in summer it would be better not to wear it at all, because it shelters flies.[19]

However, I don't intend to speak against other ladies in this book, but instead to speak to my own daughters, and the women and servants of my house, to whom I may say what pleases me, according to my own will.

You can be sure that no serving women at La Tour Landry attracted summer flies with furry collars or heels—it would have been Jeanne de Rougé's duty to instruct them about appropriate attire. Her daughters would have learned from her example—and their father's words—how to manage the serving women in their own homes, once they were married. Servants needed minding in bourgeois households, too. Because his fifteen-year-old wife was an orphan with no female relatives living near enough to teach her such things, it was left to the Householder of Paris to caution her about her responsibility toward her servants, some of whom would have been far older than she was. Both the younger and the older servants would have been expected to be moderate in their clothing, and it would have been up to the fifteen-year-old bride to make sure they were.

Things would have been no different in England a hundred years later. Fifteenth-century moralists cautioned young people against outlandish fashions. Like their brother Richard, our imaginary sisters Katherine and Elizabeth Goodwyn would have favored scarlet, blue, and green cloth for their headdresses and their gowns, which they would have preferred to be cut low at the neck and trimmed with fur the way all the other ladies were wearing them. Not that their parents would have allowed such a display. Their father might also have had a word with his wife when he noticed that the some of the servants were wearing their "sleeves so long that they dipped in the soup."[20] He would expect her to reprimand the servants and bring order back into the household.

Into the previous story, like into others, Sir Geoffrey drops the names of powerful lords and ladies. The lord of Beaumont whose wife wore tastefully expensive clothing held the rank of *maréchal de France*, or Marshal of France, one of the highest positions in the French army. He married twice, first to Thiphaine, a woman from the town of Chemillé—about eight kilometers from La Tourlandry—and later to Marguerite de Rohan. The "present lord" of Beaumont, whom the story mentions, was Jean IV, who died in 1385, about twenty years after his father.[21] Like many of Sir Geoffrey's stories, this one takes place a generation earlier and we might wonder whether Sir Geoffrey's daughters ever wearied of hearing how things were back then.

Elsewhere, Sir Geoffrey discusses the lecherous daughters of Moab, who adorned themselves in fine clothing in order to infiltrate and tempt the soldiers of the enemy army. In that passage, Sir Geoffrey not only cautions his daughters against wearing finery, he also upbraids the kinds of captains "who allow a great number of harlots within their armies."[22] Although he has no fear that Jeanne, Anne, and Marie might turn to that profession, prostitutes did regularly follow soldiers, who gave them so much business. Joan of Arc demanded that her army be free of prostitutes.

Perhaps these women of ill repute were the first to begin wearing embroidered edges and slit skirts, but if, as Sir Geoffrey reports, princesses and noble ladies also wear dagged fabric and embroider the edges of their clothing, wouldn't other aristocratic ladies want to follow their example? Unwittingly, Sir Geoffrey offers fashion advice to ladies who have been wondering just what to wear—as he will at the end of the next story, too.

How a hooly bisshop reprysed and taught many ladyes
(How a holy bishop reproved and taught many ladies)
    I'll tell you how a bishop, who was a very good scholar, preached recently. There were many ladies at his sermon, some wearing the new headdresses that are shaped like two horns. Their gowns were also fashionably made. The good man marveled at their clothing and began to reprove them. He told them the gathering of waters in the days of Noah took place because of the pride and over-elaborate clothing of men and especially of women. When the enemy saw those people's great pride and their fashionable clothing, he made them fall into the filth of the stinking sin of lechery. This was so displeasing to God that he caused it to rain forty days and forty nights without ceasing, so that the waters were ten cubits higher than the highest mountain. The entire world perished. No one survived except Noah, his wife, his

three sons, and his three daughters, and all of this happened because of that sin.

The bishop told them many other stories, and then he said the women wearing the headdresses looked like horned snails and deer and unicorns. He also mentioned men who wear their gowns so short that their breeches show, which is shameful.[23] Both the men's clothing and the women's horns mock God. The horns make women like deer, who put their heads down to drink. When the women come to church and holy water is cast on them, they cast their faces down. Why? "The devil," said the bishop, "sits between their horns and forces them to bow their heads for fear of the holy water."[24]

The bishop reproved them so sorely that they were full of shame and afterwards, many of them cast away their horns and dressed simply. He said that such fancy clothing could be compared to the spider who makes his net to take flies. In the same way the devil uses the fashionable clothing of men and women to tempt people to lechery. He takes them and binds them the way the spider does the flies in her net.

The sin lies with those who first wear such clothing. Good and wise women should fear wearing such fashions until everyone wears them commonly because according to the word of God, the first will be the most blamed but the last will sit on the high seat.

My fair daughters, if some foolish woman full of her own will takes up every novelty and new fashion, all the other women will soon say to their lords, "Sir, I heard that so and so has a fancy item that's very becoming, and I pray you, good sir, that I may have one, too, for I am as good and as noble of blood. You are as noble as she and her lord are and have as much to pay with as she has." She'll find so many reasons to have her will, or else her home will be full of quarreling and strife all day, and there will be no peace until she has what she wants, whether it's right or wrong. She won't look to see if any of her neighbors has the item she wants, nor will she wait until everyone has one, but she'll get it and wear it as fast as she can. In fact, great scholars say that seeing men and women so outlandishly dressed and taking on new fashions every day, they fear the world will perish as it did in the time of Noah.[25]

Don't imagine Jeanne or Anne arguing with their father about the dubious reasons he gives for Noah's Flood. Even if the family owned a copy of the Old Testament, the girls wouldn't be able to read the Latin it was written in, so they could hardly look up the text in Genesis. Besides, they would have encountered biblical stories in the same way their father had, embedded in sermons or in other tales like this one, tales whose primary purpose was to promote a moral, which sometimes necessitated changing a few details. For the teller of such a story, there would have been the feeling that, as one scholar puts it, "any saying with a lofty moral content could be confidently attributed to" Scripture.[26]

A visiting friar embarking on such an example during a sermon might glance around with a disapproving eye at the ladies gathered in the chapel, Jeanne and Anne proudly wearing the headdresses their young and fashionable aunt has helped them construct. No friend to frippery, the friar might mold his story into a cautionary tale, using biblical details when they suited his purpose, shifting them slightly when they didn't.

As their father continues his story, he leaves the Bible behind and takes up an example from his own life.

And now I'll tell you a marvel which a good lady told me this year. She said that she and many other ladies came to a feast of St. Margaret, where, like every year, there was a great assembly. A finely dressed lady arrived who was more fantastically dressed than anybody else there. And because of her unfamiliar garb, everyone looked at her as if she were a wild beast, for her clothing and accessories were like nothing they had ever seen.

Then the good ladies said to her, "My friend, tell us, if it please you, what you call your headdress."

She said it was called the gallows adornment.

"God bless us," said a good lady, "that isn't a very nice name. I don't know how such an adornment pleases you."

The news of this headdress and its name went everywhere, and everyone scorned and mocked her for it, and people came to look at her.

I asked the good lady what the headdress looked like, and she told me, but I don't remember it very well. But as far as I can remember, it was raised high with long pins of silver on her head like a gibbet or a gallows, and very strange to see. In good faith, after that time the foolish young lady who wore that decoration on her head was mocked and scorned and not well-regarded.[27]

The lady may have been mocked and scorned, but the story may also have inspired at least one provincial fashion maven to have found herself some long pins of silver to make a gallows headdress for herself, since the style was being worn in the 1370s.

For Sir Geoffrey, as for many medieval preachers, one sin leads directly to others. Pride causes women to don new fashions, which in turn open the door to lechery. Later, Sir Geoffrey says that the novelties that women wear are signs of great evil to come, such as war, famine, and pestilence. However, his marriage of fashion and morality isn't always as extreme as the preachers would have it; sometimes he just wants other ladies to test the waters first before his own women adopt new styles.

The parish priest Katherine and Elizabeth Goodwyn listened to on Sundays would have also preferred that women choose modest clothing. He might remark that women rarely adorn themselves to please their own husbands, for as preachers were quick to point out, women are faithless and lecherous. And what of the cosmetics women wear? the priest might ask. As he warms to his theme, he points out that women who give themselves a new complexion "desire along with Lucifer to be equal with the All-highest; and for this reason the unnatural colour on their face makes them grow old before the proper time, and in the future they will be punished for it as well."[28]

The priest might well have delved into a collection such as *The Mirror for Good Women* for this kind of material—and some of its stories about clothing and cosmetics make their way into Sir Geoffrey's book, too. According to *The Mirror*, just before the Flood "women began to call attention to their bodies by means of cosmetics and clothing. They thus caused lust in men. For this reason, God shortened the life span of men and brought about the great flood."[29] Sir Geoffrey echoes this view in the passage above.

Preachers and other moralists didn't like stylish fashions for a number of reasons. Practically, it was a sin against charity to own too many expensive clothes while poor people in your own neighborhood starved. In addition, you committed the sin of pride when you were unsatisfied with the body given to you by God, a body made in God's image. Finally, women who indulged in the luxuries of tight-fitting clothing and cosmetics might lead men into the sin of lechery—is it any wonder that the Latin word for lechery is *luxoria*?

The Good Knight and his Three Wives
Of the good knyght that had thre wyues and of their lyues
(Concerning the good knight who had three wives and of their lives)

Once there was a good knight who lived honestly. His uncle was a hermit, a good and holy man of a religious life. This knight and his first wife, whom he loved greatly, were together for only a little while before death, which consumes and destroys all, took her. The knight was so sorrowful that he nearly died. He didn't know where to seek comfort except from his uncle, the hermit. He came to him mourning and weeping for his wife.

The holy man comforted him as best he could. Finally, the knight asked him to ask God whether the wife was damned or saved. The holy man had compassion for his nephew and went into his chapel and prayed to God that if it pleased him he might show where the wife was. And after he had been in prayer a long time, he fell asleep, and soon it seemed to him that he saw the wife's soul before Saint Michael the Archangel, with the Fiend on the other side. She was standing in a balance, her good deeds beside her. On the other side of the scale was the devil with all her evil deeds—like her gowns made of very fine cloth and furred with Calabrian fur, grey squirrel fur, and ermine.

The devil cried out in a high voice, "Sir, this woman had ten pair of gowns, long and short, and you know well half of them would have been enough, that is a long gown, two skirts, and two short gowns. She might have been satisfied with those. The value of one of her gowns was too much by half compared to poor people's coarse woolen clothes. They suffer such cold and hardship, yet she never took pity on them."

Then the devil took the gowns and rings and jewels that men had given her for love, and also the vain and evil words she had said about others because of envy, and taken away their good reputations. Leaving behind no sin that she had done, he put them all together in the balance and weighed them compared to her good deeds. They weighed much more than all the good she had ever done.

Thus the devil took her and forced her to put on her gowns that were now burning like fire, and he took her to Hell, the poor soul crying piteously.

Then the holy hermit woke up and told the knight his vision. He commanded him to give all her gowns to poor people, for God's sake.

Of the second wyf
(Concerning the second wife)

Afterwards, the knight married another woman, and they lived together for five years before she passed out of this world. If the knight had grieved for his first wife, he was even more affected by his second wife's death. Weeping, he came to his uncle and asked for the same thing—to know where she was. Again, the hermit took great pity on his nephew, seeing him in such sorrow.

Alone in his chapel he prayed to God, and it was revealed to him that the knight's second wife might yet be saved, but that she must spend a hundred years in the fire of Purgatory because of certain faults. While she was married, a squire had lain with her, and there were other great sins, as well. Nevertheless, she had confessed these sins many times. If she hadn't done so she would have been damned without a doubt. The hermit told the knight that his wife was saved, and he was joyful and glad.

Here you can see that for one deadly sin she suffered so long in the fire of Purgatory. For every deadly sin confessed the soul shall be punished in Purgatory the time and space of seven years. Fair daughters, take good example of how dearly bought foul and false delight is, and how men must give account. And take note of those who have so many gowns and who waste their goods in order to be finely dressed and adorn their body so they can have the attention of the world.

Now see how it happened to the knight's first wife that because of her pride and her gowns and jewels she was lost and damned forever. And yet many people in this world have such proud spirits that they dare to buy gowns of three or fourscore crowns and think it of little price—yet if they had to give two or three shillings to poor people, they would think that too much. Behold how much those who have so many gowns will have to answer for them. Every good woman of estate and degree ought to behave herself simply and honestly in her clothing and in the quantity of it, and give a part to God so that she may be clothed in joy and glory in the other world, like the holy ladies and holy virgins whose stories you have heard. Saint Elizabeth, Saint Katherine, Saint Agatha, and others gave their gowns to poor people for the love of God and so ought every woman to do.

Now I've told you about the first two wives of the knight, and afterwards you shall hear of the third.

Of the third wyf of the knyght
(Concerning the third wife of the knight)

Soon after that the knight took a third wife and they lived together a long time. But at last she died, and the knight nearly died for sorrow. When she was dead, the knight came to his uncle and asked him for the same thing as with his first two wives.

As the holy man was in his prayers, he saw in a vision an angel, who showed him the torment and pain that the poor soul of the knight's third wife suffered. He saw clearly how one devil held her firmly with his claws by her hair, like a lion holds his prey, so she couldn't move her head. Then the devil put burning needles through her brows, which went as far into her head as he could thrust them. Every time he pushed a needle in, the poor soul cried horribly.

This lasted a long time, and then another hideous devil came with great brands of fire and thrust them into her face. In this way he tormented and burned her all over, so that the hermit trembled for fear. But the angel assured him that she had well deserved it.

"Why?" the hermit asked.

The angel said she wore cosmetics and smoothed her face to seem more beautiful to the world, and that was one of the sins most displeasing to God. She did it because of pride, by which men fall to the sin of lechery, and finally to all the other sins. Above all things it displeases the Creator for one to have by craft more beauty than nature has given him. One should be content to be made in the holy image, of whom all the angels in heaven take their joy and delight. If

God had wanted, they would have been dumb beasts or serpents instead of women. Why then do they take no heed of the great beauty with which their creator has provided them? Why do they put anything on their faces other than what God has given them? It is therefore no marvel if they suffer such penance.

"She well deserved it," the angel said. "Go to where her body lies and you will see her hideous and terrified face, because she was always busy dressing and painting her brows and her temples and forehead so she would look fair and pleasing to the world. It's right that in every place where she plucked a hair from her face, a burning brand will be put every day."

"Sir," said the hermit, "will she be in this torment for a long time?"

"Yes, a thousand years." More than that the angel wouldn't say.

But as the devil put the brand on her face, the poor soul cried sorely and cursed the hour that she was born. The holy hermit woke up full of fear and told the knight his vision.

The knight was sorely distressed. He went to see the body men had thought so fair, but the face was black and hideous and horrible to see. Then the knight believed everything his uncle had told him. He had such great horror and abhorrence and pity that he left the world and wore a hairshirt every Friday and every Wednesday, and gave up a third of his estates and property for God's sake. And from that day forth he led a holy life and had no more care for worldly pleasures, since he was so fearful about what he had seen of his last wife, and of what his uncle had told him.

From these stories, Jeanne, Anne, and Marie—as well as their fifteenth-century English counterparts—would be expected to think not only about the faults of fashion, they would also be reminded about the importance of confession. Although the first wife's sin of owning too many dresses may seem less egregious to us than the second wife's adultery, the fact that the second wife frequently went to confession saved her from eternal damnation. Nevertheless, the length and severity of her suffering in Purgatory is sobering.

Despite such explicit warnings about the perils involved in doing so, ladies continued to wear extravagant clothing and to pluck the hair from their eyebrows, foreheads, and temples, the better to create the smooth dome of a forehead that made the whole effect of their headdresses so fashionable. And—like the lady in the next story—they colored both their faces and hair with cosmetics and dye. Sir Geoffrey looks to his own life to warn his daughters about hair dyeing—his personal example emphasizes that the tale of the Knight and his Three Wives is far more than fiction for him.

Of the lady that blanked and popped her
(Of the lady who powdered and painted herself)

To affirm how true this example is, I'll tell you something that happened recently. I saw a baroness, a lady of very high and noble lineage, whom men said powdered and painted herself. I also saw the man who gave her the cosmetics, for which he took a large yearly pension from her, as he said in private. This lady was once very honored and very powerful. When her lord died her estate began diminishing day by day. There was a time when she had more than sixty pair of gowns, men said, but in the end, she had scant enough. And I heard that after she was dead, her face and body took such a form and disfigurement that men couldn't say what it was, and no one was able to look at it, it was so horrible. But I know well that the painting of her face, which she often did when she lived, and also her great pride and the great waste of her gowns, was the cause of this terrible disfigurement.

Therefore, my fair daughters, I pray you that you will take this example and remember it within your hearts, and that you will wear no cosmetics on your faces but leave them as God and nature has ordained them. Don't pluck your eyebrows, nor your temples, nor your foreheads, and don't wash your hair in anything but lye and water. You can see the miracles that happened in the church of Our Lady of Rocomadour—the ladies who washed their hair in wine and other things to color their hair other than the way God had made it and who came there on pilgrimage were unable to enter the church until they had cut their hair, which now hangs before the image of Our Lady. This is true and has been proven, because many people who have been there say so. So leave off such folly like powdering and painting yourselves, because doing so causes pride and lechery, which destroyed the world in the time of Noah.[30]

The Tour Landry priests might have woven this story into their Sunday sermons. In so doing, they would have joined a host of preachers who faulted women for wearing make-up. Writers sometimes satirized the habit, too. In *The Romance of the Rose*, Jean de Meun details the wiles women use to capture men, from the "moist unguents" they use to brighten their faces to the hairpieces with which they hide their thinning tresses. He suggests that many women's hair color may have been enhanced:

> And if she should have need to dye her hair,
> There's many an herb with which it may be tinged,
> For root and bark and stem and leaf and fruit
> Possess the qualities of medicines.[31]

For Jean de Meun, as for the priests, the links between fashion and lechery were clear.

In another story, the biblical tale of the daughters of Lot, this link is equally explicit.[32] In Sir Geoffrey's telling, the details don't follow Genesis very closely—probably because he has heard the story this way in sermons or read it in other anthologies—but the changes help the story illustrate his moral. This kind of misinterpretation is one of the reasons the Church didn't want the Bible translated into vernacular languages: it's a complex and mysterious text that needs expert explication to be understood, they believed (and with good reason—Chaucer's Pardoner uses the same biblical story to condemn drinking, twisting the details to fit his own purposes).

Sir Geoffrey's story is based on Genesis 19, in which the daughters of Lot believe they are the last people on earth after they escape the destruction of Sodom. In order to produce children to inhabit the earth, and with no evil intent, they get their father drunk so he'll have sex with them. The result? Two sons, Moab and Amon. In Sir Geoffrey's version, however, Lot's daughters are filled with lechery when they see their father without his breeches. That's why they get him drunk and have sex with him, and from these unions come two sons from whom, according to Sir Geoffrey, sprang the "pagans and the false law," as well as many evils. This all came about, Sir Geoffrey adds, because Lot's daughters wanted to dress elegantly, and that led the devil to tempt them with the foul sin of lechery. The close connection between fashionable clothing and sin, be it pride or lechery, should remind Jeanne and Anne to wear simple, moderate gowns and headdresses. An unhealthy attention to fashion can lead to other ills, as well, as the daughter of Jacob learns to her peril in the next story, a blame-the-victim tale if there ever was one.

Of the doughter of Iacob that was depuceled or her maydenhode taken fro her
(Concerning the daughter of Jacob who was deflowered, or had her maidenhood taken from her)

I'll tell you the story of the daughter of Jacob, who because of her frivolity and lightness of heart left the house of her father and brothers to go see the headdresses and fine clothing of the women of another country. It happened that Shechem, the son of Hamor, who was a great lord in that land, saw her, coveted her, asked for her love, and finally took her virginity from her. When her twelve brothers discovered how this lord had shamed and deflowered their sister, they slew him and most of his kin.

Look on this example and see how many evils and misfortunes are caused by foolish women. Because of her youth and her frivolous spirits a great deal of blood was shed.

In the biblical version of this story, the Rape of Dinah (Genesis 34), Jacob's bloodthirsty sons trick the prince who, having already slept with her, wants to marry Dinah. You can't, you're not circumcised, her brothers say. So the prince and all his men submit to circumcision, and when their pain is greatest, Jacob's twelve sons kill them and abduct their women and children, their revenge for the prince's rape of their sister. Jacob is furious. "You have made me hateful to the inhabitants of this land, who will kill me," he tells his sons.

Nowhere in the biblical story does Dinah go off to a fashion show. In fact, she isn't even accused of frivolity. But, as happened with the story of Lot's daughters, and as so many preachers discovered for themselves, a shift in the emphasis of a tale can make it fit your theme ever so much better.

In the next story, Jeanne and Anne learn more about the connection between fashionable clothing and morality: *when* you wear something is just as is important as *what* you wear. Both men and women should wear their finest clothing on Sundays and other holy days, but there are times when it is less appropriate.

Of them that wylle not were theyr good clothes on hyghe festes and holy dayes
(Of those who will not wear their good clothes on high feasts and holy days)

Once there was a lady who had good, rich gowns, but she wouldn't wear them on Sundays or feast days unless noblemen would be present. Once, on a feast of Our Lady, her damsel said to her, "Madame, why don't you wear your good gown today for the love of Our Lady?"

"Because I see no men of good estate here," she said.

"Ah!" said the damsel. "God and his mother are greater and ought to be honored more than any worldly thing, for God may give and take away all things at his pleasure. All good and all honor comes from him and from his blessed mother dear, and we ought to dress well on their holy days."

"Hold your peace," said the lady. "God and the priest and the people see me all day long, but folk of high estate don't always see me. Therefore it's a greater honor to me to dress well for them."

"Madame,' her damsel said, "that is ill spoken."

"It is not," said the lady, "whatever may come of it." Just as she spoke, a hot wind blew around her, striking her so that she couldn't move.

Then she confessed and repented and vowed to take many pilgrimages. Afterwards, she was carried around in a litter and she told all the honorable men the cause of her malady—it was the vengeance of God. She told them how she had previously found greater joy in pleasing people of high estate than she had in her devotions at the high feasts of our Lord and his saints.

She also spoke with gentlewomen, as she was getting dressed. "My loves, here you see the vengeance of God. I used to have a fair, noble body (that's what all the men said about me), and because of my pride, I wore the richest clothes with fancy fur on them, and I showed them off at feasts and jousts. At that time everything I did was for the glory of the world. I would hear people say, in order to please me, 'Lo, here's a well-made woman who is worthy of some knight's love,' and my heart would rejoice. Now you can see what I've become; I'm bigger than a barrel. Now the expensive gowns and robes that I loved and wouldn't wear to honor God will never serve me. My fair loves and friends, God has shown me my folly about sparing my fancy clothes on holy days in order to have them fresh for men of high estate. Take example of me."

This good lady was sick and swollen for seven years. Afterwards, when God had seen her contrition and repentance, he sent her health for the rest of her life. She was always humble towards God and gave the greater part of her goods for God's sake. She lived simply and didn't set her heart towards the world the way she had been accustomed to earlier.

Therefore, my fair daughters, remember from this story how you ought to dress and to wear your good clothes on Sundays and feast days for the honor and love of God who gives all, and for the honor of his sweet mother and the holy saints, instead of for worldly people who are nothing but filth and earth. People who do things for the regard and praise of earthly people displease God, and he will take vengeance on them in this world or in the next, like he did with this lady.

Although the lady says she has learned her lesson about pride and humility, after her illness she seems to take great pride in being humble. Her constant reminders to others about how God chose her as an example and about how beautiful she used to be must have caused many a knowing glance among her visitors and her ladies-in-waiting. When Saint Michael weighed her sins against her good deeds in her final hour, would her pride make the sinister side of the scale sink too low to ensure her a place at God's right hand?

Yet when Sir Geoffrey relates the episode, he infuses it with no sense of irony or play the way Geoffrey Chaucer or Jean de Meun might have done; his tone is perfectly straightforward and serious. As Jeanne and Anne sit side-by-side after the pages have cleared away the serving bowls and brought around the scented water for hand washing at the end of the midday meal, one of the two clerics who helped their father compile the book might read this story aloud. The girls, like the rest of the audience, would probably focus on the moral, not the way the lady was characterized.

As for the moral, Sir Geoffrey is nothing if not moderate. He doesn't expect Jeanne and Anne to give away all their fine gowns, only *most* of them. They may be able to make do with fewer fine clothes, but he expects them to be well dressed for God, for distinguished visitors, and certainly, for suitors—especially rich ones.

In the end, Sir Geoffrey ties together his two great themes: this world and the next, worldliness and spirituality. Dressing well at the appropriate time is important in order to honor God and your human superiors—except, of course, when it's important *not* to dress well. He wants his daughters to spend eternity in the Heavenly City of Jerusalem, but while they're trapped in their earthly bodies, they should be wrapped in the finery their social status entitles them to.

CHAPTER 10

HEARTS SET ON THIS WORLD — ACTING FASHIONABLY

Fashion is about behavior, not just clothing. In *The Canterbury Tales*, Chaucer's Prioress is as fashionable as a nun can be, and far more fashionable than she *should* be. She pays quite a bit of attention to her clothing, she wears jewelry that she shouldn't (including that famous brooch with "Love conquers all" inscribed on it), and she keeps little dogs whom she feeds *wastel bread*, the finely milled white bread available only to the rich. (Ironically, today's expensive whole-grain bread would have been peasant fare in the Middle Ages, whereas medieval aristocrats would have appreciated the texture and color of WonderBread.)

Like owning sixty expensive gowns but sharing nothing with the poor, giving fine food to dogs when people around you are dying of hunger and the plague is an offense against charity, especially when such an act is committed by a member of a religious order. Chaucer's Prioress, like a fourteenth-century convent of English nuns who were admonished for bringing "birds, rabbits, hounds and such like frivolous things" to Mass with them, should have been thinking of poor people, not of her plump puppies. The nuns were told that their animals disrupted services with their noise, ate up the alms that should have gone to the poor, and kept the nuns from paying attention to the psalms — and to their souls.[1]

The nuns, who came from wealthy aristocratic backgrounds, were acting like sophisticated secular women, women such as the lady in the next story. She probably brought her lapdogs into church with her, as fashionable ladies often did, to the consternation of priests. Men acted the same way; knights sometimes came to mass with hawks riding on their wrists.[2]

Of the woman that gaf the flesshe to her houndes
(Concerning the woman who gave meat to her dogs)

I'll tell you a story about a lady who gave meat and fine food to her little dogs, whom she loved dearly. Every day she made them dishes of broth and delicacies. One time a friar told her it was evil to give such food to the dogs, who were fat, when there were many poor people, lean and withered from hunger. Although he preached this, the lady wouldn't stop. A little while later, she became deathly ill. And a marvel happened: two little black dogs came onto her bed, and when she drew near to death and was in a trance, they came near her mouth and licked her lips. Wherever they licked her, she became black as a coal. I heard this from a damsel who said she had seen all this, and she told me the lady's name.

Women like this don't understand the word of God in the Gospel where God says, he who does well to the poor does service to me. Such women don't resemble Good Queen Blanche, the mother of Saint Louis, who gave food to the needy. Afterwards, Saint Louis did likewise, visiting poor people and feeding them with his own hand. The pleasure of every good woman should be to nourish and clothe the fatherless and motherless children and little poor children, like the Countess of Mauns did. Out of compassion, she nurtured thirty orphans and poor children. That was her pleasure, and therefore she was loved by God and had a holy life and a good end. At her death a great radiance all full of little children was seen. These were hardly the little black dogs that were seen with the other lady, as you have heard above.

Of the Countess of Mauns, no trace remains except what Sir Geoffrey says about her goodness. His daughters probably recognized her name, and they certainly knew about Good Queen Blanche and her son, Saint Louis, who were famous for their almsgiving. On August 25, Saint Louis's feast day, the midday meal at La Tour Landry might have been accompanied by stories of Quinze-Vingts, the institution Louis founded for 300 blind and poor people. The alms-dish might have been heaped especially high as Jeanne and Anne looked down at their rich food and—for the sake of Saint Louis and his mother—decided to forgo eating it. Unlike modern American children, who are told to clean their plates because children are starving elsewhere, Jeanne and Anne could more easily feed the hungry by leaving their plates full. The almoner would collect their leavings to be distributed to poor people who sat outside the nearby church, hoping for just this sort of charity. Further, in honor of Saint Louis and Queen Blanche, Jeanne and Anne's mother may have ordered an extra loaf of bread to be placed in the alms dish.

Saint Louis—or King Louis IX of France—lived from 1214 to 1270. The famous Sainte-Chapelle in Paris is one of his foundations—he had it built to house what he thought was a piece of Christ's crown of thorns. His life illustrates one of the troubling paradoxes of medieval Christianity. Loved for his impartial justice as well as his charity to his fellow-Christians, Louis was also a Crusader, a soldier for God, who slaughtered non-Christians in an attempt to free the Holy Land from the hands of the infidel. Although the killing in the Crusades is probably negligible compared to twentieth-century genocide, it gives modern readers a view of the Middle Ages as particularly violent and bloodthirsty, which Louis IX probably wasn't. Even during the Crusades, he tried to control both violence and injustice, although without success.[3]

In addition to fighting, ruling, and praying, Saint Louis also wrote two courtesy books for his daughters Isabelle, Blanche, and Marguerite. In both works, he stresses religion first, followed by a young woman's duties as a wife and a daughter. At the very beginning of the sixteenth century, his great-granddaughter Anne of France wrote yet another courtesy book for her daughter Suzanne, who was about to marry Charles de Bourbon (the wedding took place in 1505). Anne owned two copies of Christine de Pizan's *Book of the Three Virtues*, and she drew on it in her work. But none of them focused on fashion and fashionable behavior quite as much as *The Book of the Knight of the Tower* does.

Chide to This Wisp of Straw—Arguing

The physical trappings of wealthy households in fourteenth- and fifteenth-century France and England sometimes contributed to dicey social situations, the kind in which reputations were at stake. Consider, for example, the bed. In a noble lady or gentleman's chamber, it would often be the only piece of furniture, and during the day, it served as a place for people to sit when the chamber was used as a room for receiving guests or conducting business.[4] At night, the curtains around the bed would be pulled closed to help keep out the cold, which was particularly important since people often slept naked. In *Sir Gawain and the Green Knight* the curtained bed becomes a battleground for Sir Gawain's considerable virtue. Each morning, the lord of the castle where Sir Gawain is staying goes off hunting, and after he's gone, his wife conducts some hunting of her own. She lets herself into Sir Gawain's chamber, sits beside him on his bed (presumably inside the curtains), and coyly asks him to show her the kind of love games they practice in King Arthur's celebrated court. Sir Gawain, lying naked under the coverlet, resists the lady's advances as they become more and more blatant over the course of three days, giving her only a demure kiss or two instead of the sex she all but demands ("You are welcome to my body," she says at one point). After each encounter with her, Sir Gawain springs out of bed, throws on his clothes, and races to the chapel to hear Mass.

In a household such as Sir Geoffrey's, tales of this sort—albeit French ones, starring Sir Lancelot, not the Scottish knight Gawain— would have been recited to the assembled guests at a feast. While their mother kept a strict eye on her daughters' reactions to the entertainment, other ladies' and gentlemen's eyes might have flickered across the room at each other—those knowing glances people shared as they thought of decadent ladies and gentlemen they knew who remained long abed, perhaps receiving visitors in their chambers instead of rising for an early morning prayer service. Discussions of the knight's dilemma—how could he be courteous to both the lord of the castle and the lord's wife?—would have continued after dinner was over and couples drifted to window seats to sing or tell stories or play board games.

At the beginning of the next story, a knight and a lady who have little else to do with their time are playing at tables, a game similar to backgammon. As with backgammon, two people sat together to play each other, throwing dice onto an expensive, beautifully decorated board. You can imagine how ladies and gentlemen, sitting in pairs apart from the group to play board games, might be carefully watched by those who delighted in gossip. And you can see how playing such games could lead to arguments like the one here, and to the loss of a lady's honor. A lady's reputation is as fragile as fine china, and Sir Geoffrey and Jeanne de Rougé must have feared that their young daughters wouldn't realize that until it was too late.

Of them that ben chydars or scoldes
(Of those who are chiders and scolds)

Fair daughters, don't ever start an argument with a fool or somebody who is quick-tempered—that's a great peril. I'll tell you about something I saw happen in a castle where many ladies and damsels lived.

A damsel, the daughter of a very noble knight, got very angry when she was playing at tables with a quarrelsome gentleman. They argued about a throw of the dice, which she said hadn't been done fairly. Their words got hotter and angrier until she called him a coward and a fool.

I said to the damsel, "My fair cousin, don't be angry about what he says. You know he has only proud words and foolish answers. For the sake of your honor, I pray you, don't argue with him."

I spoke to her like I would talk to my sister, but she wouldn't listen, and she kept chiding the gentleman, telling him he wasn't worth anything.

He said he was a better man than she was a woman, and she said it wasn't true. Their argument kept escalating, until he said, "If you were wise and good, you wouldn't come into men's rooms at night without a candle and kiss them and embrace them."

"You lie," she said, thinking to avenge herself.

He denied it, saying that so and so had seen her doing this.

Well, there were many people listening who hadn't known anything about her before this.

She wept and said he defamed her. In front of everybody, she assailed him again, so he said more terrible, shameful things that dishonored her so much that she'll never regain her honor. Her arrogance brought her nothing but shame, and people said she had been beaten by her own staff—by her tongue, that is.

This is an example of how women should eschew fools or proud people instead of arguing with them. The way to treat them is to speak courteously to them and then leave, like a knight did to a lady I know. The lady said many outrageous things to him in front of everybody. He spoke politely to her, but she kept right on talking. When he saw that, he found a wisp of straw and set it in front of her, saying, "Madame, if you chide more, chide to this wisp of straw. I'll leave it here in my place." Then he left. After that, people considered him to be a reputable man, but she was held to be a fool.

The wisp of straw the knight set in front of the fine lady was a deadly insult. The lady, like all the gentlemen and ladies who were watching this argument, would know that bits of straw were used to rebuke "common scold[s]."[5] Shakespeare was still using the phrase that way when he wrote, "Woman . . . whose tatling tongues had won a wispe" in *Henry VI, Part III*.[6] The knight in this story implicitly compares the lady to a common woman in front of everybody. Yet the honor of the lady in the previous example was even more grievously besmirched when the knight said she had been seen creeping into men's rooms. It doesn't matter whether or not she's really done anything wrong. The rumor has been started, and it will fly far before it rests. You can just hear other ladies tittering and see the men hiding their smiles behind their hands, while Sir Geoffrey and Jeanne de Rougé frown with disapproval at the entire event, just as they would at the scene described in the next story.

How no woman ought to chyden or brawle with folk whiche ben braynles
(How no woman ought to chide or argue with folk who are brainless)

It's a great folly for any woman to chide or argue with brainless people. I'll tell you about something I witnessed. A gentlewoman was arguing with a man who was mentally unbalanced. I said to her, "My lady, I pray you that you won't answer this fool, because he's always ready to say more evil than good."

She wouldn't believe me, but argued more than she had before, saying that he was worthless. He replied that he was as good a man as she was a woman. Their words went back and forth, and then he said he knew a man who kissed her both night and day, whenever he wanted to.

I called her aside and told her that it was folly to heed the words of a fool and to argue with him. His words were foul and dishonest and because many people heard them, she was dishonored. Because of her arguing, she caused many people to know something they hadn't known before.

From time to time we put ourselves into great wrong by our own words. Further, it's a bad thing for any gentlewoman to argue with any man. Let me give you an example of the behavior of certain beasts. Think of the huge dogs that men call mastiffs who bark and show their teeth. However, a well-bred dog will not do this. Likewise it should be with gentlemen and gentlewomen.

At sixteen, Jeanne de la Tour might witness some of these kinds of exchanges between men and women when she attended social gatherings. Although it might be fun to banter coquettishly with a young knight who was teaching her the words to a new song, pretending to misunderstand an innocent expression of his as something shocking, Jeanne's marriageability could be put at risk by such behavior. The knight wouldn't suffer; only Jeanne would. Think back to Sir Geoffrey's encounter with the young woman he was courting—he instigated a flirtatious conversation about prisoners of love, but when she joined in, he crossed her off his list of eligible partners. Arguing was even worse. Jeanne's parents had good reason to warn her to avoid public squabbles and to steer her away from men who are known for their witty repartee, such as Clermont in the next tale.

How we ought not to stryue ayenst them that ben langageurs and full of wordes
(How we ought not to argue with those who are fast talkers and full of words)

Fair daughters, it's perilous to argue with worldly, quick-witted people, because men will win little if they banter and jest with them. One time many lords and ladies were at a great feast, including the Marshal of Clermont, who had experience of the world, especially when it came to fair speech and subtle lies, and who cut a fine figure among the knights and ladies. One lady said to him in front of everyone, "Clermont, in good faith you ought to praise God because you're such a good, handsome knight, and it would be so much better if you wouldn't mock people with your evil tongue, which is never quiet."

"Now, Madame, is this the worst flaw I have?" he asked her.

"Yes," she said.

"Then," he said, "we can see here that I don't have as evil a tongue as you because you have reproved me and told me my worst flaw, but I haven't mentioned your worst flaw. What wrong have I done, then, Madame, being not as swift to speak as you?"

The lady held her peace and wished she hadn't said anything to him, but some people said it would have been better if she had been quiet.

The quick-witted Clermont was probably Jean de Clermont, Seigneur of Chantilly, who became Marshal of France in 1352. He died four years later at the battle of Poitiers.[7] On the day before the battle, Clermont crossed paths with an Englishman, Sir John Chandos, when both of them were out reconnoitering. According to Froissart's *Chronicle*, "some strong words and very ugly insults were exchanged," but not because the men were in opposing armies. Rather, it was because they were both wearing the same love token on their left arms, "a lady in blue embroidered in a sunbeam." Froissart says each man always wore the emblem, whether or not he was encased in his armor. They argued over who had the right to wear it, but because there was a truce between the armies, they couldn't fight. When the truce broke, Clermont fought gallantly but finally fell in battle. Some attributed his death "to the angry words he had exchanged the day before with Sir John Chandos," Froissart writes. Chandos not only survived the battle but distinguished himself by exhorting his prince, "Ride forward, sir, the victory is yours! Today you will hold God in your hand."[8]

No such gallantry is recorded for Boucicaut, who appears in the next story, although Froissart distinguishes him with the words, "the great Boucicaut."[9] Like Clermont, whom he succeeded as *maréchal de France* in 1356, Boucicaut is something of a lady's man. Despite the threat men like this pose to his daughters, Sir Geoffrey admires him, and in chapter 14 of this book, he refers to Boucicaut as a valiant, honored military leader.

Of thre ladyes that aresonned Boussycault
(Of three ladies who rebuked Boucicaut)

Boucicaut was a wise man and well thought of by the other knights. One time at a feast, three great ladies sat together for a long time talking about the fun things they had done. One of them said to the others, "May it go ill to the one of us who won't tell whether a man has desired her this year."

"Truly," said one of them, "I have been desired this year."

"By my faith," said the second, "so have I."

"And I also," said the third.

"Now," said the one who was the most pert, "May it go ill to the one of us who won't tell the man's name."

"By my faith," said one, "if you'll promise to tell, so will we."

The pert woman agreed. "It was Boucicaut," she said.

"Yes," said the second, "he was the one who desired me."

"He desired me, too," said the third.

"Ha," they all said, "is that so? Certainly he isn't as loyal or true as we had supposed. He is a mocker and a deceiver of ladies. Let's send for him."

Immediately, he was fetched. When he came he said to them, "My ladies, how may I please you?"

They said, "We have to speak to you. Sit down here by us."

They wanted him to sit at their feet, but he said, "Since I came when you called me, let me have a chair or a stool to sit on. For if I should sit so low, I might break my points and laces."

When he was sitting, the well-born ladies said, "How is it, Boucicaut, that we have been so deceived by you? We thought you were faithful and true, but you're nothing but a mocker of ladies."

He replied, "My ladies, have I deceived anyone?"

"Yes," said the first. "You desired my fair cousins here, and me as well, and you swore to each of us that you loved her best above all creatures. This was a great lie. You are false and deceitful and you ought not to be counted among good knights."

"Now, my ladies," he said, "you may have spoken, but you aren't in the right, and I'll tell you why. At the time that I said so to each of you, it was the truth. And therefore you're wrong to think of me as deceitful. But I suppose I must bear with your judgment."

When they saw that he wasn't abashed, they asked each other what they should do. "Let's draw lots for him, and the one with the shortest straw will have him," one of them said. "If I lose I shall quit my part truly."

"And I mine," said the second.

But Boucicaut said, "Nay, my ladies, by the sacrament of God, I am not to be dealt with this way. There isn't a woman here with whom I'll tarry."

He rose and went his way, and they were more ashamed than he was. It's dangerous to argue with men who know the world, and sometimes the people who think they know the most are the ones who are most deceived.

Jean le Maingre de Boucicaut is a subtle lover, not the kind of knight Jeanne and Anne de la Tour should even speak to, let alone banter with, the way the foolish ladies do here. In the story, the elegant Boucicaut demands a chair because if he sits on the ground at the ladies' feet both his dignity and his points and laces might snap. He's referring to the laces that attach his hose to his doublet; should they break, his hose would fall, exposing his legs. You can imagine the embarrassment for Boucicaut, and the delight of the three ladies, should that happen. Instead only the ladies end up being embarrassed.

In their mother's chamber, where the girls take turns reading tales aloud to the ladies assembled for the endless task of needlework, their mother might remark on this story, telling them that their father heard it from someone who had been present at the actual feast An older cousin, visiting from Brittany, nods vigorously, saying that she has heard the story before, too—in fact, she even knows who the three ladies were who rebuked Boucicaut.

Jeanne and Anne listen with interest, hoping their cousin will say more. But she doesn't, and the sisters know better than to ask her in their mother's presence. The message, not the gossip, is what they should attend to, although they can hope to hear more of the details later from a lady-in-waiting.

Although the girls' father might have secondhand information about the incidents in this story, he certainly wasn't close to the events in the next one. It has the feel of a folktale to it in the way it recasts the biblical phrase, let him among you who is without sin cast the first stone.

Of thre ladyes that accuseden one knyght
(Of three ladies who accused one knight)

One time three ladies accused a knight of lying and shut him alone in a room. They condemned him to death saying that never again would he deceive any lady, woman, nor maid. They were so angry toward him that each of them held a knife to slay him. Then he said, "My ladies, since it pleases you that I shall die without mercy, I pray that you grant me a boon." They agreed and he said, "Do you know what you have granted? I want the greatest whore among you to strike the first stroke."

Then they were all ashamed and each looked at the others and thought to herself, "If I strike first, I will be dishonored and ashamed."

When he saw them so astonished and abashed, he ran to the door, opened it, went out, and so departed from them. And thus the knight saved himself and the ladies were all mocked.

Now I leave this subject and turn to those who have their hearts set on the world, and who want to attend feasts, jousts, and dances, and to go on pilgrimages more for fun than for devotion.

When the Dancing and Singing Begins—Jousts and Feasts

Jousts were rituals by the Late Middle Ages, not the grand melees that tournaments had been earlier in the era where one army fought the other across wide areas. By the thirteenth century, tournaments had rules, referees, well-defined locations, and sometimes blunted weapons. Nevertheless, they were still dangerous, and excellent training for young knights who needed practice fighting within a group of soldiers, handling their horses in battle, taking captives for ransom, and being taken captive. And of course, knights won honor and fame, as well as material wealth—the horses, armor, and ransoms of the knights they captured, as well as prizes—in tournaments. Often, the tournament was preceded by individual jousting, where two knights at a time, wearing heavy plate armor, tried to knock each other off their horses. Although men were injured, few of them died at this kind of tilting.[10]

Some jousts weren't associated with tournaments at all, but were held to celebrate a knighting or, like in the story in chapter 8, the birth of a child. And like in that story, the jousting might be followed by a feast and perhaps a dance. During the jousting, while the knights galloped at each other, lances lowered, ladies and gentlemen watched from the gallery, cheering on their favorites. For girls like Jeanne and Anne, dressed in their finest, the excitement must have been intense. As they sat in the wooden gallery, rather like the football fans on bleachers at small-town homecoming games, Jeanne and Anne would have been carefully watched by their ladies-in-waiting, who had experienced enough of the world not to be overwhelmed by the sights, sounds, and smells that so thrilled the girls. Horses' hooves clattered, minstrels sang songs of love and war, and hawkers sang of steaming pies for sale, pies whose meaty aroma rose in the cool air to tickle Anne's nose. Down on the jousting field, bright banners fluttered in the breeze, and in their gaily colored pavilions, knights armed themselves. As the combatants, anonymous behind their armor, solemnly processed into the lists, the sisters would strain to hear the heralds crying out each knight's blazon in the formulaic language of heraldry— "*Argent*, a chevron gules with three besants gules"—and identifying the man by name and rank.[11] As their favorite knights' names were called, they might clutch each others' hands with anxiety—especially when Sir Bertrand hove into view. Their own brother, Charles, served as Sir Bertrand's squire, and although she had rarely seen him when he wasn't encased in armor, Jeanne thought she just might be able to give her heart to Sir Bertrand—if her parents required it of her, that is.

As the knights made ready to joust, there was plenty to be anxious about. Not only did Jeanne and Anne want Sir Bertrand to acquit himself well, they wanted him to do so without getting hurt. The expectant hush that fell over the crowd when he was unhorsed would have caused Jeanne's heart to skip a beat—until, with the help of Charles, his squire, Sir Bertrand rose and limped from the lists to the cheers of the onlookers. He would have been completely unaware of the prayers Jeanne had been saying on his behalf, but he might have heard Anne calling out, "Charles!" before Dame Agnes hushed her.

After the jousting ended and the prizes had been awarded, spectators and knights would gather for the feast, and it was here where Jeanne hoped her parents might introduce her to Sir Bertrand. Might she even be seated beside him, to share his cup and plate? But the long table Dame Agnes guides the sisters to is far from the high table at which the knights sit, and it's filled with other damsels who eye Sir Bertrand with just as much hope as Jeanne holds in her heart. From afar, she can see him being served by a page who proudly wears the livery of the Craon household. It's a moment before she realizes that the page is her own little brother Arcades.

Of course feasts weren't only associated with jousts; they might be held to commemorate a Church festival or a secular occasion such as a military victory, the return of an army, or a marriage. Because conversation was one of the main forms of entertainment at feasts, rumors flew, and reputations could be ruined. Sir Geoffrey doesn't speak idly when he warns his daughters about the dangers.

Whom you were seated next to was very important, since you shared not only gossip, but a platter and a cup with your neighbor. Beware drinking after the man with meat grease on his lips! Seating arrangements were strictly determined according to rank, and woe to the host who insulted a baron by placing him below an abbot. A list of rules printed by Caxton's successor Wynkyn de Worde tells who sits where, starting with a pope, who "has no peer." Then comes an emperor, a king, a cardinal, and a king's son. They are followed by an archbishop, and then a duke, who comes before a bishop, who precedes a marquis, who is before an earl. The earl is followed by a viscount, a baron, an abbot with a miter, the three chief judges and the mayor of London, an abbot without the miter, a knight bachelor, a prior, and so on down the line. The usher, an aristocratic servant in charge of the seating, would be expected to know all these ranks to avoid embarrassing his lord or causing a political debacle. He would also have to know who could share a table or a cup, how many people of each rank could be seated together, and many more distinctions that Wynkyn de Worde and other writers recorded.[12]

Conversation was not the only entertainment at the feast. Before and after dinner as well as between courses, musicians sang and played harps, horns, lutes, and pipes while professional dancers showed off the latest steps from the royal court. Traveling entertainers juggled, performed acrobatic tricks, and amazed the audience with their trained dogs, monkeys, and birds. Storytellers told tales of love and valor, sometimes episode by episode after each course. Hired actors might perform skits or plays in between courses or at the end of the meal. Sometimes the aristocratic hosts and guests themselves performed for their peers, dressing up in costumes to take part in an early sort of *tableau vivant*.

Not to be outdone by these performances, cooks labored for days over elaborate dishes that were more to be seen than eaten. Called *entremets* in France, *subtleties* in England, they were spectacles to be oohed and ahhed over by the guests: roasted swans or herons with their feathers dyed in the colors of the guest of honor's coat of arms and reattached so they looked like living birds, or boar's heads with gilded tusks. One Christmas feast featured three subtleties, food formed into the shape of Gabriel visiting Mary, the angel appearing to the shepherds, and the three kings honoring baby Jesus. Introduced by trumpet fanfares and paraded in by servants wearing the host's livery, the dishes might be set on the high table, or rolled in on a cart if they were too big for the table.[13] By the time the food got to the tables, it was no longer hot. That hardly mattered next to its tastelessness. With subtleties, appearances were far more important than taste. In fact, feasts were all about appearances, both of people and of food. Rare was the medieval guest who assumed she was in for a gustatory delight when she attended a feast.

Just because they were not members of the aristocracy doesn't mean that Katherine and Elizabeth Goodwyn wouldn't have attended a few feasts and jousts. In many towns the wealthy bourgeoisie, who were already imitating the aristocrats in so many other ways, began to stage their own jousts and even to form jousting societies. The fighters weren't only rich merchants and public officials (who looked remarkably like nobles once they were encased in armor). In the fourteenth and fifteenth centuries, jousting societies were often able to attract knights with aristocratic names but small pocketbooks to their contests by offering large prizes to the winners. The nobility reacted by restricting entrants in their own jousts and tournaments to those whose lineage contained no commoners. Heralds became increasingly important; it was their job not just to recognize men by their coats of arms, but to check each knight's credentials, to see whether or not he was noble enough to participate in an event. However, these restrictions didn't stop the upper middle classes from holding their own extravaganzas.[14]

Upper-middle-class feasts might also be impressive affairs, although many of them were far less sumptuous than the Christmas feast described above. Take, for example, a feast celebrating the marriage of the London wool merchant George Cely to Margery Punt of Little Over, Derbyshire, on a Tuesday in May 1484. George—not the bride's family—spent over twelve pounds on the celebration, which one scholar estimates equaled six months' worth of his normal household costs. In addition to wine, beer, and ale, he bought wheatmeal for bread, salt fish, mackerel, plaice, veal, mutton, two pounds of figs, and a hundred oranges. Some of the wedding guests stayed for several days and George was obligated to provide them with dinners and suppers. His other purchases from the same week include "seven gallons of raw cream, one gallon of 'sodden' (clotted) cream and eight gallons of curd" as well as butter, vinegar, honey, mustard, 480 eggs, chickens and pigeons (a dozen each), herons, geese, wrens, and six rabbits. For the wedding celebration, he also bought another three live rabbits to be turned loose for the amusement of the guests as "a symbol of fertility."[15] Impressive as these purchases may be, they imply nowhere near the pageantry associated with the feasts of wealthy nobles.

The expense of feasts and jousts can't be measured in money alone. Reputations, honor, even marriages might be squandered if young women weren't ever watchful, as we see in the next story.

Of them that gladly go to festes and Ioustes
(Of those who gladly go to feasts and jousts)
    I'll tell you about a lady who got great blame and slander at a great feast during a joust. She was young and her heart was set on singing and

dancing, which is why the lords and knights liked her so well. Her lord and husband was not at all pleased about this, but she often asked his permission to go to jousts and he agreed so he wouldn't be out of favor with the other lords, and so they wouldn't accuse him of jealousy. And for the sake of honor, he spent a lot at the feasts. But his wife could easily have seen that if she wanted to please her husband, she shouldn't have gone.

One time she planned to dance at a feast all night long until day broke. But suddenly, while she was dancing, the torches and lights were all quenched and there was a great hue and cry. When lights were lit again, her husband's brother saw a knight holding the lady, and they were standing a little to the side of the crowd. In good faith, I don't think much harm was done. Nevertheless, the brother-in-law told the lady's husband, and for the rest of her life, he mistrusted her, and he never loved her the way he had before. He was a fool, and so was she. Ever after that, each of them snarled at the other like hounds, and all their household went to nothing, and all for this little thing.

In a break from custom, Sir Geoffrey assigns the blame in this case to both the lady and her husband. The husband was cowardly to care about what other knights would think if he didn't allow his wife to attend feasts and jousts, and by not ruling his wife firmly, he brought about the downfall of their marriage. But his wife should have recognized that he didn't approve of her behavior. In fact, she should have known that all that singing and dancing with other knights was bound to lead to trouble. Sir Geoffrey continues his remarks about those who gladly attend feasts and jousts with a cautionary tale about a lady of his acquaintance.

I also know very well another fair lady who enjoyed going to feasts. She and a great lord got so much blame and slander that she become very ill for a long time and became nothing but skin and bones. She began to draw towards her death and they brought the sacrament to her. Then she said in front of everyone: "My lords and my friends, behold the condition I'm in. I used to be white, pink-cheeked, and well-shaped, and the world praised my beauty. Now look at what I've become. I used to love feasts, jousts, and tournaments, but now that time is past and I must return to the earth from which I came."

She continued, saying, "My dear friends, much has been said about me and my lord of Craon, but by that God whom I must accept, and on the damnation of my soul, he never had more to do with my body than did my father who engendered me. Although he did lay on my bed, it was without any immoral conduct."

Then people who had thought it was otherwise were ashamed, because they had blamed and slandered her and damaged her reputation.

For these reasons it is great peril to all good ladies that have their hearts set too much on the world. Don't be overdesirous of going to such feasts, because feasts and revels have been the cause by which many good ladies and gentlewomen lose their reputations. Of course, sometimes they must obey their husbands and their relatives and go to feasts. But my daughters, if you do go because you can't easily refuse, when night comes and the dancing and singing begins, keep yourselves away from it and always have some of your relatives or servants by you. Then if the torches or lights are quenched, they will stay by you to protect you from evil eyes and evil tongues who spy and say more harm than exists. Then you will keep your honor, your name, and your good reputation against liars who will always say evil things and forget the good.

Like so many of the ladies Sir Geoffrey mentions whose reputations have suffered, this one remains nameless. No need for his daughters to spread gossip; it's more important that they learn the tale's moral than its cast of characters. Of course, they couldn't have helped wondering who the lady was, especially since their father was so well acquainted with her. However, neither Jeanne nor Anne needs to be told who "my lord of Craon," with whom the lady in this story did *not* have an affair, is, since their brothers serve in his household. When the well-known Craon family is mentioned, the girls feel a sense of pride and just a hint of superiority.

At the end of the story, their father cautions them to keep their friends or servants by them when darkness descends on the feast. Although servants can protect you and your reputation, they must be chosen very carefully. Consider the lady-in-waiting in the following story, taken from the midst of a much longer tale, who is easily bribed with a hood. In contrast to the greedy and duplicitous lady-in-waiting, the lord's servant is trustworthy.[16]

> I want you also to have in your thoughts the example of the wicked damsel who for a hood that a knight gave her, and because of other gifts, promised that her lady would do his will and become defamed and dishonored. Great trouble came of this. For a servant of her lord, who had been brought up by him from his youth, perceived what was happening and told his lord. Afterwards the lord found the knight with his wife and killed him, and had his wife shut in prison perpetually, where she died in great sorrow.

Once before she died her lord came to the prison. He stood still and listened to her, and she mourned sorrowfully and cursed the one who counseled her to do this. The lord sent somebody to find out who had counseled his wife, and she said it was her damsel. The lord made the damsel come before him and commanded her to tell the truth. At last she confessed that she was the cause of the trouble, that she had counseled the wife, and that for her labor the knight gave her a hood.

The lord said, "For a little thing you have undone yourself and have been a traitoress to me. Therefore I judge that your hood and neck be cut off together."

And that was her sentence. Now you can see how important it is to keep good company, including your servants—take good and true ones who won't be blamed by any living man. The aforesaid damsel wasn't wise, but you should take wise servants and not fools, for fools and wicked servants are sooner brought to do some evil and to give evil counsel to their lord or lady than others. This damsel received the reward that she deserved.

The ladies-in-waiting, the ushers, the chamberlains, and other servants who spent their time in the actual company of their noble patrons were members of the upper classes, not peasants chosen to be raised in the noble household, as fairy tales would have it. Only the highest nobles were picked to be the servants of the king's chamber, and only daughters of gentlemen served noblemen's wives. The social rankings of servants in a household mirrored the rest of society. The laundress was probably from the lowest social class, whereas the lady who waited directly on the countess, sharing her meals and her chamber with her, might have almost equaled the countess in social rank.

Ladies-in-waiting were not all young, unmarried women, by any means. They might have been widows, or they might have been married women. Geoffrey Chaucer's was a two-career marriage; his wife Philippa was a lady-in-waiting to the queen, a position of no little prestige. Although they were much further down on the social scale than queens, or even than the Chaucers, the Goodwyn family would also have had servants, but not ladies-in-waiting. Like the Goodwyns themselves, some servants came from the middle class, girls and young women who worked in other people's houses to earn dowry money. Middle-class families recognized not only the money earned, but also the household and social skills young people learned by serving in houses of slightly higher-class people, as valuable commodities—they made these young people more attractive as marriage partners.

Not all the servants in the Goodwyn household came from the middle class, of course. The laundresses and scullery maids would be far below Katherine and Elizabeth in social station, never even sitting in their presence. Yet Joan, the servant with whom Katherine and Elizabeth shared gossip, joined them when they sat at their needlework, listening to stories from the book their father bought them. When they walked to church or neighbors' houses, she might accompany them as a chaperone, echoing the way the higher-ranking ladies in the next story would have been accompanied by ladies-in-waiting, who would hover silently in the background, just beyond the story's margins.

Once again, the setting is a feast, but the tale isn't really about going to feasts. Instead, it's a vehicle for Sir Geoffrey to warn his readers to obey their elders and not to behave too fashionably. The action takes place at a wedding feast, and although we don't hear what was served, there might have been an *entremet* such as one that was served at a fifteenth-century English wedding, in the shape of a woman lying in childbed, presumably to wish good luck in children to the newlyweds.[17] For the bride, however, the message might have been a little too immediate, since she would now be spending many of the years to come either pregnant or suffering the dangers and pain of childbirth.

How the yong ladyes were scorned and mocked of the olde & Auncyent
(How the young ladies were scorned and mocked by the old, wise ones)

Once many ladies and damsels came to a maid's wedding. As they were going towards the place where the dinner would be, they came to a very foul way in a meadow. The young ladies said, "We will go through this meadow and leave the high way."

The old, wise ladies said they would take the high way, for it was surer going and drier. The young ladies were willful and wouldn't follow them and thought they would arrive before them. And so they took their way through the meadow which was full of crumbling clods of dirt. As they walked, the clods broke under their feet and they fell into the dirt and the mire up to their knees. With great trouble they came out again to the high way and cleaned their hose and gowns with their knives as best they could.

It took so long to clean their hose and gowns that they didn't arrive at the beginning of the dinner. Everyone asked about them, but nobody knew where they were. At last, just as the first course was finished, they arrived. After they had eaten and drunk something, they began to tell how they had fallen into the mire.

"Yes," a good and wise old lady said, who had come by the high way. "You thought to take the shortest way, so that you might be there sooner and you wouldn't follow us. I'll tell you: some who think to advance themselves only hinder themselves. And one who thinks to be the first often finds herself the last of all."

The lady gave them these two ideas so they should know their faults. For as the holy man says, thus it is of this world: they who are first to have novelties of the world think to do well and be enhanced and held before others. But as for one who holds it well done, there are ten who mock it. For such a one praises them in front of them, but behind their backs puts out his tongue scorning and mocking them.

The young ladies in this story carry their tableknives with them, as was the medieval custom. Although manuscript images demonstrate that forks already existed and were used for activities such as turning the meat on the spit, they weren't common table utensils in England and France until the seventeenth century.[18] On the table at the wedding feast, the ladies would have found only spoons and napkins. They would spear their meat with the small knives they carried with them, the very ones they had used to clean the muck from their gowns.

If you visit La Tourlandry today, you'll find a path overgrown with cow parsley and lined with hedgerows running alongside the château, that opens onto a wide meadow dotted with buttercups. It's an inviting meadow, and you can see why the young ladies might be drawn to it, instead of the high way. Yet if you cross the meadow in the early summer, you'll find yourself tripping over clods of earth, sinking into mud, and wondering why you didn't take the road, instead. But when you stop to listen to the wind whistling across the fields and feel the sun shining down at you from a blue sky, you, like the young ladies of the story, might decide muddy shoes are a small price to pay for such a sense of freedom.

Not for Fun, but for Devotion—Pilgrimages

Medieval pilgrims expected to trek through muck and mire, since no highway systems or paved roads linked towns and cities. Despite the promise of discomfort, pilgrimages were common throughout the medieval period, from the early Middle Ages to the end of the era. People of all classes ventured to shrines a few miles from home, or they covered vast distances, crossing mountain ranges and wide bodies of water to visit shrines such as the one to Saint James in Compostella, Spain, or even further, to the Holy Land. Pilgrimages might take a day, a month, or years. Chaucer's pilgrims are traveling about seventy miles, from London to Canterbury, to visit the cathedral where Saint Thomas was martyred, but the Wife of Bath has already been on much longer journeys. She's visited Jerusalem three times, as well as Compostella, Rome, Boulogne-sur-mer, where she would have worshipped at a shrine to the Virgin Mary, and Cologne, with its shrine to the Three Kings.

For many medieval pilgrims, motivations were complex—piety can sit side by side with a desire for adventure without making the religious longing less real. Yet some pilgrims, like the Wife of Bath, may have traveled "more for fun than for devotion," as Sir Geoffrey puts it. Christine de Pizan warns women not to "use pilgrimages as an excuse to get away from the town in order to go somewhere to play about or kick up her heels in some merry company," suggesting that they did that very thing.[19] Sometimes pilgrims take to the road because it's spring and the air is finally warm and bright after a long, miserable winter. Some are looking for love, some for new experiences. Other pilgrims have been sent on pilgrimage as penance for their misdeeds. And then there are the many travelers who are motivated by their religious devotion to visit a place housing a saint's relic or gravesite, or a place where a miracle took place. When their son was sick with the plague in the fifteenth century, Richard and Agnes Cely "went on daily pilgrimage to a local shrine" in London to pray for him.[20] They probably gave offerings of money, as well, in hopes that the saint would intercede with God for their son. These offerings meant that attracting pilgrims could bring a lot of money to a shrine, so the Church's promotion of pilgrimages is hardly disinterested.

Despite the Church's approval of pilgrimages, many people— including John Wycliffe's followers—spoke out against them. The following story suggests one of the reasons pilgrimages were undertaken, and one of the reasons some people disapproved of them. As Sir Geoffrey coyly puts it, these pilgrims "intended to do other things than to say their matins."

Of a yong amorouse lady and of an esquyer
(Concerning an amorous young lady and a squire)

I'll tell you about a young lady who had her heart set on the world. A finely-dressed squire loved her, and she didn't exactly hate him. So that they could more easily be together, she told her lord and husband she had vowed to go on a pilgrimage. Her husband, who was a good man, allowed it because he didn't want to displease her, so she and the squire went on a pilgrimage to a monastery of Our Lady. On the way, they enjoyed speaking to each other, for they intended to do other things than to say their matins.

When they got to the church and were in the middle of the Mass, the foul fiend, who always lies in wait to enflame and tempt men and women, found them. He tempted them with pleasures so that they spent more time watching each other and making little love-signs to each other than they did paying attention to the divine service or saying their prayers.

Suddenly, by a miracle, the lady swooned. Some great malady took her and they didn't know whether she was dead or alive. Men carried her back to town as if she was dead, and her husband and friends were very sorrowful, not knowing whether she would live or die.

The lady was in great pain, but she saw a marvelous vision. It seemed to her that she saw her father and mother who had long been dead. Her mother showed her her breast saying, "Fair daughter, love and honor the husband and lord the Church gave you just as you loved this breast which nurtured you."

Then her father said to her, "Fair daughter, why have you given more pleasure and love to a man who isn't your own lord and husband? Behold this pit beside you, and know for certain: if you fall in this evil fire, you will abide therein." She looked and saw a pit full of fire so near to her that she almost fell in. She was very afraid.

Then her mother and father showed her a hundred priests that she had clothed in white for the souls of her parents, and they thanked her for it. After that it seemed to her that she saw the image of Our Lady holding a dress and a shift and saying to her, "This dress and shift will keep you from falling in the pit even though you have defiled my house and mocked it."

Then she woke up and gave a great sigh, and her lord and friends were joyful when they saw she wasn't dead. The lady felt all weary from her vision and her dread of the fiery pit. She asked for a priest, and immediately a holy man who wore a hairshirt and lived a holy life was brought to her. She confessed to him and told him her vision and the great fear she had of falling into the pit. She told him all her sins and about her wanton life.

The holy man said, "Dame, you are beholden to God and to his sweet mother who don't want you to be damned. They have shown you your peril and your salvation." Step by step, he explained her vision to her, showing her that the dress and shift Our Lady offered to her signified the charity she had shown when she clothed two poor women, giving one a shift and another a dress. "God sent you this sickness to show you your sin, but Our Lady saved you for your charity," the cleric said.

Once she had confessed, the lady regained her strength. She thanked God and left behind her foolishness.

About half a year later, the squire who loved her returned from a military expedition and expected her to take up where they had left off. He bantered and played as they had before, but she was standoffish. When he asked her why, she said, "That time is past. As long as I live I will never have love or pleasure with anyone but my lord and husband." Then she told him about her vision. He coaxed her, but she wouldn't change her ways. Finally, he left her and told others how constant and steadfast she was, increasing her praise and honor.

And therefore, this is a good example about how we ought not to go on holy pilgrimages for pleasure, but only for divine services and for the love of God. Also, you see here how good it is to pray and to have Masses said for the souls of your father, mother, and relations, because they pray and garner grace for those who are alive who remember them and do good for them. Further, it's good to give alms, for those who give alms get the grace of God.

Although Sir Geoffrey would disagree, on short trips to local shrines or long ones to distant lands, pleasure and prayer might mingle with no diminution of a pilgrim's piety. And having been on pilgrimage could bring solace and honor—as well as powerful prayers—to the pilgrims and their kin. Even Sir Geoffrey couldn't argue with that.

The idea of praying and giving alms might have been foremost in the minds of Katherine and Elizabeth Goodwyn when they, their mother, their neighbor Mary Rawson, and her mother all decided to trek across London to St. Giles, Cripplegate, on a fine spring day when white clouds were sailing across the sky and the air smelled of lilacs. When it was discovered that there was no room for Joan, the maidservant, inside the carriage with the rest of the party, she might climb up cheerfully beside the driver, pleased to be out of doors. It would be Joan's task to set out the picnic lunch they had brought with them when they found a grassy meadow along the way. However, the party atmosphere might have quieted as they neared St. Giles, especially when Katherine suggested they go the last mile on foot, to feel properly penitent.

Although pilgrims on their way to a nearby shrine wouldn't need them, those heading to Rome or the Holy Land might do the same thing modern travelers do—consult a travel guide. A particularly compelling medieval Fodor's is the Pilgrim's Guide to Santiago de Compostella, the shrine of Saint James in Spain that's still visited by thousands of people every year. The Pilgrim's Guide is filled with fascinating details about how to get there and what to avoid if you want to survive your journey, from horseflies and quicksand to a river whose water will poison your horse. It remarks on the languages, customs, and clothing of the people whose lands you'll pass through, such as the Basques with their barbarous speech and the Navarrese who disgustingly eat with their hands, not with spoons, and whose shoes are made of "uncured, hairy leather" that only covers the bottoms of their feet.[21] Pilgrims learn of an eight-mile high mountain they'll have to climb, the forests they'll have to battle their way through, and the fruits and fish they can expect to find on their way.

If you make it to your destination alive, the guidebooks tell you what to visit. Instead of attractions such as the Eiffel Tower and the Louvre, pilgrimage guides describe the Christian monuments to visit. In *The Solace of Pilgrims*, his fifteenth-century guidebook to Rome, the Englishman John Capgreve points out the pillar on which Jesus leaned when he preached to the people and on which he rested when he prayed to the Father of Heaven, and a guide to Jerusalem—written by a friar named Felix—tells pilgrims to watch for the descendents of the dogs who licked Lazarus's wounds. The Pilgrim's Guide takes readers through the city of Compostela with its ten churches, and then focuses on the basilica of Saint James, including its sixty-three stained-glass windows, its ten doors, and of course its miracles. By praying to Saint James in his church, the Guide says, the blind have had their eyesight restored, the deaf and dumb their ears and tongues, the lame have walked again, and those possessed have been delivered of their demons.[22]

Modern college students on Eurailpasses often adorn their backpacks with pins and patches advertising the places they've been, and similarly, medieval pilgrims could buy metal badges at the most famous shrines. At Canterbury the badges were in the shape of Saint Thomas, at Saint James in Spain, they were scallop shells, and in Jerusalem, they were palm leaves, which gives us the word *palmers*, a synonym for pilgrims.[23] Like modern college students, many medieval pilgrims sought the sights and adventures they could find at distant shrines. The records they left us make Sir Geoffrey's admonition to his daughters that "we ought not to go on holy pilgrimages for pleasure, but only for divine services and for the love of God" seem particularly apt. Adventure rivaled piety as an inspiration for many pilgrims' journeys.

CHAPTER 11

AS FIRE KINDLES STRAW—
LOVE AND ITS GAMES

Nineteenth-century scholars invented the phrase "courtly love" to describe an old idea: the stylized love affairs found in medieval literature, such as those in the stories of Lancelot and Guenevere, or Tristan and Isolde—stories that Jeanne and Anne de la Tour and Katherine and Elizabeth Goodwyn would have grown up hearing. According to the strict rules of the game of courtly love, the lady is distant and idolized, ruling her knight with a mere word. The knight's entire existence is devoted to serving his lady, and she inspires him to fight brilliantly in tourney and joust by allowing him to wear her favor on his helm. According to Andreas Capellanus, the twelfth-century author of *The Art of Courtly Love*, "A true lover is constantly and without intermission possessed by the thought of his beloved."[1]

Courtly love turns the usual relationship between medieval men and women topsy-turvy. No matter how high the knight's social position, he is always inferior to the lady, performing deeds to demonstrate his devotion to her. Instead of being subservient, the disdainful woman haughtily rules her lover, who grows pale and emaciated with love-longing. Whatever test she requires, he performs without hesitation. In contrast to the woman who jumped on the table when her husband asked for salt, the women in courtly love affairs are the ones making capricious demands.

This convention, which medieval writers sometimes called *fin'amors* (or "pure love"), began in French courtly literature before spreading to other parts of Europe. The twelfth-century Provençal troubadours sang about it, and in the same century Chrétien de Troyes included this kind of love in his long Arthurian tales. He was the first to involve Lancelot and Guenevere in an adulterous relationship in *The Knight of the Cart*, but the romantic liaisons associated with courtly love weren't always adulterous. In Chrétien's *Eric and*

Enide, the ideal relationship is between a husband and wife. From the twelfth through the fifteen centuries writers from Chrétien to Sir Thomas Malory composed tales that incorporated elements of courtly love; however, they were far more popular on the continent than in England.

Was courtly love a purely literary convention? Or did it reflect actual social behavior? It's difficult to know. Even the Latin treatise on the subject by Andreas Capellanus (or Andrew the Chaplain) is open to question because we can't know for sure whether he was being satirical. (Andreas's own title for his work wasn't *The Art of Courtly Love* but the more general *De Amore*, or *Concerning Love*.) Andreas writes about "courts of love," where questions of love affairs were judged by Eleanor of Aquitaine and her daughter, Marie of Champagne. But these courts may have been pure fiction. Furthermore, in the last section of his book Andreas condemns the very love affairs he describes in the early parts.[2]

Whether or not the complicated rules of courtly love ever found their way into the world outside fiction, affairs of the heart certainly existed. Christine de Pizan devotes two chapters of *The Book of the Three Virtues* to the chaperone of the young noblewoman involved in a "foolish love affair." In the second of these chapters, she provides a model letter that a chaperone might write to the lady advising her against such entanglements. Of course, the chaperone can only write such a letter after she has resigned from the lady's service, and she has to have a priest deliver it. Before then she must act discreetly, carefully guiding the lady away from folly, all the while knowing that sometimes a headstrong young woman won't listen to her. Instead the girl will talk with the attendants her own age who will agree with her about the chaperone: "The devil take the old bat! What a sourpuss! We're stuck with her until she fries in Hell!" they'll tell her, or even, "So help me God, Madam, you should scatter peas on the steps so that she'll break her neck!" No matter what happens, Christine says, the chaperone will get all the blame. If she simply can't convince her lady to give up the affair, it's time to quit—discreetly and without ever revealing the true cause of her resignation.[3]

Christine's descriptions of love affairs emphasize how foolish and wrong they are, and how much harm they can do to a lady's reputation. She doesn't make them sound like the courtly love affairs of the French romances where the lady becomes the sovereign lord of her subservient lover. Neither does Sir Geoffrey. He devotes twelve chapters to the topic of love affairs, styled as a debate between himself and his wife about whether their daughters should take paramours. Sometimes the lovers they discuss are suitors with marriage on their minds; at other times the relationship takes place outside of marriage. However these liaisons are portrayed, the men are hardly pale, wan lovers doing whatever they can to earn a mere glance from their ladies. Instead, they retain their superiority over women. And women, instead of being distanced and idolized, try their best to please their lovers. Nevertheless, the debate does incorporate a few aspects of the courtly love ideal, especially the notion that the lady's love can inspire a knight to heroic feats. The idea was prevalent not only in romances, but also in works written for knights such as Geoffroi de Charny's *Book of Chivalry*, which is as contradictory in its messages about chastity and love affairs as Sir Geoffrey's book seems to be—when we take Sir Geoffrey's role in the debate at face value, that is.

In this section of the book, his words clash with those in his prologue, where he says his fellow soldiers used "fine language to deceive the ladies and damsels" when they asked for their love. In fact, his fear "that some men are still like this nowadays" impelled him to make this book for his daughters in the first place, yet here he argues in favor of love affairs. Or at least he seems to. Like his prologue, Sir Geoffrey's love debate is a literary formula filled with conventional, literary ideas. The main message, voiced by Jeanne and Anne's mother, Jeanne de Rougé, echoes many other admonitions in the book: women should be very careful with their reputations and they should be cautious in matters of love. Sir Geoffrey's opinions throughout the rest of the book suggest that here he's merely playing devil's advocate.

The Argument of the knyght of the Towre and of his wyf
(The argument between the Knight of the Tower and his wife)

My dear daughters, as for loving paramours, listen to the great argument between your mother and me. I said to your mother, "Lady, why shouldn't ladies and damsels love paramours? For it seems to me that in good, pure love there may be nothing but honor, and it makes the lover better, more gay and jolly, and it encourages him to exercise himself more often in arms and to be better in all ways in order to please his lady. And in the same way, she of whom he is enamored tries to please him more as she loves him more. I tell you that it's a great act of charity when a lady or a damsel makes a knight or a squire good. These are my reasons."

The knight's reasons echo Charny's; the latter devotes a section of his *Book of Chivalry* to what his modern editors call "Deeds

Undertaken for the Love of a Lady." Charny argues that some knights achieve great deeds "because they put their hearts into winning a lady. . . . [T]hese ladies," he says, "urge them on to reach beyond any of their earlier aspirations."[4] Elsewhere in the book he advocates secret love affairs, saying: "men should love secretly, protect, serve, and honor all those ladies and damsels who inspire knights, men-at-arms, and squires to undertake worthy deeds that bring them honor and increase their renown."[5] With his focus on knights, Charny is silent when it comes to the dangers these affairs pose for young women. Jeanne de Rougé, on the other hand, is not.

The answere whiche the lady of the towre maad vnto her lord
(The answer the Lady of the Tower gave to her lord)

Then your mother answered me, "Sir, I'm not surprised if among yourselves men tell themselves this is why all women ought to love paramours. But since this argument comes before our own daughters, I'll answer according to my own advice and intention, for we must hide nothing from our children. You say, and so do all the other men, that loving paramours gives a lady greater worth and cheerfulness, that it makes her lovely and courteous, and that she does a great charity by making a knight good. These words are nothing but the sport and amusement of lords and their companions. They say that all their honor comes from their paramours, and that their lovers encourage them to go on voyages and to please them by deeds of arms. But these words cost them little in order to get the good will and grace of their paramours. Many of them use such words, saying they have done these things for their lovers. In good faith, however, they have done it only to enhance themselves and to get the notice and vainglory of the world.

Therefore I charge you, my fair daughters, don't believe your father. I pray that you'll hold yourselves pure and without blame and that you won't be amorous for many reasons. First, I'm not saying that a good woman of age may not love one person more than another, that is to say, some honorable person. People ought to love one person more than another in this way. But a lady shouldn't be so enamored that this love masters her and makes her commit some foul and shameful delight, either rightfully or wrongfully. People will watch this shameful deed, and the dishonor and gossip won't easily disappear because false backbiters would rather talk about evil than good. Thus the reputation of many a good lady is ruined. Therefore all women who are not married should keep themselves from taking paramours."

From her own experience, Jeanne de Rougé knows that the lords and their companions who amuse themselves with love games are the very ones who ruin ladies' reputations, soldiers like those with whom her husband rode in his youth. Their own reputations can't be easily tarnished, but those of her girls are as fragile as spidersilk. A man could blunder right through the web without ever noticing he'd done so, whereas the spider loses her home and all her hopes.

Although we hear Jeanne de Rougé's voice only through her husband's words, it's hardly inconceivable that conversations between wife and husband about the ideas in works such as Charny's led to this section of Sir Geoffrey's book. In this way, we might think of Jeanne de Rougé as a collaborator, not just a character, in her husband's book for their daughters.[6] And of course, by attributing these ideas to his wife, Sir Geoffrey avoids having to publicly disagree with Charny, a man he admired, and whom he will mention later in his book. Charny was as pious as Sir Geoffrey—he even owned the Shroud of Turin— and in his description of a knighting ceremony he emphasizes a knight's chastity, symbolized by a white belt with which the new knight is girt.[7] Charny seems to see no contradiction between his focus on a knight's piety and chastity on the one hand, and his encouragement of love affairs on the other. However, with three daughters' marriages to consider, Sir Geoffrey has a more practical approach.

The essentials of his argument, presented through his wife's moderate, reasonable voice, are contained in these two paragraphs, but Jeanne de Rougé continues at length, putting the ideas into a Christian context and drawing comparisons with classical literature, all of which Jeanne and Anne would have heard before.

Further, a woman who is enamored of a man may not serve God with as good and true a heart as she did before. I have heard many who were amorous in their youth say that when they were in church, their thoughts turned to their melancholy, their delights, and their paramours more often than God's service. The art of love has such a nature that when one is in church to hear Mass and the divine service, evil and foul thoughts come to mind even as the priest holds the body of Our Lord between his hands. This is the craft of the goddess called Venus, who has the name of a planet, as I heard a good and true man say. He preached that once the devil entered into the body of a damned woman who was happy and very amorous. The devil who was in her body caused her to do many false miracles, which is why the pagans considered her a goddess and worshipped her.

This was the very Venus who counseled the Trojans that they should send Paris, the son of King Priam, to Greece, and she made him abduct Helen, the fairest lady of all Greece. Because of this deed, more than forty kings and twelve hundred thousand others were slain. Venus, the evil goddess, was the principal cause of this calamity. She is the goddess of love who kindles and inflames amorous hearts and makes them think both night and day of the joy and foul delights of lechery.

Classical literature and mythology, and especially the Troy story, were well known and loved in the medieval period. The Lady of the Tower takes her metaphors from *The Iliad*, and she and her daughters have heard all about Greek and Roman gods and goddesses, whom poets such as Chaucer included in their works. Sometimes they are portrayed as instruments of the devil, as they are here. At other times, stories about them take place in a secular context, the way Chaucer's *Knight's Tale* does, while still promoting Christian ideas. In that poem, set in ancient Athens and Thebes, Mars, Venus, Saturn, Diana, and other classical deities play roles, but the underlying tenor of the story is Christian, as is Jeanne de Rougé's.

The debate continues as she gives her daughters an example of the way the devil tugs hearts toward love affairs—and away from God—even during the Mass.

I'll tell you a story about this. There were two queens on this side of the sea who took their foul delights and pleasures inside the church, during the divine service, on Holy Thursday during Passion Week. They didn't stop their folly until the service was almost done, and therefore God, who was displeased with them because of their enormous and foul sin, made their deed openly known among the people. They were placed under a heavy vault of lead, and there they died a horrible death. And the two knights, their seducers, were flayed alive. Now you may see how Venus, the goddess of love and the lady of lechery, tempted them so much that she made them take their foul pleasure in such a holy time, on Thursday and Holy Friday in Passion Week. From this example you can easily see how every amorous woman is more tempted within the Church than in any other place. And this is the first reason why a young woman must keep herself from such foolish love and not be in any way amorous.

The second reason is because many gentlemen are so deceitful that they desire every gentlewoman they can find. They swear they'll be true to them and love them without falsehood, and they say they'd rather die than think any villainy or dishonor. They tell the gentlewomen that they shall be praised because of their love, and any honor will come from them. These gentlemen tell them so many lies that it's a great marvel to hear them speak. And further, they give great, feigned sighs, acting as if they were thoughtful and melancholy so the good and the opposite of true lovers, for he who loves with good and true love fears doing anything that might displease his paramour. He isn't bold enough to say a single word, and if he truly loves her, I think it will be three or four years before he tells her his secret.

False lovers don't act this way. They don't fear saying anything that comes to their false tongues, and they have no shame of it. They tell their fellows everything they find out about their paramours, and they laugh and mock and scorn the ladies, making up gossip and lies about them. Those with whom they gossip use it in some evil way so that many ladies and damsels find themselves blamed.

Knights and squires found plenty of encouragement to urge young women into having affairs with them. Geoffroi de Charny's book was moderate in its approach to love when compared with other works that circulated in fourteenth-century France. Raoul de Hodenc went much further in his treatise on knighthood, arguing that "the knight should be a lover, loving truly for the sake of love and gaining all its benefits."[8] Arthurian romances also portrayed exciting adulterous affairs. Yet some romances and treatises on chivalry promoted virginity—the story of the Grail-quest in particular demonstrated the importance of chastity. Because of his affair with Guenevere, Lancelot is denied the Grail, whereas—in the thirteenth-century French *Quest of the Holy Grail*—Perceval's virginity allows him to achieve this highest honor. (In English versions, Lancelot's son Galahad is the Grail Knight. Even Sir Bors, who was, in Sir Thomas Malory's words, "a virgin save for one," can't compete.) And Ramon Llul's widely known *Book of the Order of Chivalry*—written in Catalan in the thirteenth century, but translated into French and English and later printed by Caxton—advocated purity in thought, word, and deed. Like Saint Augustine with his famous "give me chastity but not yet," Ramon came to this stance on chastity late in life, after he had become a Christian missionary. In his youth, he devoted himself to "chivalric pursuits," which may or may not have included love affairs.[9] By the time he wrote his book, Ramon found some of the same vices in knights that Jeanne de Rougé fears. In her next section, she recognizes that it's up to her daughters to be wary of men's words, instead of trusting in knightly virtue.

How a woman ought not to here the wordes or talkynge of hym that requyreth her of loue
(How a woman ought not to listen to the words or the speech of him who asks for her love)
  So that you won't be deceived, keep yourself far from that kind of talk. If someone starts to talk with you about such matters, leave him

alone or else call somebody else to be with you. In this way you will avoid and stop his talking. And know for certain that if you do this once or twice, he won't speak to you like this any more, but in the end he'll praise and fear you and will tell people you are assured and firm. In this way you will avoid being the subject of their gossip, and you will have no blame nor defame in the world.

Despite his wife's firm stance, Sir Geoffrey is unwilling to drop the subject of love affairs. His next question reflects the emphasis on class distinction that was so important in the medieval period; he suggests that if a man is of high enough social status, his word is to be trusted. Jeanne de Rougé's answer reminds her daughters that from viscount to villein, the promises of all men are suspect.

How the knyght answereth to his wyf
(How the knight answers his wife)
Then I answered, "Lady, you are very hard for not allowing your daughters to be amorous. If it happened that some noble, honorable and mighty knight, one of high estate, had set his heart on one of them and was willing to love her and take her for his wife, why shouldn't she love him?"

"Sir," said his wife, "I'll answer you. It seems to me that every woman, maid, or widow might as well beat herself with her own staff, for all men are not alike. Some take pleasure in the great courtesy shown to them, and think only honestly. There are some who are more anxious to ask their paramours to be their wives. But there are many others who are not like this at all, but completely to the contrary. When they see that their paramours take pains to be pleasant, they praise them less and within their hearts they doubt them. When they see them so enamored, they leave them and don't ask them to be their wives. And thus many a lady, because she seems too amorous and too open, loses her marriage, while those who keep themselves simply and who don't favor one man over another are the most praised and the soonest married.

"You once told me something that happened to you concerning a lady I won't name. You went to see her, willing to take her in marriage. She knew a marriage between the two of you had been discussed. She greeted you familiarly, as if she had loved and known you all the days of her life. You asked her for love, but because she wasn't wise enough to answer you courteously and well, you didn't ask her to marry you. If she had been more demure, more private and less forward, you would have married her. I have since heard it said of her that she was dishonored, but I don't know for certain if it was so. And certainly, sir, you are not the first to whom such a thing has happened. For many women have lost their marriages because of their coy, amorous looks. Therefore it's good for every unwedded woman to behave herself simply and purely, especially in front of those of whom marriage is spoken for her. I don't say, however, that men shouldn't be honorable to everyone."

Jeanne and Anne would well remember their father's story, which is recounted in chapter 6. Like their London counterparts, Katherine and Elizabeth Goodwyn, they would probably have agreed that the blame lay with the lady, not with Sir Geoffrey, even though he instigated the flirtation.

Social class is again the subject in the next part of the debate. Whereas climbing to a higher status is lauded in modern America, medieval Europeans believed you should cleave to your own class. Sir Geoffrey opens with another question for his wife.

How men ought to loue after his estate and degree
(How men ought to love according to their own estate and degree)

"What say you, lady? Would you have them kept so strictly that they should never show more pleasing manners to one man more than another?"

"Sir, I do not want them to take pleasure with those who are of lower estate or degree than they are. No unmarried woman should set her love on a man of lower rank than she is. If she did, her family and friends would consider her degraded. Those who love such people act against their honor, for people ought to desire nothing as much as honor and the friendship of the world. That's all lost as soon as she takes herself away from their governance and counsel. I could tell you examples of many who have been dishonored in this way and hated by their relatives and friends.

"And therefore, Sir, I, their mother, forbid them to set their love on one of a lower degree than their own. Nor should they have as their lord one of higher estate, for the great lords won't take them as wives, but they deceive them to have the delights and pleasures of their bodies, and to bring them to the folly of the world."

Despite the social gulf between aristocrats such as the Tour Landry family and the mercantile Goodwyns, the latter would have agreed wholeheartedly with the Lady of the Tower's ideas about marriage and class. Consider the example of Margaret Paston, another member of that rising middle class in England. In the 1460s, her daughter Margery fell in love with Richard Calle, who was a long way from being a gentleman. He came from a family of shopkeepers, and he managed the Paston family's estates. Richard returned Margery's affections and they made a private marriage agreement. In the eyes of the Church, this meant they were married. Gone were Margaret's plans to wed her daughter to a wealthy member of the gentry (she had been negotiating possibilities for several years). The erring daughter's brother revealed his feelings about the union when he wrote contemptuously that Margery would be selling "candles and mustard in Framlingham." It must have galled the Pastons even more to know that their trusted servant Richard had betrayed them this way. Although Richard was older than Margery, she was at least twenty when they married, so he was hardly robbing the cradle. And judging from a tender letter he wrote her soon after their secret wedding contract became known, he married her not out of some mercenary goal but because he loved her. He writes of the "great love that . . . is between us, and on my part never greater."[10] Later, the family had the bishop of Norwich examine the marriage vows to see if they could be dissolved, but because the Church recognized the private vows spoken by a couple as binding, the merchant family unhappily found itself forevermore related to a tribe of vulgar shopkeepers.[11]

If she had heard this story, Katherine Goodwyn might have found it appealing, with its emphasis on love. And this was exactly why her parents worried—what if she and John Plowryghte, a handsome new apprentice from a lower class than the Goodwyns, caught each others' eyes, or worse—hearts? Or did Katherine harbor any unsuitable feelings for George Rawson, the son of their neighbor, the less-than-exalted glover? Like the Pastons, the Goodwyns had higher hopes for their daughters' marriage prospects. So did Jeanne and Anne's parents. The rules about class and station continue, in the voice of Jeanne de Rougé.

How wedded wymmen whiche haue sette theyr loue to some of lower degree than they be of are not worthy to be callyd wymmen
(How wedded women who have set their love on someone of a lower degree than themselves are not worthy to be called women)
   Concerning women who set their love on three kinds of men—that is to say married men, priests and monks, and servants or people of no estate—I hold them of no esteem or value. They are greater harlots than those who are daily at the bordello, for many women of the world commit that sin of lechery out of need or poverty, or else because they have been deceived about it by the false counsel of bawds. But all

gentlewomen who have enough to live on and who still make the kind of people mentioned above their paramours do it when they are in great ease and because of the burning lechery of their bodies. They know well that according to the law of their marriage they may not have for husbands men of the church nor men of no value. This love has nothing to do with honor, but only dishonor and shame.

Although the speaker here is still Jeanne de Rougé, her voice is filtered through her husband's. He reveals an astonishingly lenient attitude toward prostitutes, acknowledging the role social conditions play in their lives. The contrast with Christine de Pizan's opinion in *The Book of the Three Virtues* is striking. In a short chapter addressed to prostitutes, Christine says she can speak to them, telling them to turn from "their disreputable lives" because Jesus did so, but her words are hardly as mild as Sir Geoffrey's. She calls them "miserable women so indecently given to sin," without recognizing the extreme poverty that may have driven them to their profession. Although she acknowledges the brutality of their lives and the danger they are constantly in from men's violence, she attributes the prostitute's choice of career to perversion and a sinful nature.

Following these sections, the debate returns to its primary topic, love. Sir Geoffrey reintroduces one of the points he began with, a woman's ability to enhance a man's honor through her attentions. He also repeats several of his wife's arguments, stressing that taking paramours brings a woman blame, shame, and defame. Although he frames these ideas as his wife's opinions, we can assume from his description of "over-false men" in his prologue that he shares her views. The soldiers of the prologue pretended to be in love with the young ladies they met. Although they spoke to the ladies in fair language, they desired only pleasure and didn't care about the ladies' reputations. Sir Geoffrey wants to protect his daughters from this kind of treacherous behavior. He is the speaker in this short chapter, and his wife replies at length in the next.

How hit is almesse to enhaunce a man in to grete valour
(How it is a charitable act to advance a man to great worthiness)

"Since you won't allow your daughters to love any paramours while they're unmarried, will you at least allow that when they are married they might take some pleasure in love by behaving themselves gaily and joyfully among honorable people? I have said before that it is a great happiness and honor to them to raise up a man who is of no esteem or worth."

The answere of the lady of the Towre
(The answer of the Lady of the Tower)

"Sir, I answer you this way. I am content for them to make good cheer with all honorable men, more to some than to others (that is, those of greater name and esteem). After they honor them, they may sing and dance before them virtuously. But as for loving paramours, I believe that no lady nor damsel, wedded or not, should put her honor in this balance for many reasons.

First, as I told you before, no amorous woman will be devout in her prayers or in hearing the service of God. From love springs many thoughts and melancholy, and many a one is so inflamed by love that if they heard the last peal of Mass ring and they knew that their paramour was coming to see them, they would miss Mass in order to please their paramour. Such is the temptation of Venus, the goddess of lechery.

Secondly, think of a mercer who weighs his silk, which is fine and light. Yet he may put so much of it on the balance that it will weigh more than the weight on the other side of the balance. This is like the woman who is so enamored of her paramour that she loves her husband less. She takes the love, honor, and fortune which he should have and gives it to another. A woman can't have two hearts any more than a greyhound can run after two beasts. Therefore it's impossible that she might love both her lord and her paramour with true love and without any deceit.

But God and natural reason constrain her. For as the scholars and the preachers say, God began the world by marrying man and woman. And when God himself came into this world, he spoke about it in a sermon about marriage, saying that marriage is a sacrament, and man and woman are joined by God. They are but one body, and they ought to love each other more than father and mother or any other creature. And therefore since God has put them together, no mortal man ought to separate them or take away the love that is between them. God said this from his own mouth. And therefore, the priest makes them swear at the door that they shall love and keep each other in both sickness and health, and that they shall not leave each other for any other, better or worse. And therefore I say, since the creator of all the creatures said there is only one thing and one body for which men ought to leave all other worldly love in order to take the love which ought to be in marriage, how then should the married woman give her love nor make any oath to some other without the consent of her lord? I believe that according to the will of God and the commandments of Holy Church, this may not be done without breaking faith on one side or the other. In good faith, I don't doubt that those who are amorous and who give their faith to other men love their own husbands little or not at all, and that they are cursed by God."

Chaucer's Wife of Bath is famous for the five husbands she's had at the "chirche dore," and like the Lady of the Tower, who mentions

Christ's sermon about marriage, the Wife of Bath also refers to the marriage at Cana of Galilee, found in John 2:1. However, the Wife of Bath twists the biblical text to her own purpose, which is to justify all five of her marriages. The Lady of the Tower is more circumspect, reading the biblical text as a defense of marriage vows. Many of her words in this section—in William Caxton's translation—mirror phrases found in modern wedding ceremonies: "since God has put them together, no mortal man ought to separate them"; "in both sickness and health"; "they shall not leave each other for any other, better or worse." Compare a certain English groom's words to his bride in the year 1456. He, too, uses phrases familiar to us:

> Here I take thee, Jennet, to my wedded wife. To hold and to have, at bed and at board, for fairer for lather, for better for warse, in sickness and in heal, to death us depart. And thereto I plight thee my troth.

(A modern scholar points out that after the word "depart" lost the meaning "separate" [making the phrase read "until death separate us"], the words were changed to "do part."[12])

A manual in the Hereford Cathedral Library suggests another set of words a medieval couple might exchange, and again, we can recognize at least one line:

> Wyth this gold ryng I thee wedde
> Gold and silver I thee give,
> And with my bodi I thee worship
> And with all my worldly goods I thee honoure.[13]

Both publicly acknowledged vows and those taken privately, such as Margery Paston's and Richard Calle's, were usually solemnized with a ceremony in front of the church. The couple exchanged vows and sometimes rings, the bride's dowry was guaranteed, as was the dower promised to her: the third part of her husband's property, which would be hers when he died (the kind of arrangement that gave the Wife of Bath such a strong impetus to marry rich old men). Afterward, everyone moved inside the church to hear the nuptial Mass. And then there was the wedding feast, a sometimes raucous affair with lewd songs and games.[14]

If the couple made their desires known more publicly than Margery and Richard did, the banns would be posted on the church door three weeks before the ceremony. This gave people who knew an important reason for the marriage not to take place time to object—if one member of the couple was already secretly married, for example, or if the pair were too closely related.

It's not prenuptial behavior but rather, how a woman acts after she is married that concerns Jeanne de Rougé in the next section. She mentions romances in which marriages—and even lives—come to tragic ends when women take paramours.

How a woman whiche wylle kepe her honour must doo ne shewe no maner of semblaunt to none
(How a woman who wants to keep her honor must make no outward display of emotion to anyone)

There are still more reasons to keep the love of her lord pure and far from the danger of envious people with cursed tongues who make false reports. If any woman makes a show of love to a man, and if her servant or somebody else sees it, when they leave her they will immediately talk about it in front of other people. The words will race so far that in the end men will say she has done dishonorable deeds. In this way, a good and true woman is blamed and dishonored. If her lord gets any knowledge of it, he'll never truly love her again, but will always speak ill of her, and they'll lose their happiness and the true love of their marriage. It's perilous for any married woman to put her lord and his estate and wealth and the joy of her marriage in this balance. I counsel that no good woman should have a paramour, for one word can cause a hundred evils.

I'll tell you an example of those who died because of the perils of foolish love. The Lady of Coussy and her paramour died from love, as did the Châtelaine of Vergi, and after her the Duchess of Burgundy, and also many others. Most of them died without confessing, and because of that, I don't know how they are getting along in that other world, but I don't doubt that the delights and pleasures they took in this world will be dearly bought. The delights of those who have been amorous are such that for one joy they received, they suffer a hundred pains, for one honor, a hundred shames. I have always heard it said that an amorous woman will never afterwards love her husband with a good heart, but she will ever suffer melancholy and anxiety.

The two romances mentioned here were often confused with each other even though their stories are very different. Froissart refers to both tales and compares their lovers to Tristan and Isolde. The first romance, of the Lady of Coussy, is better known as *Le Roman du Castelain de Couci et de la dame de Fayel.* It came into English as "The Knight of Curtesy and the Fair Lady of Faguell," and survives as a wretched sixteenth-century poem of sing-song quatrains, beginning:

> In Faguell, a fayre countrè,
>> A great lorde somtyme dyd dwell,
> Which had a lady so fayre and fre
>> That all men good of her dyd tel.

Even those desperate "dyds" don't make the lines any smoother.

In the poem, a married lady takes a courteous knight as her chaste paramour, "Hym for to love wyth herte and minde, / Nat in vyce but in chastytè." But a spying courtier tells the lady's husband about the relationship without bothering to mention its chaste nature. To get the knight away from his wife, the lord of the castle sends him out questing and then to the Crusades. When the Knight of Curtesy takes leave of his lady, "The teres ran from theyr eyen twayne." She cuts off her blonde hair for him to wear on his helm as he journeys forth; presumably her lavish headdresses would hide her shorn locks.

The knight performs brave deeds for his lady, first killing the dragon that's been harrying both man and beast in Lombardy, and then joining the Crusades. In Rhodes, he smites off the head of a Saracen before twelve infidels rush him—he manages to kill four of them before he, too, is slain. As he dies, he tells his loyal page to take his heart from his body, wrap it in his lady's yellow hair, and deliver it to her, all the way back in France. The audience is clearly expected to overlook the gory logistics of this feat. The page almost carries out the knight's last request, when he is waylaid by the lord of the castle, who squeezes the truth from him.

If you thought the story was taking a turn toward the macabre, read on. The lord of the castle takes the heart to the kitchen and tells his cook to dress and spice it delicately. He serves it to his wife and watches her eat it. Then he tells her what it is:

> Your knight is dead, as you may se,
>> I tel you, lady, certaynly,
> His owne hert eaten have ye.

Shouldn't she be horrified or enraged? Instead, she's sad. Very sad. So sad that she takes to her bed, gives up all food, and dies. As she takes her last breaths, she calls on Jesus to have mercy on her.[15] True, as Sir Geoffrey (or his wife) says above, she didn't confess to a priest, but neither did she die in great sin.

You can just hear Anne sighing as she listens to a traveling entertainer singing the final stanza. She's still mourning the Knight of Curtesy when the singer plucks his harpstrings and begins a new romance.

In this one, the Châtelaine of Vergi has no time to confess or to call on Jesus before she dies. And certainly the Duchess of Burgundy, who plays a role in the same story, doesn't. The thirteenth-century poem was popular at the fourteenth-century court of the Dukes of Burgundy,[16] so the Tour Landry family would have welcomed the chance to hear it, despite its immoral characters.

The Lady of Vergi, unlike her counterpart in the previous story, was unmarried when she agreed to a secret affair with a knight. Theirs was hardly a chaste romance. The knight would wait in an orchard until the lady sent her little dog as a signal that he could come to her chamber, where he would spend the night with her.

Alas for the lady and her knight—the Duchess of Burgundy falls in love with him. When he politely rebuffs her, she takes the role of Potiphar's wife when Joseph refused her advances: she marches directly to her husband and tells him that the knight propositioned her. The Duke is astonished and speaks to the knight. After much anguish, the knight finally reveals his secret love to the Duke, who accompanies him on a tryst in order to test him. Although the lady the knight is sleeping with is the Duke's own niece, the Duke still promises the knight that he would have his teeth "pulled out one by one" rather than reveal the knight's secret.

But he's not counting on his wife's wiles. Through some deceitful behavior, she worms the truth out of the Duke, who swears her to secrecy. Of course she agrees, but at the next opportunity, a dance at the Duke's court, she speaks to the Châtelaine of Vergi about her clever little trained dog.

What is the lady to think? She assumes her knight has told the Duchess about their affair. Furthermore, she assumes that he loves the Duchess more than he loves her. So great is her anguish that she falls down dead. The knight finds her, kisses her dead lips, and runs a sword through his own heart. The Duke finds the dead lovers and a maid tells him everything that has happened. Furious, the Duke seizes the knight's sword and in the middle of the dance, swaps his wife's head off. He has the lovers buried in a single grave, and then the Duke takes ship for the Crusades. He becomes a Knight of the Temple and never returns to France again.

Like Sir Geoffrey's stories, *The Châtelaine de Vergi* ends with a moral. However, although Sir Geoffrey would have used the story to warn against taking paramours, the lesson in the romance is to keep your love a secret so "false and inquisitive felons who pry into the loves of others" won't discover it.[17] Geoffroi de Charny would agree—he advises knights to guard their lovers' honor by keeping affairs secret.

In the next story, Jeanne and Anne's own mother has to deal with men who want her as a paramour. The girls may have enjoyed hearing these sad romances, but they would have been expected to model their behavior on their mother's, not on the Lady of Coussy with her chaste love, and certainly not on the Châtelaine de Vergi, who consummated her love for the knight. Far better to be thought distant and cold, as the Lady of the Tower is accused of being, than to be dishonored. Sir Geoffrey continues to play devil's advocate in the sections below, but in truth he and his wife are in firm agreement about appropriate behavior for young ladies.

How a knyght loued the lady of the toure
(How a knight loved the Lady of the Tower)

"Lady, you cause me to marvel because you so strongly caution them against love. Should I believe from your words that you have never been amorous? Certainly I have heard the laments of some people whom you never mention."

"Sir," said the lady, "I think you would not believe me if I told you the complete truth of it, but to say that I have been asked for love— well! I have often perceived that some men were about to speak to me about love, but I always stopped their words and called somebody over to me. One time, when many knights and ladies were talking with me, a knight told me he loved me more than all the ladies in the world. I asked him if it was very long since that sickness had taken him. He said he hadn't dared to tell me for two years. I told him that was hardly any time at all, that his was nothing but a temptation. He should go to church, cast holy water on himself, and say his Ave Maria, and his temptation would immediately leave him, for the love was new.

"He asked me why and I said that no paramour should tell his lady he loves her before seven and a half years have passed. When he started to argue with me, I called out, 'Everyone, listen to what this knight says, who's loved a lady for only two years.'

"Then he asked me to keep my peace, and said in good faith he wouldn't speak to me about it. But in the end he said, 'Lady of the Tower, you are distant and cold and your words about love are too full of pride. I think you've always been this haughty. You're like the Lady of the Fucille, who told me she would never listen to anyone's words or read their notes, except for one time when a knight sought her out.

But she hid her uncle behind her to hear what the knight would say, and in doing so, she did great treason, because the knight didn't think anyone else had heard him except for her alone. I dare say that you both speak well, but you have little compassion towards those who require mercy and grace. And she holds your opinion that no ladies or damsels may disport themselves with anyone other than their lord.' "

"But, Sir," the Lady of the Tower said to her lord, "as for your daughters, I pray to God that they may come to honor as I desire. My intention is not to give orders to any lady or damsel except my own daughters, of whom I have the charge. If it please God, every good lady will govern herself well according to her honor without my meddling, for I have very little wit and understanding of such matters."

In a chapter that Caxton omits (it may not have been in the manuscript he worked from), Sir Geoffrey tells his daughters that while they need to be wary of love affairs, they also shouldn't be too hard with men. He mentions a lady who, like his wife, tested paramours by making them wait for seven years. This lady, Sir Geoffrey tells his daughters, was too hard. Of course when his wife uses the seven-year rule, Sir Geoffrey has no objection at all. The hypothetical ladies he keeps bringing up, as in his following answer, are sometimes held to a different standard than are his wife and daughters.

In his next speech, he repeats the idea so many knights were enamored of: a lady's love brings honor to a knight. A fifteenth-century knight named Jacques de Lalaing wrote in his *Chronicles*, "Know that few gentle men come to high estate of prowess and good renown, save if they have some lady or damosel of whom they are amorous."[18] The Lady of the Tower wasn't fooled by this reasoning at the beginning of the debate, and she isn't here, either. Nor does she allow her daughters to fall for this false counsel, in her closing arguments in the question of love affairs.

Yet speketh the knyght of the Toure
(The Knight of the Tower continues)

"And yet, my lady, I will still argue with you saying that a lady may bring honor to someone who wasn't bold enough to have it, except from the love and pleasure of his lady. His confident expectation of obtaining the honor and grace of his paramour could make him a good knight, renowned among the valiant and hardy. For just a little kind treatment, a man of low degree might be enhanced by his love and counted among the worthy and the valiant."[19]

How one must be wyly and subtyll for to discouere his loue
(How one must be wily and subtle in order to make his love known)

"Sir, it seems to me that there are many kinds of love, and men say one is better than the others. If a knight or a squire loves a lady or damsel honorably, and wants her to keep her honor and her courtesy, and loves her because of the good she does to him, such love is good, when it comes without prayer or request."

"What, lady, if he asks her to kiss or embrace him? Surely it doesn't matter; the winds blow it away."

"Sir, concerning my daughters and others, I consent that they may behave courteously towards men, and that others may kiss in front of everybody as long as it's done honorably. But as for my daughters who are present here, I forbid kissing and all such manner of play. For the wise lady Rebecca, who was very noble, says that kissing is the near cousin of the foul act. Sybil says that the first token of love is the look, and after the amorous look they come to kissing, and then to the act. That act takes away God's love and honor, as well as the world's, and thus they go from one thing to another. It seems to me that as soon as they allow themselves to be kissed they put themselves in the subjection of the devil, who is very subtle. At the beginning one thinks to keep himself firm and strong, but the devil deceives by his subtle craft. One kiss draws the person towards another, just as fire kindles a straw, and that straw kindles another, and at last the bed is on fire and the house as well. Love is the same way.

And so I charge you, my fair daughters, don't gamble this way. For such playing often leads to foolish looks, and from that blame and a bad reputation may come.

I once heard a tale about the Duchess of Bavaria. People said she had at least twenty subjects who loved her, and she gave each of them tokens of her love. She played tables with them and won coursers and hackneys and expensive fur and rings and precious stones from them, as well as many other jewels. But it couldn't last and in the end she was blamed and defamed. It would have been better for her honor if she had bought and paid for everything she won from them, because it was twice as expensive as it was worth. It's perilous for any good and honorable woman to live this way. In the end, even the wisest find themselves mocked, blamed, and foully defamed for such dallying. Therefore my fair daughters, take example here, and don't be too curious to play or to win such brooches or clasps. Because of greed to have such jewels for no money, many a woman puts herself in subjection, and they are often deceived. Thus it's good to be on guard before the coming of the stroke."

The stroke the Lady of the Tower ends with is God's punishment, and it's far better to guard against divine wrath than to enjoy the transitory pleasures of the world. After all, as Jeanne de Rougé says, just as fire kindles straw, finally burning both the bed and the house, the fire of love likewise leads from innocent pleasures to deadly sin. And as we see in chapter 12, the devil knows exactly how to tempt an unwary Christian across the stepping stones of sin, one leading directly to the next.

The blame and defame the Duchess of Bavaria gets for herself result from her attachment to worldly pleasure—like taking paramours. In the love debate, the Lady of the Tower is allowed the last word. Although other women may have paramours or kiss men in public, her own daughters may do no such thing. Despite the romances they've heard or the arguments Sir Geoffrey and other knights put forth about the ennobling facets of affairs, in the end, there's no question about what's expected of Jeanne, Anne, and Marie. Both their father and their mother want them to spurn fashionable love games, before and after they're married.

CHAPTER 12

THE DEVIL'S SUBTLE CRAFT—VICE AND SIN

"**T**he devil deceives by his subtle craft," the Lady of the Tower says when she connects love with lechery. The tools of the devil's trade—the Seven Deadly Sins—would have been well known to Katherine and Elizabeth Goodwyn. They would have seen them personified in morality plays, the allegorical entertainments that taught medieval audiences of all classes about salvation. The sisters—like their French counterparts Jeanne and Anne de la Tour—would also have heard about those sins in song and verse, in story and in Sunday sermons. They knew that pride was the principal sin, just as surely as they understood how closely the sins were intertwined. As we've seen in the chapter on fashion, pride may lead people to don fashionable clothing, but the route from there to lechery is direct. How easy it was for the devil to trap unsuspecting sinners into committing sins of greed, envy, gluttony, anger, and sloth—yet if she only remembered in time, it was equally easy for a sinner to disentangle herself from those nets. The way out? Confession, Sir Geoffrey tells them.

Of the vyces that renne & ben in many one
(Concerning the vices that assail many people)
My fair daughters, he who sees the good but chooses the evil must repent. In this world we have examples of evil, and more people choose the bad than the good. Those who do so are fools because they take themselves from the commandments of God from which salvation comes. We hold little store by his law because we see that for the most part, the world rules itself according to carnal desires and is full of vainglory. One person is proud of his knowledge, another of his riches, one of his nobility, while some are envious of other people's wealth and honor. Some are full of anger and hold evil will in their hearts towards other people. Some are so full of the stinking fire of lechery that they are worse than wild beasts. Others are gluttons, drinking too much wine and eating fine foods. Some covet other men's goods, or are

thieves, usurers, plunderers, traitors and backbiters. These people are disciples of the devil. They follow the doctrines of their master by whose counsel they are joined with sin and lie in the way of damnation. The devil holds them bound fast until the time of true and pure confession. In this way most of the world is overcome.

Most of the world may be overcome by sin, but there's hope for Jeanne and Anne de la Tour, as their father means to show them. Not for them the torments of Hell, if they will only hear his words, and heed the lessons of the ladies in his tales. He begins with Eve.

Listening to the Serpent—The Nine Follies of Eve

Jeanne and Anne know how wily and corrupt Eve is—a judgment they shared with most medieval Christians. In fact, their father takes his nine chapters about the follies of Eve—which I summarize here— directly from *The Mirror for Good Women*. Because many preachers borrowed from this collection when they composed sermons, these stories would have been familiar throughout France. And because the book was available in Sir Geoffrey's library, the Tour Landry priests would have spiced their sermons with its tales.

On an early summer afternoon, the Tour Landry ladies might picnic in the park outside the château walls. After the meal, the ladies gather on the grass and try to pay close attention as Jeanne reads aloud from her father's book. But sometimes a flicker of sunlight in the bright green chestnut leaves, or the buzzing of a honeybee seeking pollen, or the sweet scent of the last lilacs draws their attention away from Eve and out into the world.

When he blames Eve for evil in the world, Sir Geoffrey echoes Church authorities and legions of medieval writers. Following his source, he writes, "If Eve hadn't fallen into the sin of disobedience, there wouldn't have been a fish in the sea nor a beast on the earth or bird in the air that wouldn't have been under her command." If Eve hadn't broken God's commandment, childbearing would have been painless and people would never have suffered in any way, "not hunger nor thirst, cold nor heat, work, sickness, sadness, nor earthly death."

The ladies shift on their grassy seats, making themselves comfortable. Such suffering as Sir Geoffrey writes about exists all around them, but on a day as fine as this, it hardly seems to matter.

Jeanne looks up from the page as a saucy crow calls from a nearby branch. Then she turns back to her father's words: Eve's first foolish act was disobedience. She listened not to God but to the serpent—which had a face like a woman's. Sir Geoffrey wasn't the only one to see the serpent as feminine; medieval artists sometimes gave it the head of a woman. The serpent deceived Eve with its blandishments, which led to her second folly: instead of asking her husband's opinion, she foolishly and easily agreed with these pleasing words. For Sir Geoffrey, Eve's second sin implies a clear moral that ties this story to his tales about wifely obedience: always ask your husband instead of making up your own mind.

By the third folly, Sir Geoffrey has identified the serpent with Lucifer. Just exactly what the third act is, however, isn't clear. At first it's simple: you must obey God's prohibitions, which Eve did not do. But then we learn that she didn't merely disobey, she also equivocated, telling Lucifer that if she and Adam ate the fruit, they *might* die, but they might not. This gave the serpent the opening he needed to cajole Eve with flattery, just as men do when they try to get women's love dishonorably. Like Eve, the women who give in to these temptations end up "shamefully defamed."

The ladies-in-waiting exchange a meaningful glance, both of them reminded of the recent gossip about a fine lady from a nearby château who has allowed herself to be flattered into a shameful liaison from which her reputation will never recover.

Jeanne reads on, reaching the fourth folly, foolish beholding. If Eve hadn't looked at the forbidden fruit, she wouldn't have fallen into foul thoughts, and if she hadn't fallen into foul thoughts, death would never have come into the world. Man's worst enemy, Sir Geoffrey says, is the eye, which deceives. It leads to temptation, especially in love, and thence into all kinds of trouble, including fornication and even murder.

Like Eve's fourth folly, her fifth and sixth are also associated with the senses. The fifth folly was touching the fruit, the sixth, eating it. "It would have been better if she had had no hands," Sir Geoffrey says. Because of this deed, "we and all the world were given up to the peril of death and hell and made strangers to the great joy of paradise." In the same way, touching other people and eating and drinking delicacies and "strong and sweet wines" lead directly to lechery—and lechery leads the soul to hell.

When God told her she would die, Eve didn't believe it: her seventh folly. For this, she and Adam suffered for 5,000 years until the Harrowing of Hell. Then, after dying on the cross, Christ descended into hell to defeat evil and deliver those who suffered there. Like Eve,

Sir Geoffrey says, sinners nowadays don't think about death, which follows them as closely as the thief that comes in at the back door to rob and cut men's throats. No man knows when it will come.

The eighth folly Eve shares with Adam. When she gave the fruit to her husband and asked him to eat it, he did. "Therefore," the text says, "they were both partners in our great sorrow and evil." Husbands should never take their wives' counsel without careful consideration, because women's advice is often foolish. As further evidence, Sir Geoffrey includes the example of a baron he knew who died because he believed everything his wife said. However, the circumstances surrounding the baron's death are left unstated, and Sir Geoffrey quickly shifts the focus back to women, who should counsel their husbands wisely instead of giving foolish advice the way Eve did.

Eve's ninth folly was the most serious: when God asked her why she broke his commandment, she made excuses and blamed the serpent. In the same way, people rationalize their sins when they go to confession, but doing so is no confession at all. Yet here is a reminder of the importance of confession, Sir Geoffrey's emphasis from the very beginning of his section on sin and vice.

Katherine and Elizabeth Goodwyn would have been just as familiar with Eve's sins as were the Tour Landry sisters. They would have heard the catalogues of virtuous and sinful women that medieval writers were so fond of. In Sir Geoffrey's book, the Nine Follies of Eve are followed by a section of tales about wicked women, many of them from the Bible, and another section about good biblical women, all taken from *The Mirror of Good Women*. These tallies might have made the Goodwyn sisters think of Chaucer's works; he includes a short catalogue of virgins who preferred death to dishonor in *The Franklin's Tale* and a long list of virtuous ladies in his poem *The Legend of Good Women*. But his most famous catalogue appears in *The Wife of Bath's Prologue*, where Jankyn, the Wife's fifth husband, makes her listen to him read from his book of "wikked wyves." Starting with Eve and moving on to examples such as Socrates's famously shrewish wife Xanthippe, and Clytemnestra, who murdered her husband Agamemnon, Jankyn reads tale after tale until, in a rage, the Wife of Bath rips three pages out of his book and punches him on the cheek so hard she knocks him down. He hits her back, but she tricks him to win the fight and then demands that he burn his book. After that, she says, they never had any arguments, and she was as kind to him as any wife from Denmark to India, and as faithful as he was to her. Chaucer leaves it to his readers to decide just how faithful that might be.

Katherine and Elizabeth might argue that very point, the older sister taking Chaucer's words at face value, the younger disagreeing. But they would have no such disagreement about the stories in Sir Geoffrey's book—ambiguity isn't his style. Many of his tales are as familiar to modern readers of the Bible as they were to his medieval audience, so here I include only a selection of the less well known ones, leaving out for example the story "Of the Jew and the pagan who were skewered with a sword" (a retelling of Numbers 25), and the tales of Tamar, of Joseph and Potiphar's wife, of the daughters of Moab, and of the daughter of Jacob. In most of Sir Geoffrey's biblical stories about women who committed deadly sins, the sinner comes to a very bad end. Of course, he counters these examples with ones about biblical women who demonstrate virtuous behavior.

Juggling Coal into Beauty—Flattery

Some stories illustrate not the Seven Deadly Sins but the follies Eve committed, especially that of listening to flatterers, who "are like jugglers who will make a piece of coal seem like a fair thing." Sir Geoffrey writes, "Such flatterers deceive rich men just like the man did with a woman who sold cheese and who was foul of face. He told her she was fair and pretty, and the old woman was so foolish that she thought he spoke truthfully. She gave him a cheese, and after he got it, he mocked her behind her back." To this tale he adds another scene about flattery that he himself witnessed during his soldiering days. Jean, the Duke of Normandy (later Jean le Bon), whom Sir Geoffrey speaks about here, led the army that recovered the town of Angoulême from the English in 1436. Then the French held Aiguillon siege for four months before they finally retreated.[1] In Sir Geoffrey's view, women have no monopoly on flattery—either giving or receiving it.

> I want you to know the example that I saw in the town of Angoulême as the Duke of Normandy came before Aiguillon. Several knights were shooting at a mark for sport. When the duke came into the park, he demanded that one of the knights give him a bow and arrow to shoot. After he had drawn his arrow, two or three knights near him said, "Certainly my lord shoots well." Another knight said, "Holy Mary, how well he aims," and another said he wouldn't want to have to take arms against the duke. In this way they praised him, but it was nothing but flattery, because he shot worst of all the others. Flatterers are always agreeable this way, pleasing lords and ladies and making them believe they are stronger and wiser than they are, and causing them to become arrogant.

Concerning flattery, medieval writers agree: rich and powerful people have to be more cautious of it than do the poor, because the rich have more to lose. The flattery can come from men and women who are their social equals, but also from their servants, who might have both something to gain from flattering girls such as Jeanne and Anne—as well as plenty of opportunity to whisper into their ears. Flattery may lead to the deadliest of the sins, pride, but for Sir Geoffrey, lechery merits even more attention. In the following stories, he illustrates the perils of anger, greed, and gluttony before settling into the subject of lust.

Like a Toad on the Heart—Anger

Of the Burgeys whiche wold neuer pardonne her euylle wylle to one her neyghbour wherfore she was dampned
(Of the Burgess who would never pardon her evil will to one of her neighbors and who was therefore damned)

My fair daughters, beware that the sin of anger doesn't overcome you. On this topic, I'll tell you a story I heard in a sermon, about a great burgess who was very rich, charitable, and highly praised as a good Christian. Through a severe illness she was brought to her deathbed. Her parson, an honest and holy man, came to hear her confession. He spoke about the sin of anger, telling her she must pardon all those who had done her wrong. When she heard that, she said that a woman who was her neighbor had done her so much wrong that she could never forgive her with a good will.

The holy man tried to teach her through stories. He reminded her of Jesus Christ, who forgave those who killed him. Then he told her the story of a knight's son whose father had been slain. This knight's son came to a hermit and confessed to him. When he got to the sin of anger, he said that he could never forgive the one who had slain his father. The holy hermit told him many moral stories, including how God forgave his own death, until finally the young knight forgave his father's death with a good will. When the young knight came to kneel before the crucifix, the cross bowed to him and a voice was heard saying, "Because you have humbly forgiven for my love, I forgive all your sins and misdeeds and you shall have grace to come to me in celestial joy."

The parson told this story and many others to the burgess, but nothing he could say would cause her to give up her ill will. That night, the parson had a vision in which he saw devils taking the burgess's soul away with them. He saw a huge toad on her heart.

In the morning, people told him she had passed out of this world. Her children and relatives came to speak with him about her burial, asking that she might be laid to rest within the church. But the priest said she couldn't be buried in any holy earth because she would never forgive her neighbor, and therefore she died in deadly sin. When her friends and family argued with him about this, he told them if they had her belly opened they would find a huge toad on her heart. "If you don't find what I say, I am content for her to be buried where you want her to be," he said.

They spoke to each other, mocking the parson's words and saying it wasn't so. She should be opened up, they said, so they could mock the parson even more. But when they had her body opened they found an enormous toad, very foul and loathsome, crouching on her heart.

Then the priest questioned the toad, asking him why he was there and what he was. "I am the devil who has tempted this woman these twenty-five years," the toad said. He told the priest he had had the best advantage in the sin of anger, ever since she got so angry at her neighbor that she wouldn't forgive her. "The other day when you confessed her," the toad said, "I kept my four feet on her heart clutching her with my nails and enflaming her anger so she would have no will to forgive. Nevertheless, there was an hour when I feared you would have her from me, and that you might convert her with your preaching. But in the end I had the victory so that she is ours for ever more."

When all those who were there heard these words, they marveled. Never again did they speak of burying her in holy earth. And so here is a good example about how one ought to forgive others, for the one who doesn't forgive with a good will shall have forgiveness from God only with great pain. And perhaps it might happen to that one as it did to the aforesaid burgess.

The toad crouching on the dead woman's heart may be a devil, but the sin of anger could bring out the animal in humans, too. Take, for example, this passage from the *Ancrene Wisse*, or *Guide for Anchoresses*, a thirteenth-century work of spiritual guidance written at the request of three aristocratic female recluses.

> Anger is a shape-changer, as we are told about in stories, for it deprives a man of his reason and entirely changes his disposition, and trans-forms him from a man into the nature of a beast. An angry woman is a she-wolf; a man is a wolf, or a lion, or a unicorn. While there is ever anger in a woman's heart, if she is saying versicles, or her hours, *Aves*, *Pater nosters*, she is doing nothing but howling. It is as if she has changed into a she-wolf in God's eyes.[2]

The great burgess may have seemed like a good Christian outwardly, but the anger she held toward her neighbor turned her prayers into nothing more than wolf's howls, as the author warns the young anchoresses in *Ancrene Wisse*.

Embedded in Sir Geoffrey's story of the burgess's anger is another tale, one about the virtue of forgiveness: the example of the young knight who forgave his father's murderers. As an indication of how important the knight's change of heart is—and how closely he imitated Christ by his actions—the crucifix bows to the knight.[3] Unlike the knight, the angry burgess never balanced her wrath with forgiveness, although she—like Jeanne and Anne—would have been taught that each sin has a corresponding virtue. In the next story, charity, or a sense of generosity, could have kept the lady from the torments of hell. Instead, she allowed herself to be ruled by greed. To make the connections between the vices and virtues explicit, Sir Geoffrey counters her story with one about a widow whose humility and whose charity toward others surely led her to heaven after she died.

Gold, the Devil's Servant—Greed

How the deuylle tempteth many one of the synne where as he fyndeth them most wyllynge and redy to
(How the devil tempts many a one with sin, and finds them most willing and ready)

I'll tell you about a great lady who was married to a baron. She had long been widowed and she had only one daughter, who was married to a great lord. When she became very ill and lay in her deathbed, she had her treasure chest sealed and the key brought to her. She put it in a linen cloth under her back. Death ran fast upon her, and she, who kept thinking of her treasure, raised her hand to signal that no one should come near her back. She continued in this way until she died and her soul left her body.

Then her daughter, who was a great lady, came and asked those who were present at her death if she had any treasure. They weren't certain, but if she had any, it was hidden somewhere near her bed. They told her how her mother acted, how she wouldn't allow anybody to come near her, and how she had ordered a chest to be sealed and the key brought to her.

The body was moved, and the key found. Then her daughter went into a tower where the chest was kept and opened it. Inside she found in coin and plate more than thirty thousand pounds, but the gold was wrapped in cloths and balls of thread and wool. Everyone who saw this marveled and was taken aback. The daughter made the sign of the cross and said that in good faith she hadn't thought her mother so rich by twenty-five times as she was, and she was astonished. Recently, she said, she and her lord came to her mother and asked her to lend them some money until a certain time when they would be able to return it to her, but she swore great oaths to them that she had no money or silver, but only such plate as they saw sitting out—a cup and one piece only.

The people who were with her said, "Madame, don't marvel so much, because we are more amazed than you. If your mother wanted to send a message or do some other thing, she borrowed money from the servants and said that she had no money, by her faith."

The daughter took all these goods with her and went back to her lord, to whom she was welcome. And of all this treasure, they gave not a halfpenny for their mother's soul, but they soon forgot her.

Not very long ago I was in the place where she was buried and I asked the monks of the abbey where she lay why she had no tomb over her or any token. They told me that since she had been buried there, no Mass or service or anything else had been done for her. And so you can see that the devil is subtle in tempting people into sin wherever he sees them the most attached. He holds them so firmly in it that they may not leave it unless they confess it. He makes them his servants the way he did with this lady—she was his subject and his servant through her gold since she never used it to do any good.

And therefore, my fair daughters, if God through his grace sends you any great treasure, you should give most of it to the poor, in the love and honor of God. Especially give it to your poor relatives and neighbors, and don't leave it to be divided by the hands of your heirs as this lady did, for whom no Mass or any other good thing was done after her death.

Unlike the greedy lady in this story, for whom no Masses had been said, Sir Geoffrey and Jeanne de Rougé ensured Masses for themselves when they endowed religious establishments. Their charity in providing places for clerics and priests reflected back on them when prayers were said in their names. The Goodwyn family might have been equally charitable, endowing an altar in their parish church, for example, and leaving money in their wills for priests to sing memorial services. These services would be in addition to the ones their family provided: the funeral Mass with its hundreds of candles made of expensive beeswax, not tallow, its feast, the month mind, the year's mind, and the third year's mind. Each of these occasions was marked by Masses, by feasts, and by alms being distributed to the poor, all in honor of the dead. Because of her greed, the lady in the story forfeited any such remembrance.

The charity of the good widow in the next story provides a much better model for Jeanne and Anne to follow, especially if they expect to be memorialized in prayer after they die—even charity can take on a certain mercantile quality in Sir Geoffrey's telling, as it still can, in the case of tax-deductible contributions.

Thexample of a good wydowe
(The example of a good widow)

I'll tell you another story contrary to this one about a good lady who was also widowed for a long time. She lived a holy life and was very humble and honorable. Every year she kept a feast on Christmas day with her neighbors, both far and near, till her hall was full of them. She served and honored each one according to his degree, and she gave especially great reverence to the good and true women and to those who deserved to be honored. She had a custom that if she knew any poor gentlewoman who ought to be wedded, she dressed her in jewels. Also, she went to the funerals of poor gentlewomen and gave torches and as much other material for lights as were needed.

Her daily ritual was simple: she rose early and always had friars and two or three chaplains who said matins before her within the oratory. Afterwards, she heard a high Mass and two low, and said her service very devoutly. Then she walked in her garden or else inside saying her other devotions and prayers. When it was time, she went to dinner. After dinner, if she knew any sick people or women in their childbeds, she went to visit them and had her best food brought to them. If she couldn't go herself, she had a suitable servant ride on her little horse and carry with him a great plenty of food and drink to give to the poor and sick folk wherever they were. After she had heard Evensong, she went to her supper, if she wasn't fasting, and at the proper time she went to bed. She had her steward come to her to know what food they should have the next day. She lived such an orderly life, and provided all the things that were necessary for her household. She was very abstemious, and wore a hairshirt on Wednesdays and Fridays.

How do I know this? I'll tell you. This good lady died in a manor which she held in dower which belonged to my lord my father. When my sisters and I were young, we came to live there, and the bed on which this good lady died broke into pieces and under the straw was found a hairshirt which a damsel took. She told us it was the hairshirt of her lady, and that she wore it two or three days a week. She also told us about her good life; how she rose three times every night and kneeled to the ground beside her bed and gave thanks to God and prayed for all Christian souls, and how she gave great alms to the poor. This good lady ought to be named and praised: she was called my lady Olive de Belle Ville.[4]

And yet I have heard it said that her brother might spend eighteen thousand pounds in a single year, notwithstanding that she was the humblest, best and most courteous lady that I ever knew in any region. She had the least envy and would hear no evil spoken of anybody. Instead, she prayed to God that they might amend themselves. She blamed those who spoke evil of other people, and made them ashamed by reproving them. Much of the fair and profitable speech of this good lady is in my memory, notwithstanding how young I was when she died, for I wasn't older than ten. She had a very noble end, and I think it was very agreeable to God. As men commonly say, a good end comes from an honest and virtuous life.

The admirable widow of this tale is none other than Sir Geoffrey's grandmother, who died when he was nine. He grew up hearing stories about her virtue, so it was only fitting that he include her in his book for his daughters. Jeanne and Anne must have perked up when they came to her story mixed in with all the tales of hypothetical widows and Biblical ladies. They would probably have heard about their great-grandmother from their aunts—the ones who were with Sir Geoffrey when the hair-shirt was discovered—as well as from some of their other relatives, because she seems to have made quite an impression on people.

Olive de Belleville may have been Sir Geoffrey's grandfather's second wife, not his first, but either way, the quondam Dame de la Tour Landry was known both for her piety (in the French version she wears the hairshirt three days a week, not just Wednesdays and Fridays) and for her patronage of the arts. After her husband died, she retired to la Gallouère, a fief she had received as part of her dowry from her husband. There, she surrounded herself with churchmen as well as with poets, singers, and traveling minstrels, whom she often hired to sing at her court.[5] The minstrels loved her for her generosity and composed a song for her, a "chanson de regret d'elle," when she died. In a passage Caxton omits, Sir Geoffrey quotes the song's refrain:

> Helas! À la Galonnière
> N'avons nous plus bel aler,
> Comme endroit ma dame chière,
> Qui tant nous souloit amer.[6]

It means something like, Alas, at the Galonnière we no longer have good cheer as we did with our dear lady who used to love us.[7]

After reading this story aloud to Anne, Jeanne—in a youthful passion for piety—may have asked her confessor for permission to wear a hairshirt, just once a week, just on Fridays, in honor of her great-grandmother's goodness. The priest recognizes her ardor, and he gently reminds Jeanne how subtle the devil is, and how even piety can lead to pride. He suggests saying an extra paternoster each day, or setting aside a little of her dinner for the almsdish, instead. That way she can practice charity without inviting the devil to worm his way into her heart.

Jeanne's great-grandmother's generosity contrasts sharply with the greed Sir Geoffrey finds so common. He has his final say about covetousness at the end of the tale of "Dalida the evil wife" of Samson.[8] In this passage he exhibits none of his former compassion for prostitutes, saying that greed leads them to their trade, not poverty. But those who really define greed for Sir Geoffrey are lawyers. Their avarice and dishonesty leave him without a single positive comment.

> A covetous heart will do great evil, for it makes noblemen tyrants over their subjects. Covetousness also makes many thieves, usurers, and murderers; it makes many maidens and widows become harlots; and many secret murders are committed because of the vice of covetousness. Children desire the deaths of their fathers and mothers in order to have their property after their deaths. Judas betrayed our Lord Jesus Christ because of his desire for silver. In the same way, advocates and men of law these days sell their speech. They turn their words from the truth and plead against it. They cause the rights of the good man to be delayed in order to take more silver from him. Many of them even argue for both parties. They sell the speech which God gave them to profit the common good.

Living like a Beast—Gluttony

As charity balances greed, so abstinence overcomes gluttony. But it's an uphill battle for virtue, vice being so much more attractive. And whereas the vices all skip merrily to hell, hand in hand, rarely do you read that one virtue leads to another. For Sir Geoffrey, avoiding vices might help you get what you want in this life, not just the next one.

> You should fast and be abstinent if you want anything from God, for confession and fasting cause the request to be granted by God. For by the sin of gluttony, men fall into all the other six deadly sins, as you will more plainly know in the book of your brothers, where it is told how a hermit chose the sin of gluttony and indulged in it so much that he became drunk. And soon afterwards because of this sin he committed all seven—he, who was supposed to have been the best of them all.

Although we no longer have "the book of your brothers," the story of the hermit survives in Latin, French, and English versions, most of which accuse the hermit of committing only three sins, not all seven. So it is in the tale the English preacher John Bromyard used in one of his sermons. And in a Latin version, the devil himself gives the hermit (who had long lived a holy life) three sins from which to choose one, but of course the poor hermit ends up guilty of all three. The fullest surviving version of the story is told in French verse, summarized here by Thomas Wright:

> The hermit, obliged to choose one of the three sins, selected drunkenness as the least criminal: he visited a neighbouring miller, with whom he caroused till late in the evening: being drunk, the miller's wife goes with him to show him the way to his cell, and in a lonely part of the road, excited by his previous excess, he commits the sin of adultery: meanwhile the miller, uneasy at the long absence of his wife, sets out in search of her, with his axe on his shoulder, and arrives just in time to be a witness of his own disgrace, when the hermit, in a moment of anger, seizes the axe and kills its owner. He was thus led on, by indulging in one sin, to commit the two which it was his desire to avoid.

An English version of the story ends with the hermit's lament: "While that I was sober, sin ne did I not, / But in drunkenship I did the worst that might be thought."[9]

Although gluttony includes more than intemperance, medieval sermons and stories frequently equated gluttony with drunkenness. So did the Householder of Paris, in his recital of a glutton's hours (prayers): For Matins, she says, "Ha! What shall we drink? What's left from last night?" Then comes Lauds, when the glutton says, "Ha! We drank good wine yesterday evening." Her orisons, the Householder adds, sound like this: "My head aches—I won't feel better til I've had a drink."[10]

Sir Geoffrey continues with more evidence of the close relationships of the sins, citing Solomon, the prophet who embodied wisdom, as his source.

> I'll tell you what Solomon says in the book of instruction about this. First he says that too much wine troubles the sight and makes the eyes grow red; it enfeebles the brain, makes the head shake, takes away the hearing, stops the conduits of the nose, makes the face become red, and makes the hands shake. It mars and corrupts the good blood, makes the sight feeble, changes the body within, troubles the wits and

the memory, and hastens death. Therefore Solomon says that of thirty women who have this vice and who are accustomed to getting drunk, men won't find one of them who is good and honest in her body, nor loved by God nor by her friends. It would be better for her to be a thief or have some other evil vice than drink, because by drinking she will fall into all the other vices. For which reason, my dear daughters, beware that you keep yourself from this evil vice.

Taking refection once a day is an angel's life, twice is a man's life, but eating many times a day is a beast's life. This goes according to custom and habit, for in your old age you will desire the diet you are accustomed to in your youth. Thus it's in your power to remedy it if need be.

Although Solomon's "book of instruction" is probably Proverbs, this passage isn't taken from scripture. It's the kind of thing a preacher might include in a sermon, and it's reminiscent of the Pardoner's tirade against what were known as "the tavern sins," gambling, swearing, and drinking. The Pardoner, probably the most cynical of Chaucer's pilgrims, sits drinking in a tavern as he fulminates against the evils of gluttony. He even blames the fall from Eden on gluttony, saying it was what drove Adam and Eve to eat the forbidden fruit. Like Sir Geoffrey in the passage above, the Pardoner lists the physical and mental ills that result from drinking: the disfigured face, the sour breath, the clogged-up nose, the loss of discretion, the confused thoughts—and the acts of lechery committed by the drunken man.

Joined like a Dog to a Bitch—Lechery

Sir Geoffrey's take on lechery may seem a bit extreme to us because his tales often involve not only ordinary laypeople, but also priests and monks, who were sworn to celibacy. Or he sets his stories within church walls, where the lecherous couple wrangles under the very altar. Because his examples are so far-fetched, they seem unlikely to teach his daughters what they really needed to know about lechery. Jeanne and Anne needed to be wary of fine men such as Boucicaut and Clermont, whom they would encounter at social gatherings— men who might find it amusing to trifle with the affections of an unsuspecting young girl.

For the Goodwyn sisters, other sorts of social gatherings might lead to compromising behavior. Although good girls such as Katherine and Elizabeth never went to wrestling matches or cock fights, they could get themselves in trouble on more innocent occasions if they weren't watchful. On Midsummer Eve, for example, the bustling London streets became even busier as people decorated their houses with garlands of flowers and greenery. The Goodwyns and their wealthy neighbors would set up outdoor tables filled with food for the poorer inhabitants of the neighborhood. Katherine and Elizabeth's father would don the bright livery of the Worshipful Company of Mercers and join the procession through the streets.[11] As people drank the abundant ale, beer, and wine, tongues and morals got looser, and their neighbor Mary Rawson's older brother George might suddenly find Katherine Goodwyn the prettiest sight he had ever seen as he tried to get her off into a dark alley. If not for the watchful eyes of Joan, her mother's maid, Katherine could find her own reputation ruined. Her opinion of the handsome George would certainly be sullied by this episode. Flustered and ashamed of his attempt to kiss her, Katherine might vow never to see him again, and certainly never to think of him as a possible beau.

Despite this near-encounter with George, it's hard to imagine either Katherine Goodwyn or Jeanne de la Tour ever being accused of behavior as egregious as that in the next two stories. These examples, and the others that follow, hardly seem to us to be appropriate material for young girls. Yet in Sir Geoffrey's view, it's far better to frighten his daughters with such tales than to fear for their immortal souls once they are dead. An unsavory story may cause passing displeasure, but the pain of hell is forever.

Of the man and woman that made fornycacion within the Chirche

(Concerning the man and woman who fornicated inside a church)

Now I'll tell you something that happened at the church of Notre Dame de Beaulieu. During the Vigil of Our Lady, Perrot Lenard, who was sergeant of the church that year, lay with a woman under an altar—and a miracle happened: they were joined together like a dog to a bitch. They were knitted together this way a whole day, so that everybody in the church and in the whole region had time to see them. When they couldn't get free of one another, the people made a procession and prayed to God for them. Finally, in the evening, they got loose from one another. Afterwards, they had the church newly-hallowed before any Masses were said there. For his penance, Perrot had to go all around the church naked for three Sundays beating himself and telling his sins to everybody. Now, isn't this a good example about how every man should live purely and honestly according to Holy Church? And I'll tell you another story like this that happened in Poitou, not three years ago.

Of a Monke that made fornycacion in his Abbeye
(Concerning a monk who fornicated in his abbey)
    In Poitou there was an abbey named Chievrefaye, and the church of
the abbey had been damaged by war. The prior had a nephew called
Pygrere, a monk in the abbey. One Sunday after Matins, as the monks
readied themselves for High Mass, this Pygrere couldn't be found.
When they searched, they found him inside the church lying on top of
a woman. He was in great distress because so closely were Pygrere and
the woman joined to one another that they couldn't get away from
each other. They stayed that way so long that all the monks came in
before they got loose. When poor Pygrere saw his uncle and all the
other monks with him, he was so full of shame and sorrow that he fled
the abbey and joined another one somewhere else.

    Notre Dame de Beaulieu, from the first story, was a priory near Sir
Geoffrey's château at Bourmont, a holding he acquired when he married Jeanne de Rougé. In one French manuscript, Sir Geoffrey calls it
"a church on my land," so Jeanne and Anne would surely have visited
it when the family was staying at Bourmont. For them, the stories
would gain a sense of immediacy when they remembered the church's
altar and thought with fascinated horror of what had happened
beneath it. They might even have heard other people talking about
Perrot Lenard, the sergeant of the church, or Pygrere and the abbey
of Chievrefaye, in the second story, but now these names survive only
in Sir Geoffrey's book.[12]
    Other stories are more distanced, with no clear setting. The one
that follows is a digression within a long passage about Lot's sinful
family.

    I want you to know the example of the lady who left her lord, who was
    a fair knight, and went with a monk. Her brothers pursued her and
    found her that night lying with the said monk. They cut off the monk's
    genitals and cast them in their sister's face. Then they put both of them
    together in a sack with many stones and cast them into the deep water.
    Together, the monk and the lady drowned. For from an evil life comes
    an evil end, and all sins will be recognized and punished in the end.[13]

    This brutal little tale might remind readers—both medieval and
modern ones—of what happened to the twelfth-century Parisian
scholar Peter Abelard. As a young man he was chosen to tutor the
extremely well educated Heloise, the seventeen-year-old niece and
ward of a church official. They fell in love, and she became pregnant
with their son, Astrolabe. Heloise's uncle ordered his henchmen to

cut off Abelard's genitals, which they did. However, the lovers hardly ended up like the lady and the monk in this story, drowned in the river. Abelard became an abbot, Heloise an abbess. Nevertheless, Heloise was a true lover. She continued to write love letters to Abelard, who answered them with pious sermons. Heloise never wanted to marry Abelard because doing so would keep him from being a teacher and a philosopher (how can a philosopher think with babies crying and maidservants gossiping? she asks). In fact, she says she would rather be his whore than his wife. Alas, she ended up locked in her convent, forced to be a nun when she had no vocation for it. Nevertheless, she made a more than competent abbess.

This chapter ends with yet another story of clerical incontinence. Although the tale begins amusingly, it descends into the same kind of brutality seen in the story above. The she-wolf, which we have already seen as an image of anger, appears at the very end. Here, it emphasizes the medieval association of physical beauty with moral goodness, an idea that hasn't yet died the death it is due.

Of the roper or maker of cordes and kables and of the fat Pryour
(Concerning the ropemaker and the fat prior)

A ropemaker had a wife who was neither wise nor honorable. She paid her friend, a bawd, a little silver to set her up with a rich, lecherous prior. Because she coveted the little gift and jewel, the evil bawd made the ropemaker's wife fall into a wicked deed.

One time the prior came by night to lie with the wife. After he had done his foul delight and was leaving the room, the fire sprang up in the chimney, and the ropemaker saw him going out. He was afraid and told his wife he had seen a man in the room. His wife pretended she was afraid, too, and said it must have been the devil or else a goblin or a spirit. But despite her saying this, the good man felt sadness and great melancholy, fearing that his wife had done amiss.

The wife, who was subtle and full of malice, went immediately the next morning to her gossip and neighbor, the bawd, and brought her home with her. The bawd saw how the goodman walked around the house carrying with him the cord from which he made his ropes. She took in her hands a distaff with black wool and began to spin. Before he turned towards her again, she replaced it with white wool. Then the good man, who was plain and true, said to her, "My friend, it seemed to me that right now you span black wool."

"Ha," she said, "My friend, truly I didn't." Then he went from her and when he turned toward her again, she had taken the distaff with the black wool. He watched her and said, "Fair gossip, you just had a spindle with white wool."

"Ah, dear friend, what ails you now? In good faith, it isn't so," she said. "I can see that you're dazed and deceived in your sight and your wits. Truly, men sometimes think they see something they don't see. You're thoughtful and pensive. Something must be bothering you."

The ropemaker thought she said the truth and replied, "By God, gossip, last night I thought I saw a black thing, I don't know what it was, coming out of our room."

"My good friend," the old, false woman said. "It was nothing but the day and the night that strove together, and there was great lightning." The good man was contented by the old woman's falseness and thought she spoke truly.

Another time the ropemaker rose early to go to the market three miles from his house to bring home some fish. He had put a sack at the foot of the bed and when he reached for it in the morning darkness, he grabbed instead the prior's breeches. When he got to the market and took out his sack, he found not the sack at all, but the breeches. This troubled and angered him greatly.

Meanwhile, the prior, who had hidden between the bed and the wall, reached for his breeches but found only the sack, and realized that the husband had his breeches. The ropemaker's wife didn't know what to do. She went to her gossip again and told her what had happened and asked her for God's sake to find some remedy.

Her friend said, "You put on a pair of breeches and I will, too, and we'll tell him that all women wear them." And so they did.

When the false gossip saw the ropemaker coming, she went and welcomed him and said, "What cheer, good gossip? Did you lose something? You look so sad."

"Truly," said the good man, "I haven't lost anything. Something else is bothering me." She kept at him until he told her how he had found a pair of breeches at the foot of the bed, and what he feared.

When she heard him say this, she started to laugh and said, "Oh, my friend, you are very much deceived about your wife. For truly, in the whole town there's no one better than your wife, no one who keeps herself more faithfully and purely towards her husband than she does to you. In fact, she and I and many other good and honest women in this town have taken to wearing breeches on account of those lechers and seducers who do their will with good women. And just so you can know whether I lie or speak truly, look to see whether I wear them or not." She pulled up her clothes and showed him the breeches. And he looked and saw that she spoke truly, and believed her. And so by such a manner the false gossip twice saved the wife.

But in the end, evil will be known. One time the good man saw his wife go in to the prior's house alone, and he got very angry. Immediately he warned her, on pain of losing her eye, that she should never be so bold as to go into the prior's house. Nevertheless, she couldn't keep herself away because the Fiend tempted her so greatly.

One time the ropemaker pretended to go out, but really he hid himself in a secret place. Soon afterwards his foolish wife went to the prior's house, and her husband followed her step by step. He hauled her home, saying, "You have broken my commandment." Then he went to town and found a surgeon who would heal two broken legs. When the agreement with the surgeon had been made, he came home again and took a pestle and broke both of his wife's legs, saying to her, "At least you'll hold my commandment for a little while and you won't go far." He laid her in bed and she couldn't get up for a long time.

In the end, however, the Fiend mocked her and made her seek foul pleasures again. When her legs were almost healed, she had the prior come to her secretly, even while she was in bed with her husband. But the good man heard the prior come in, so he snored and pretended to be asleep. When they were in the midst of their foul sin of lechery, he got so angry that he almost lost his memory and wits. He drew out a long knife with a sharp point, cast a little straw on the fire so he could see, and killed them both in the bed.

Then he called his household and his neighbors and showed them what he had done. He also sent for the judge, by whom he was excused and had no harm. The neighbors marveled how his wife had turned her heart to love such a prior, who had such a great belly and was so thick and fat and so dark and so foul of face and so unrefined, when her husband was so fair and good, wise and rich.

But many women are like the she-wolf who chooses for her love the foulest of the wolves in the wood. And likewise this foolish woman was tempted by the devil, who stays ever and incessantly around the sinner, man or woman, to make them fall into deadly sin. And the greater the sin, the more power he has over the sinners. Therefore I pray that you, as my very dear daughters, think on this night and day, for many great and evil temptations will assail you. Be strong then, and valiant to resist and overcome them. Remember your place and think of what dishonor and shame might come to you.

Despite murdering both his wife and the prior, the ropemaker is absolved of any guilt—by his neighbors, by the judge, and by Sir Geoffrey himself. He continues his discussion of dishonor and shame by reminding his daughters of the estimable behavior of the virgin martyrs, Katherine and Margaret. Although the stories of both of these saints stress their virginity, for Sir Geoffrey they are also models of "wifely chastity."[14]

In chapter 13, he gives other examples of good women his daughters can emulate, some of them saints, some of them ordinary Christians.

CHAPTER 13

TRUE WOMEN AND GOOD LADIES—VIRTUOUS LIVING

Balancing the Seven Deadly Sins are the Seven Virtues—faith, hope, charity, justice, prudence, temperance, and fortitude. Of these, *The Book of the Knight of the Tower* emphasizes faith and charity with a little temperance thrown in. And of course, Sir Geoffrey is very concerned with his daughters' chastity—as his focus on lechery in chapter 12 indicates. Before he tells stories about good and wise women from the Bible, from classical literature, from saints' lives, and from stories about "good women of the present time," he introduces the subject of virtuous living to his daughters—taking as his source *The Mirror for Good Women*. A virtuous life in fourteenth-century France and fifteenth-century England is indistinguishable from a good Christian life: good Christians don't stop at practicing the virtues; they also avoid sinning.

After reminding his girls of this, Sir Geoffrey suggests that those who live virtuous lives imitate Christ, "our model of life and of lasting joy." He promises stories of "the true women and good ladies whom our Lord God praises so much in his Bible, whereby you may take example of honest and pure living." However, if you count them, you'll find many more tales of wicked women than of good ones. Nevertheless, the knight does find some positive stories, many of them about the Virgin Mary's obedience, charity, humility, and devotion to God. Likewise, he lauds Elizabeth, the mother of John the Baptist, for her humility and her faith, and the three Marys who came to the sepulchre for their diligence in serving God. The sinner Mary Magdalene also earns praise for her great love and fear of God, as well as for confessing her sins with a contrite heart.

Several examples of good women come from the Old Testament; both the Goodwyn sisters and Sir Geoffrey's daughters would have heard about these women in sermons. Sarah, the wife of Abraham, kept herself pure when Pharaoh took her from her husband, and Esther never spoke back to her cruel husband. Instead she loved and honored him, just as wives ought to do. Susannah was rewarded for her purity and faith after her unfortunate incident in the garden with the lecherous elders. Isaac's wife Rebecca is praised for her humility ("she acted more like a servant than a lady"), as are Abigail and Rachel, the mother of Joseph. Rachel is as obedient as she is humble, and for her acts of faith and charity she won God's rewards for both herself and her children. Pharaoh's daughter, who found baby Moses in the bulrushes, is praised for her great charity in helping orphans, as is Saint Elizabeth of Hungary in the next story.

Saint Elizabeth lived a Cinderella story in reverse. Born a princess in 1207, she was beautiful, wise, and exceedingly generous. Her marriage not only made her a queen, it brought her exquisite happiness and three children. But when she was twenty, her husband joined a crusade and shortly thereafter succumbed to disease. Elizabeth nearly went mad with grief. As if that weren't bad enough, her wicked brother-in-law sent her away from the court. She joined a lay religious foundation, lived modestly, and served the ill and elderly poor, but her powerful and sadistic confessor treated her cruelly. He slapped her face, beat her with rods, and sent away her favorite ladies-in-waiting, replacing them with two horrid women. Elizabeth cheerfully endured all this for two years, spinning and carding wool, "cleaning the homes of the poor and fishing to help feed them," and, as we learn below, teaching orphans ways to make their living. Then, only twenty-four years old, she died. Four years later, the pope declared her a saint, and a church dedicated to her became a popular pilgrimage site.[1]

The saint was known in both France and England. Her story was told in church images, and in a fifteenth-century Middle English saint's life.[2] Elizabeth Goodwyn might have prayed especially to the saint (even if she was named for John the Baptist's mother, not for Elizabeth of Hungary). Her story must have been important to a much more modern reader, too. If you open one copy of Caxton's first edition of *The Book of the Knight of the Tower* in the British Library in London, you'll find a dark blue ribbon, flattened with age, marking Chapter lxxxvi, "Of charyte." Surely the ribbon was placed there by a nineteenth- or twentieth-century reader, but it's tempting to imagine a fifteenth-century girl such as Elizabeth Goodwyn laying it across the page before she closes the book.

Of charyte
(Concerning charity)

God never forgets the service done to him out of charity, like the helping of orphans or the fatherless. This is called misericord, and God greatly loves it. You can see it in the life of Saint Elizabeth, who helped poor orphans and taught them crafts by which they could earn their livings.

Once there was a good woman who had only one child, and he was accustomed to bathe in the river. One time he fell into a deep pit in the river and stayed there for eight days. His mother, who was charitable to God and to Saint Elizabeth, was filled with sorrow. On the eighth day, she dreamed her son was in a pit full of water, and that Saint Elizabeth was keeping him alive. The saint said to her, "Because you have always cared for orphans and the fatherless, Our Lord will not allow your son to die in this pit. Therefore, get ready to get him out." When the mother awoke, she had her son taken from the pit and they found him alive and fair in color. The child told his mother that a pretty lady had taken care of him, and had told him that it was God's will that he would be saved because of his mother's charity and compassion.

This story shows us that men ought to take care of orphans and small children in need, because great alms and charity are very pleasing to God. Also, there are many examples of beasts who, when men have slain the mother, and the cubs have been without sustenance, nourish them until they can take care of themselves.

In both the French version and the earlier English translation, the animal who takes care of other beasts' young is specifically named as the hind—a female deer. Animals were often used as examples of proper Christian living—or of sinful behavior. One type of medieval book, the bestiary, taught specific Christian lessons through descriptions of beasts. The majority of bestiaries, which were usually written in Latin and sometimes lavishly illustrated with miniatures (making them very appealing to modern audiences) were made in the twelfth and thirteenth centuries and used by clergymen, not lay readers, as sources for sermons. They described the characteristics of animals both mythical and actual—although even the real animals might be ones the European writers had never laid eyes on. Often, they included etymological information taken from Isidore of Seville's fascinating seventh-century encyclopedia, *The Etymologies*.[3] In this work, which was well known and deeply influential throughout the Middle Ages, Isidore, the Archbishop of Seville, "argues that the nature of every thing can be derived etymologically from its name,"[4] although his understanding of etymology was based on sounds, not on linguistic principles. For example, Isidore says that the eagle got its name, *aquila*, because of the *acumine*, or acuteness, of its vision.[5]

All bestiaries tend to include very similar information, in varying amounts, since they derived from a common source, the second-century *Physiologus*, a Greek text later translated into Latin. The encyclopedic information from Isidore of Seville easily merged with the original stories. The examples in bestiaries are explicit Christian allegories, explained in a moral at the end of each tale. Consider the whale, who looks so much like an island that sailors land on him. Suddenly, the whale dives to the depths of the sea, taking the unwary sailors with him. Just so, the devil lures Christians into thinking they don't need to pay attention to their surroundings. Then, like the whale, he plunges to the depths of hell, the heedless Christians in his claws.

Although some of the details about animal behavior in *The Book of the Knight of the Tower* may reflect the teachings of bestiaries,[6] the genre was no longer popular by the late fourteenth century when Sir Geoffrey was writing. Yet medieval books were made to last, so an old bestiary might have lain on a shelf in the Lord of Craon's château until Sir Geoffrey borrowed it. When he brought it to Tour Landry, the sumptuous illustrations of creatures both strange and ordinary would have tempted Jeanne and Anne into turning its pages. Unless a priest translated for them, however, they would have had to be content with looking at the pictures — they wouldn't have been able to read the Latin text. But there was plenty to look at, from fabulous satyrs, griffins, and unicorns to familiar frogs, ants, and turtledoves. They might have enjoyed the miniature of the fox, who lies on his back, his tongue out, playing dead, while birds sit on him. They wouldn't need a priest to make the connection between the fox and the devil, who lures victims in a similar fashion and suddenly seizes them in his jaws.

Of course, far more influential than the bestiary throughout the medieval period is the Bible. In fact, the purpose of the bestiary is to make plain biblical truths. Although often filtered through intermediaries, the Old and New Testaments are Sir Geoffrey's primary sources. He finds another example of charity in the Book of Joshua, where the widow Rahab saved the lives of "certain good men who had come to preach to the evil and cruel people" of Jericho. For her troubles, she and her household were saved when everyone else in Jericho was put to death. Then Sir Geoffrey moves from the Bible to stories of charitable saints, including Anastasia and Radegunde.

How the benefaytte whiche is done for the loue of god is rendred of god an C tyme gretter than it is
(How the good deed which is done for the love of God is repaid by God a hundred times greater than it is)

I want you to know about Saint Anastasia. When she was thrown into prison, God delivered her because she herself had sustained prisoners who had been wrongly imprisoned for envy or debt. Often, she gave so much of her goods that she got them out, and therefore God rewarded her double.

And also as sweet Jesus Christ said in the Gospels, at the great day of Judgment, he will have mercy on those who have visited and comforted prisoners and the sick and poor women who lay sick in their childbeds. On that dreadful day, God will ask all for a reckoning, and men must then render him a reply. And well do I know that many a one will be hard put to give a good answer.

And therefore, my fair daughters, think about this now while you live, as did Saint Radegunde, who was Queen of France. She comforted and visited poor prisoners and took care of orphans and visited the sick. But she wasn't able to do this as often as she wanted to for fear of disobeying her lord, so she left him and all the honor and vainglory of the world and secretly escaped from Paris to Poitiers where she became a nun. She left the world so she might better serve God without fear of any man.

Later, God showed a miracle for her sake. There was a tree in the middle of the cloister that had given shade for a long time but now it had become old and dry.[7] At this holy lady's prayer, God renewed the tree so that its bark became fresh and green and new branches sprang out full of green leaves. Although it seemed to go against the course of nature, nothing is impossible to God, and he did many other great miracles for the love of Saint Radegunde. And therefore you, too, should be charitable, as these two holy ladies were, and also the good lady Rahab. In the end God rewarded them for their good service.

Sir Geoffrey's explanation of the miracle God performed for Saint Radegunde's sake is as good a statement as you'll find about medieval perceptions of the miraculous: although a miracle may seem to go against nature, nothing is impossible to God. Often associated with saints, miracles were an integral part of ordinary medieval life. Nobody questioned them. No medieval church thinkers wrote treatises trying to explain them. Miracles "seemed to be contrary to nature but were in fact inherent in it," as one modern scholar puts it.[8] People understood miracles the way Saint Augustine did in his writings, especially in *The City of God*:

> God himself has created all that is wonderful in this world, the great miracles as well as the minor marvels I have mentioned, and he has included them all in that unique wonder, that miracle of miracles, the world itself.[9]

Miracles made manifest God's omnipotence. They appeared in stories for both *the lerned and the lewed*, the educated and the ignorant. Preachers in dusty village churches told miracle stories in their sermons, high-ranking ecclesiastics mentioned miracles in letters to their colleagues. At saints' shrines, monks recorded the cures and other miracles that regularly occurred, and public reports of these miracles kept pilgrims coming to the shrines, perhaps in hopes of a miraculous cure, perhaps just to be near such holiness.

The various versions of the Life of Saint Radegunde report miraculous cures taking place at her tomb shortly after her death. A sixth-century princess, Radegunde converted to Christianity as a teenager when she married Clotaire, son of Clovis, and king of the Franks. In the manner of converts, she took her vows a little more seriously than did her violent, unfaithful husband. In addition to mocking his queen for her inability to give him an heir, the king also murdered her brother. Thus, you can hardly blame her for taking the veil.

After becoming a nun, she founded the monastery at Poitiers that Sir Geoffrey mentions, where her nuns studied at least two hours every day and where Radegunde herself became known for her peacemaking between rival political factions. As a saint, she was popular in both France and England, where several churches and even a college at Cambridge were dedicated to her.[10]

Although miracles were often associated with saints, as Jeanne and Anne well knew, you didn't have to be a saint to be associated with a miracle. Their father's examples demonstrate that ordinary people— such as the good lady of Rome in the next story and the Countess of Anjou in the example that follows it—could inspire miracles, too.

How the wymmen ought to be charytable after the exemplary of our lady
(How women ought to be charitable according to the example of Our Lady)

Every good woman ought to be as charitable as the holy lady who gave the greatest thing she had for the love of God. By her example, Saints Elizabeth, Lucy, and Cecelia and many other holy ladies were so charitable that they gave most of their belongings to the poor, as you can read in their legends.

I want you to know about a good lady of Rome. While she was at Mass she saw a poor woman who was shaking from cold. The good lady had pity on her and privately called to her and took her to her house, which wasn't far away, to give her a good furred gown. While they were gone, the priest who was saying the Mass couldn't speak a word. The moment she returned, however, he spoke as he had before. Afterwards he saw in a vision why he had lost his speech and how God praised the lady's gift before his angels. Every good woman should be as charitable as this lady and not allow her poor neighbors to suffer from cold or hunger or other ills, but to help them as far as their power reaches.

How it is good to herberowe and receyue in his hows the seruaunts and mynystres of god
(How it is good to shelter and receive the servants and ministers of God in your house)

It's good to harbor the servants of God, that is to say the preachers and those who preach the faith. In the same way, we should shelter pilgrims and the poor people of God, as the Holy Gospel tells us. There it says that on the great and dreadful day—Judgment Day—God will ask whether men have visited and sheltered poor people in his name. Then every man and woman must give a reckoning of how they have used their earthly goods. Thus, it is a virtue to shelter the poor and the servants of God, for good may come of it.

Every woman ought to have pity when she sees that somebody wrongs the poor people of God, who are his servants. In the Gospels he says, that which is done to my servants in my name is done to me. And he says more: he will have mercy on those who have been full of pity. Concerning this, the sage says that a woman ought by her nature to be sweeter and more compassionate than a man, for a man should be firmer and of higher spirit. Therefore, those whose hearts are neither meek nor full of pity may be called mannish. Further, the sage says in the book of wisdom that a woman by her nature ought not to stint on things that come easily to her, like tears and a humble heart that has pity for poor parents whom she sees suffering great need.

She ought also to have pity on her poor neighbors, like the Countess of Anjou did, she who founded the Abbey of Bourgueil, where she lies buried. Men say she is still there in flesh and blood. When this good lady saw that her poor parents might not honestly keep their estate, she gave them a lot of her own property. She enhanced and had married the poor maidens, the gentlewomen who were of good renown. She sought out poor householders and gave some of her goods to them. She had great pity on women who were in their childbeds and visited them and helped them. She had her own physicians and surgeons help and heal all manner of people for God's love, and especially the poor, who didn't have to pay.

And men say that God often showed miracles for her sake. For when men took her book and her paternoster to her, they floated in the air in front of her. Many other tokens and signs were also seen which God did for the love of her. And therefore, every good woman ought to take this good example and have compassion on others, and to help and have pity on the poor. Here I leave the tale of these good ladies and this matter. But soon I shall come to it again, and shall speak of another example.

Countess Emma of Anjou, although hardly ordinary, was not a saint—yet God caused miracles to happen for her sake. The wife of William, Duke of Aquitaine and Count of Poitiers, Emma is a good illustration of Sir Geoffrey's relationship to the past. Although she founded the abbey of Bourgueil near the city of Tours in the year 990, about 400 years before Sir Geoffrey compiled his book, he speaks of her as if she was from his mother's or grandmother's generation.

He begins the story by speaking of the importance of sheltering travelers, especially members of the clergy. But not until the following tale does he give an example of this sort of behavior. Although Sir Geoffrey frames his story as one about how good it is to be charitable, his emphasis shifts a little. Instead of praising charity for its own sake, or even for its efficacy in getting a person into heaven, he suggests that being charitable can bring immediate rewards.

How it is good to aqueynte hym self with holy men
(How it is good to acquaint yourself with holy men)

Once there was a very good and honest woman whose husband was equally honest and simple. The lady was very charitable and she showed great respect to holy men. Near Jerusalem at the time there was a prophet named Elisha to whom the lady was so devoted that she asked him to come live in her house with her lord. They readied a room for him where the holy prophet could wear a hairshirt and make his prayers and suffer his afflictions alone and secretly.

The lady had been unable to have children by her lord, and she told the prophet about it. At her request, he prayed to God so long that they had a fair son who lived for fifteen years. When he was fifteen, he died in the room the prophet had lived in.

When his mother saw her son dead, she was full of sorrow and went searching the country for Elisha. When she finally found him she brought him to the chamber and showed him her dead child. "You are a holy prophet and a good man—this is the child God sent me through your prayers," she said. "He was all my joy and sustenance. I ask that you pray that it please God to restore him to life again, or else take me with him, for I will not live after him."

Elisha pitied the woman and prayed for her child, and God gave him his life again. The boy lived a long life and became a holy man.

By this example, my fair daughters, you can see how good it is to know and be acquainted with holy men, just as this good lady was. In these days God is still as mighty and gracious as he was back then to those who deserve it—the ones with meek and humble hearts. Therefore men ought to keep the fellowship of good and holy men who live holy lives, and believe them, for good may come of it, as it did to this lady.

Sir Geoffrey's attitude toward piety may seem a bit opportunistic here, but his stance is hardly unusual—either for him or for his time. Christine de Pizan, too, finds both spiritual and practical reasons to be in high favor with the clergy. Not only will priests pray for a lady, they will also praise her in their sermons and defend her if she is slandered. Christine's attitude toward religion is as businesslike as Sir Geoffrey's—even as she promotes intense spirituality, she is matter-of-fact in her cost–benefit analysis. She tells princesses to discover and befriend those priests and other religious men who have the largest following because when they speak about her, they will inspire confidence in others.[11]

Similarly, Christine advises princesses to be on good terms with high-ranking laymen, with merchants, and even with artisans, so they will come to her aid if she needs it. To this end, the princess should invite these people to court and, in fact, *court* them. If she speaks with them, advises them, and asks their advice, they will know her and her wisdom and goodness, should these ever be questioned. In this sort of scenario, virtue becomes less a quality than a commodity.

Katherine and Elizabeth Goodwyn's merchant father might have been invited to dinners in noble households for this very reason, but he would hardly complain about feeling used. His daughters wouldn't object, either; instead, they might ask him for details about who was there, what sorts of headdresses the ladies were wearing, and what romances the minstrels told between the courses. No romances at all, he tells them: instead, a friar told a very moving story about a virtuous lady who harbored a holy man—a story remarkably like the one below. Here, the holy man—who may not seem so holy to modern readers—wants his prize during this life, not after he dies; however, the lady and her husband know that virtue is its own reward.

How the holy lady approuued the Heremyte
(How the holy lady tested the hermit)

Fair daughters, I will tell you about a very good lady who is much to be praised. And this story of how the wife of the provost of Aquileia tested a holy hermit's goodness is told in the book of the lives of the holy fathers.

There was once a holy hermit who had lived in a hermitage for twenty five years, eating only bread and herbs and roots. He often fasted and lived a good and holy life. One day this good and holy hermit said, "Ah, good Lord, my creator and my maker, if I have done you wrong in any way, I ask mercy of you. And if I have done any good these twenty five years in this hermitage, what reward shall I have for it?"

Immediately he had a vision in which he seemed to see Our Lord, who said to him, "You will have the same reward as the provost of Aquileia and his wife."

After he had seen this vision he said he would never rest until he came to Aquileia to ask about the life of the provost and his wife. So he went there, and according to God's plan, the provost and his wife knew all about his coming and his reason for doing so.

As the hermit neared the town he saw the provost riding out of it with a great company of men, going to judge a squire who had slain another squire. The provost, who was riding on a fair courser, wore a handsome gown of richly furred silk and all his men were also well-clothed and decorated. As soon as the provost saw the hermit, he knew him, as the will of God would have it. He called to him and said, "Good and true man, go home to my wife and take her this ring and tell her that she should treat you as she would treat me."

The hermit asked him who he was, and he said he was the provost of Aquileia. The hermit, seeing him in such estate and so richly clothed, was abashed and marveled that he who was going to have a man hanged was so finely dressed. He didn't know what he should think or say and he was troubled. It seemed to the hermit that the provost deserved nothing from God.

Nevertheless he went to the provost's house and found there the lady, his wife. The hermit gave her the ring and told her that her lord had sent him there and had said that she should treat him as she would treat her lord. The good lady received him and had the table covered, and asked him to sit before her. She had him served a great plenty of good and delicate food and good wines. The hermit, who was not accustomed to having such food, nevertheless ate and drank. He watched how the good lady took the food that was placed before her, and how she broke and dressed the good capons and other delicacies, and then she had it all put together in a great dish and sent it to the poor people. For her own meal, she took only bread and water. She did this every day, both at supper and at dinner.

When evening came she invited the hermit to her chamber, which was richly hung with silk and nobly arrayed. She said, "Good and true man, you shall lie in the bed of my lord and in his chamber." The hermit would have refused it, but the lady said that she wanted to do the commandment of her lord, and that certainly he should lie there. She had many good spices and strong wines brought to him, and the good hermit savored them so much that he ate and drank too much.

Unaccustomed as he was to drinking, he became very drunk and full of joy in speaking.

He got in bed and the lady undid her clothes and laid herself beside him and began to embrace and touch him. The hermit woke up and his body became sorely aroused. He wanted to accomplish the act of fornication with the lady. Then she said to him, "Sweet friend, when my lord wants to do such a thing with me, he first bathes and washes himself in that tub which you see yonder full of water, in order to be more clean and fair."

The hermit, who thought of nothing but fulfilling and accomplishing his will, got in the tub and bathed and washed himself in the water, which was as cold as ice. Soon he was half dead from the cold. Then the lady called him to her, and he came all shaking, for his heat was gone, and also his evil will. The lady embraced him again so much that he got hot and was so heated that he would have done his foolish delight. And when she saw him so inflamed and so burning in that foul delight of lechery, she asked that he, for the love of her, go and wash himself again in the tub in order to be cleaner. And he who had not yet slept and was full of strong wines, rose up out of his bed like a man out of his wits and went and bathed himself again in the tub. Again the cold water made him feeble and cold. Then the lady called him to her again, and shaking, he came to her as he had before. His teeth shook and beat against each other for cold, and all his great heat had passed and gone. The lady rose up and covered him well with warm clothes and left him alone so that he could take his rest. And immediately after, when he was a little bit warm, he fell asleep, for his head was very heavy, and didn't wake until morning came.

When he rose, an old chaplain came and asked how he was. When he perceived that he lay in such a beautiful bed, he was so taken aback and surprised that he was full of shame and amazed that he had gotten so drunk and been so foolish. Then he understood that they merited a greater reward than he did. He asked the chaplain about the life and behavior of the provost and his wife. The chaplain said that for most of the year they wore hairshirts, and that they sent the good foods which were set before them at the table to the poor people, while they themselves ate black bread and foods with little flavor and drank only water. They fasted most of the week.

Then the hermit asked why the tub of cold water was set by their bed. The chaplain answered that it was there to keep them from the burning will of lechery. For as soon as she or he is warmed and their flesh is aroused to that foul delight, they get out of bed and wash themselves in the tub which is full of water on all but one day of the week. Then the hermit thought about how the provost was richly arrayed in the sight of the people while secretly, and unknown to all men, he wore the hairshirt on his flesh. He who pronounced justice and the execution of wrongdoers, and his wife as well, was worthy to have seven times more reward. Then the hermit remembered the foul act he would have done with the good lady, and how she had tested him, and he was full of shame. In his heart he cursed himself for ever leaving his hermitage. He knew he wasn't worthy to pull their shoes and hose from their legs.

He left there weeping and full of shame, saying in a high voice, "Fair God and Good Lord, I know no greater treasure, nor more noble, nor more precious than the good lady who tested me and saw my folly, and who knew my deception and error. Truly she is worthy enough to be called after the precious Margaret, which you talk about in the Gospel." Thus the holy hermit spoke all alone to himself, repenting of his wrongdoing, and humbly crying to God for mercy, and praising the lady for her good life.

A woman is to be praised when she tests herself and can resist the temptations of the devil, and the feebleness of her mortal flesh, and the foolish will of her foul delight. When they perform that act of foul and damnable delight, they repent too late, because the devil has already purchased them and brought them to where he holds them in subjection as his servants. He binds them in such a way that they may be unbound only with great pain.

The poor hermit is guilty of pride in thinking that he's better than the provost and his wife. Then he commits the sin of gluttony, which leads him directly to lechery, as Jeanne and Anne would recognize when they read the story. Fortunately for the hermit, the example of such a virtuous lady teaches him about his own sin, leading him back to the path of virtue. In the same way, the story was designed to make Jeanne and Anne realize their own sins and turn to virtue. Whether it had the desired effect or merely titillated them probably depended on who was in the room: just the girls and a few young ladies-in-waiting, or an older, more sober woman such as their mother or Dame Agnes.

Good Ladies of the Present Time

After a number of biblical illustrations of virtuous women, as well as stories from other sources, Sir Geoffrey says, "In the same way that the holy scripture praises the good ladies of that time, it is reasonable and right that we should praise some from this present time when we live. Therefore I'll tell you one or two examples from every estate." By "every estate," he means from each social class, just as Chaucer does when, at the end of the General Prologue to the *Canterbury Tales*, he says he has told "th'estaat, th'array, the nombre, and eek the cause" of each of his pilgrims. Sir Geoffrey is almost true to his word. He throws us tidbits about royals, nobles, and members of the gentry (the knight's widow in the second story). However, unlike Chaucer, he leaves out the merchant class, and he doesn't come near the peasantry, the overwhelming majority of the medieval population.

Of the quene Iohane of Fraunce
(Concerning Queen Jeanne of France)
  Good Queen Jeanne of France, who has recently passed out of this world, was wise and lived a holy life. She was very charitable and full of devotion and held herself so pure that it's wonderful to tell about it. Next to her comes the Duchess of Orleans who suffered much in her life but always kept herself pure and holy—but it would take too long to tell about her good life. Nor should we forget the good Countess of Roussillon, a widow who kept herself very pure and who brought up her children peaceably. She kept good justice and ruled her land and people in peace. I'll also tell you about a baroness who lived in our region who was widowed for thirty-five years. She was young and beautiful when her lord died and many asked for her hand, but she had secretly vowed that for the love of her lord and her children, she would never remarry. For the rest of her life she was beyond reproach, for which she ought to be praised. I'll tell you her name: it was my lady of Vertus.

The queen mentioned here is probably the third wife of Charles IV of France (also known as Charles le Bel). Widowed in 1328, Queen Jeanne was known for the good works she performed before her death in 1370.

William Caxton supplied the particulars for the next two ladies. The first is simply "la duchesse," followed by a blank space in most of the French manuscripts, while the second is "la contesse mere au conte" (the countess, mother of the count). For Caxton they become the Duchess of Orleans and the Countess of Roussillon. The first could be one of any number of women, but there really was a famously pious Countess of Roussillon: Berthe, who was married to Count Girart de Roussillon. However, the stories about her don't mention her being a widow. Finally, the lady of Vertus remains a mystery. Perhaps it was the Baroness D'Artus and Caxton misread the manuscript.[12] Perhaps the manuscript he was working from was already corrupt. Although Sir Geoffrey seems to have known her well, the lady is lost to history.

The next story helps to date *The Book of the Knight of the Tower*. The Battle of Crécy took place in 1346, twenty-six years ago for Sir Geoffrey as he finishes his book in the year 1372.

Example of many good ladyes of tyme presente
(Examples of many good ladies of the present time)

Once there was a knight's widow, a lady who was living at the time of the Battle of Crécy, twenty-six years ago. She was young and beautiful and desired by many lords and knights, but she refused to remarry. Instead she brought up her children honorably, and for this she should be praised. Yet she should be praised even more for her conduct during her lord's life, because although her lord was very small, hunchbacked, goggle-eyed, and lacking in refinement, and she was young and fair and born a gentlewoman, nevertheless she loved and honored him as much as any woman is able to love any man. She feared and served him so meekly that many men were astonished by it, and for these reasons, she should be counted among the number of good women.

Now let me tell you about a good woman who was married to a simple man. This lady was young and fair and came of good lineage, but her husband was ancient and in a state of dotage. He was incontinent, urinating and defecating on himself like a young child does. Nevertheless, the good lady served him humbly and with a good heart night and day. She showed him more courtesy than a chambermaid or a servant would have done.

Frequently, people came to take her to dances and feasts, but she seldom went with them because nothing pleased her more than to do some service for her lord. If someone said to her, as they often did, "Madame, you should take some pleasure and leave your lord sleeping, since he needs nothing but rest," she would answer, "As long as he is uncomfortable, he needs to be well served." She said her joy and pleasure came from doing things that might please him. Although many people spoke to her of pleasure, none was able to turn her from caring so diligently for her lord. And after he died, she kept herself as pure in her widowhood as she had been in her marriage. She brought up her children and never consented to remarry. Therefore she ought to be praised and set amongst the good ladies. Her goodness and generosity ought to be a mirror and an example to others—which is why men ought not to hide the good deeds of any good women.

And for this reason I have told you about some who lived recently, but if I told you the deeds of all the others I knew I would have much to do, and my matter would be long and annoying, because there are many good women within the realm of France. The good ladies of whom I have spoken are without reproof and have shown great generosity and honor in their marriages as well as in their widowhood. They have eschewed the foolish works and pleasures of the world and have held their good estate so surely that no one could gossip or say anything of them except good and honest words. They have not married again for any worldly pleasure to someone of a lower estate than their lords. For as I believe, they who for pleasure get married again to someone of a lower estate without taking counsel of their friends and relations do themselves wrong. Often, after some time has passed and the greater part of pleasure is gone, they see that the great ladies don't honor them as much as they used to. Then they become repentant but it is too late. To me it seems that those who marry these ladies and make them into their subjects do a great sin.

Of course, Sir Geoffrey himself will later remarry a widow, as will his son Charles, though none of the new spouses will besmirch the Tour Landry honor by being of a lower social rank. But in 1372, while his first wife (herself a widow when she married him, but a widow with excellent family connections) is still alive and he doesn't know what the future will bring, Sir Geoffrey views second marriages with contempt. His opinions contrast sharply with those of the Householder of Paris, who expected that his wife would marry again after he died. The Householder's wife had already allied herself to a man below her social rank, and as a member of the merchant class, she would certainly marry another merchant. Sir Geoffrey, however, seems to think it better for his daughters to remain unmarried should they become widows, unless of course they can increase the family's honor and reputation through an impressive match: "If God gives you husbands who soon leave you widows," he says, "don't get married again for pleasure nor for love, but only by the counsel and good will of all your friends and relatives."

The final story in this section is not about a virtuous woman, but a compassionate knight. Although it contradicts Sir Geoffrey's previous statements about compassion being more appropriate for women than men, it again demonstrates virtuous Christian behavior, and it's just the kind of romance his daughters (and probably his sons) would love. Katherine and Elizabeth Goodwyn would enjoy it, too, especially since it features a poisoned apple, just like in another story they might have known, Sir Thomas Malory's tale about Guenevere and Lancelot, printed by William Caxton.

Of the good knyght whiche fought ageynst the fals knyghte for the pyte of a mayde
(Concerning the good knight who fought against the false knight because of his pity for a maiden)

I want you to know the story of a knight who fought for a maiden. At the court of a great lord there was a false knight who asked a maiden for her love, but despite his gifts and promises, she wouldn't give in to him, but kept her body pure. The knight told her she would regret it.

He poisoned an apple, and a few days later, he gave it to her to give to the young son of her lord. She did, and when the child ate the apple, he died. The maiden was taken and—to make a long story short—was sentenced to burn. She wept, crying to God that she was innocent, and that the false knight who had given her the apple was guilty. He refuted her and said he was ready to prove it against any knight on the field of battle. The maiden could find no champion because the false knight was so strong and so feared in battle.

Then our Lord God, who doesn't forget the prayers of the true and the just, took pity on her. Just as men were about to have cast the maiden into the fire, a good knight named Patrides, who was noble and compassionate, beheld the maiden as she wept and made such sorrow. He took pity on her and asked her what had really happened. She told him how it had been from the beginning to the end, and most of the people who were there witnessed what she said. Patrides, moved by compassion, cast his glove against the false knight. The battle between them was hard and cruel to see, but in the end, the false knight was beaten and openly declared his treason. Thus the maid was saved.

But the good knight Patrides received five mortal wounds during the battle. And because his coat-of-arms was on it, he sent her his mail-shirt, which was broken in five places. The maiden kept it all her life. Every day she prayed for the knight who had suffered such sorrow for her.

Because of his compassion and generosity the noble knight fought and received five mortal wounds just like sweet Jesus Christ who, because of his compassion, fought for us and for all humans to come. He so pitied those who fell into the shadows of hell that he suffered alone the hard and cruel battle on the tree of the holy cross. His mail-shirt was broken and pierced in five places, that is to say, he received five dolorous wounds on his dear body because of his pity for us. In the same way, every man and woman ought to have pity on the suffering of their relatives and neighbors and on the poor, just as the good knight had for the maiden. We should weep tenderly like the good ladies who wept for the dear Jesus as he carried the cross on which he would be crucified for our sins.

In Malory's secular analogue to this story, Guenevere—falsely accused of poisoning a knight—is sentenced to burn at the stake. Like Sir Patrides, Lancelot arrives in the nick of time. Unlike poor Patrides, however, Malory's hero survives. Nevertheless, Sir Patrides is accorded the great honor of receiving wounds that imitate Christ's. As we have seen, being like Christ is the goal of every virtuous Christian, even if the nobility interpret charity in a different way than did Saint Francis of Assisi. When Saint Francis read the words of

Matthew 10:7–9, in which Jesus tells his apostles to give up their goods and to serve the sick and the poor, he took them literally, stripping off his rich robes, living by begging, and seeking out a group of impoverished lepers to serve. For Sir Geoffrey and his family, putting a cheat-loaf in the almsdish at dinner every day and endowing a chapel is plenty; as long as you avoid the other sins, that is, and embrace virtuous but moderate behavior.

Chapter 14

Praising Past Time

The love between Sir Lancelot and Queen Guenevere was the true, virtuous love of the old days, Sir Thomas Malory tells us in *Le Morte Darthur*. It's a love that recognizes God above all, from whom comes all honor. "But nowadayes men can nat love sevennyght but they muste have all their desyres," Malory writes.

> But the olde love was nat so. For men and women coude love togydirs seven yerys, and no lycoures [lecherous] lustis was betwyxte them, and than was love, trouthe, and faythefulnes. And so in lyke wyse was used such love in kynge Arthurs dayes.[1]

For Malory, and for Caxton who printed his work, the days of the legendary King Arthur were a distant ideal, a time that never actually existed but one they felt *might* have been—a time so much better than nowadays. But it wasn't only love that was better in the old days. William Caxton thought things were going to hell, and he said so in many of the prologues and epilogues to the works he printed. In his translation of Ramon Llul's thirteenth-century *Book of the Order of Chivalry*, Caxton laments that chivalry is no longer what it was in the days of "that noble king of Britain, King Arthur, with all the noble knights of the round table." He cries from the heart:

> Oh you knights of England, where are the customs and habits of noble chivalry that were common in those days? What do you do now but go to the baths and play at dice? . . . Leave these things and read the noble volumes about the Holy Grail, of Lancelot, of Galahad, of Tristram, of the Perilous Forest, of Percival, of Gawain, and many more. There you can see manhood, courtesy, and nobility.[2]

Incidentally, you could read all of these "noble volumes" in Caxton's editions—thus, this lament for past times serves double duty as an advertisement for present wares.

Nostalgia has long been with us, and its refrains can make even the young misty-eyed for a past that never was. *Ubi-sunt* passages prevail in classical literature, where poets ask "where are they?" The *they* these writers are missing are the days of an imagined golden age, the glorious past when things were better than they are now. The fifteenth-century French poet François Villon took a similarly elegiac tone when he asked, "Mais où sont les neiges d'antan?" which Dante Gabriel Rossetti translated as "Where are the snows of yesteryear?" You can find a similar line in Chaucer's *Troilus and Criseyde*, where Pandarus says, "fare wel al the snow of ferne [past] yere!" In these poets' minds, nostalgia is a sadness for losses, for a past that can never come again, like the Beatles' poignant plaint, "Yesterday, all my troubles seemed so far away."

In their works, both William Caxton and Sir Geoffrey de la Tour condemn the present, which they believe has put aside the virtues that existed in the past. They are, in the words of a Horatian epistle, praisers of past time. So is Petrarch when he writes to Boccaccio in 1366, decrying present times when the world "is perhaps depopulated of true men but was never more densely populated with vice and the creatures of vice."[3] Yet given that Petrarch writes this line fewer than twenty years after the Black Death devastated Florence, his statement may not be the pure nostalgia Sir Geoffrey's is.

Sir Geoffrey's opinions about the good old days would have appealed to Caxton when he translated *The Book of the Knight of the Tower*. Like many a modern codger in his Florida condo, who remembers all the good parts of his youth while conveniently forgetting the bad, Sir Geoffrey can precisely place his golden age: forty years ago, when he was a youth. Back then, people knew what honor was all about and the young were polite to their elders. Men knew how to treat women, and women, too, knew how to behave. Like all of us who suffer pangs of nostalgia, Sir Geoffrey doesn't recall things he's told us earlier. In fact, he seems to forget the very impetus for his book: in his prologue, he railed against the ways his fellow soldiers dishonored women back in those good old days. It's Sir Geoffrey's fervent desire that those days—at least the good parts—will return.

He wasn't alone in feeling this way. Christine de Pizan likewise laments a breakdown of the social order. In chapter 9, we saw her ruing the day when people began dressing out of their station, middle-class women wearing the clothing of the aristocracy, and aristocrats aping royals. It's not only in clothing that people disregard social distinctions so egregiously. Married women act the same way as unmarried ones; common artisans act like merchants, their obvious social superiors; ladies act like countesses and countesses like queens. Although we should all keep to our own station, Christine says, "these rules are not kept nowadays, nor many other good ones that always used to be."[4] *Helas!*

Another French writer of about 1350 also worried about trends in noble ladies' fashions. However, instead of accusing the lower classes of mimicking their betters the way Christine does, he worries about the upper classes wearing inappropriate clothing, some of it only fitting for prostitutes. Fifty years ago, Gilles li Muisis says,

> women wore white wimples, surcoats with hanging sleeves, long full skirts, and decent hoods of cloth or silk. A woman had only three dresses, one for weddings and great feasts, one for Sundays and holidays, and one for every day. Narrow laced shoes and buttoned sleeves were for courtesans; decent women tied their bodices with ribbons and sewed their sleeves, wore their belts high and plaited their hair round their heads.[5]

But no more. Luxury and flippant fashions have taken the place of the sober clothing of yesteryear, and noble ladies make a mockery of their high social positions by wearing such garments.

For us these complaints might seem trivial, but to Christine, Gilles, and Sir Geoffrey, they signal a breakdown in the "right order of things," the God-given social order established by one's birth. The English couplet, "When Adam delved and Eve span / Who was then the gentleman?" notwithstanding, acceptance of social rank was widespread throughout the Middle Ages, and changes to it meant changes to the divine order established by God. As Sir Geoffrey implies in the next tale, keeping your reputation bright and untarnished was your duty not only to your family, but also to the other members of your social class. After all, that was how it was done in the good ol' days.

How euery good woman ought wel to kepe her Renommee
(How every good woman ought to guard her reputation well)

My dear daughters, if you understood the great honor that comes from a good name and reputation, you would take pains to get and keep it, just as the good knight does who seeks honor and flies from villainy. He suffers cold, heat, and hunger, he puts his body in great jeopardy, he even risks death in order to attain honor and good repute. He makes his body feeble and weary by long voyages, battles, and other great perils. When he has suffered enough pain and hardship, he gains marvelous honor and great gifts.

In the same way, the lady who takes pains to keep her body and her reputation pure, who sets no store by her youth, and who doesn't delight in the worldly pleasures that bring with them blame, is everywhere honored. Like the knight who suffers such hardship to be numbered among those renowned for their great worthiness and valiance, every good woman ought to do this. She should remember how in doing so she gets the love of God and of her lord, her friends, and the world, as well as the salvation of her soul, for which the world and God praise her. For God calls her the precious Marguerite, the round, white pearl, bright and unstained. In the Gospel, God praises the good lady, and thus men ought to give as much honor to a lady or a damsel as to a good knight or a squire. But nowadays the world is all turned upside down, and honor is not kept according to its proper rule, as it used to be.

One time I heard my lord my father and many other good knights say that in their time men bore great reverence to good women, while unworthy women were separated from the fellowship of the others. It wasn't even forty years ago that this was the custom, and at that time a woman who was guilty of blame wouldn't be so bold as to mingle with those who had good reputations.

I'll tell you about two good knights of that time, one named my lord Raoul de Lyege, and the other Geoffrey. They were brothers and good knights in arms, and they made expeditions and never rested till they came to a place where they could prove their strength in order to increase their honor. They were so valiant that in the end they were honored above all the rest, even Charny and Boucicaut, who lived during their time. As such venerated and renowned knights, people listened to them before all others.

Even if they loved hearing about the famous knights their father knew—the Charnys, Boucicauts, and Raouls—Jeanne and Anne must have tired of hearing how things used to be. Unlike modern teenagers, however, it's unlikely that they had the freedom to talk back to their father, telling him that he was contradicting himself. Instead they might wait until they were alone in the garden with Dame Agnes—who probably wouldn't report their indiscretions—to complain.

Nor would they point out Boucicaut's questionable behavior. Earlier in the book, he appears as a ladies' man, the knight who told three different women that he desired them before shaming all three—hardly the honorable gentleman he seems here. About Geoffroy de Charny's behavior, however, Jeanne and Anne would have had no complaints. In his *Chronicles*, Jean Froissart calls Charny "the wisest and bravest knight of them all." He describes the knight's death in the Battle of Poitiers, where Charny was given the honor of carrying the oriflamme, the king's golden-red royal standard, into battle. He died heroically, the banner in his hands.[6]

Charny's long poem about chivalry (written, like his *Book of Chivalry*, for Jean le Bon's Company of the Star, a sort of round table created by the king in the 1350s)[7] ends by saying that the life of a beast of burden is less difficult than that of a man at arms. Yet his work glorifies the life of the knight, and you can be sure that Charny would have agreed with Sir Geoffrey that things just aren't what they used to be. Like Sir Geoffrey's father, Charny would have been shocked by the young man in the next story, whose clothing indicates his lack of seriousness. You can just hear Charny saying, "Back in my day, young men knew how to dress." The "German style" of the young man's outfit suggests that he was wearing striped or multicolored clothing, looking foppish and loud.[8] The fashion may have suited minstrels, but certainly not gentlemen.

How thauncyent were wonte to lerne the yonge
(How wise elders used to teach the young)

In the old days, if a young man did something dishonorable, mature men showed him his fault in front of everyone, and so young men feared them. I heard my lord my father tell about a young man who came to a feast where many lords, ladies, and damsels were dressed to go to dinner. The young man was wearing a close-fitting surcoat in the German style. After he had saluted the lords and ladies and done reverence to them, my father called him over and asked where his viol or clavichords were, and told him he should perform his craft.

The young man said, "Sir, I don't meddle with those things."

"Ah," said Sir Geoffrey, "I don't believe it, because you're dressed like a minstrel. Nevertheless, I know your ancestry well, and the good and honest men of the tower you come from. But in good faith, I never saw someone of your lineage who would dress this way."

The young man said, "If my clothing seems distasteful to you, I will amend it." He called a minstrel over and gave him his gown, and took another for himself before he returned to the hall.

When the good old knight saw him, he said, "Truly, this young man doesn't stray from the path of wisdom. He listens to the counsel of his elders."

And every young man and young woman who listens to the advice of their elders won't fail to come to honor, for what they say is only for your good. But these days young men and women won't listen. They have only scorn when they're reproved for their wickedness and folly and they think they're wiser than their elders. Such ignorance is a pity, for every noble heart and honest person ought to be grateful for being reproved for his faults.

Now that I've told you how old people chastised young men, I'll tell you how they also gave good examples to the ladies and damsels who lived back then.

The young man who dresses like a minstrel takes on different identities in different French manuscript versions of this story. Sometimes he isn't named, sometimes he's identified as a young squire, and sometimes the young man in the bright clothing is said to be Sir Geoffrey's father. This is more fitting than it might initially seem, when you consider how fond the Tour Landry family was of minstrels, but it changes the tenor of the story considerably.[9]

One might wonder just what time period Sir Geoffrey is looking back to in the next tale, which he begins by noting that it took place in a time of peace. Peace was uncommon during Sir Geoffrey's lifetime, and the story seems as far-fetched as its setting does.

How hit was wonte to departe the blamed and dyffamed women fro the felauship & companye of the good and trewe

(How it was customary to separate the blamed and dishonored women from the fellowship and company of the good and honest women)

In those days it was a time of peace and they used to hold great feasts and revels, and all kinds of knights and ladies and damsels gathered together for them. They came there with great honor, and with them came the good knights of those days. But if it chanced that any lady who had a bad reputation or whose honor was at fault walked in front of another lady with a good reputation, no matter who was more noble or wealthier, the good and wise knights felt no shame in saying in front of everyone, "Lady, don't be displeased if this lady goes before you, for although she isn't as noble or as rich as you are, nevertheless, she isn't blameworthy, and she's numbered among the good women. The same isn't said of you, and it greatly displeases me, but honor is given to those who have deserved it."

In this manner the good, wise knights of those times put the ladies of good reputation first. Those ladies thanked God who had given them the grace to keep themselves pure, for which they were honored above everyone else. The others took themselves by the nose, casting their faces downwards, and they were shamed and humiliated. Of course this set a good example for all women because they feared doing anything for which they might be blamed.

Nowadays, however, men honor those who have been blamed just as highly as good and true women, which sets a bad example. Women think to themselves, "I see men honoring ladies who ought to be blamed and defamed just as much as they honor honest women, so it doesn't matter if I do something wrong."

But this isn't true, because they only make good cheer and give honor to these ladies in front of them, but behind their backs they pull out their tongues to scorn them, saying to one another, So and so is very free with her body, or Such a man takes his pleasure with her. The foolish women don't notice this, but they enjoy themselves and think nobody knows their shame. Yes, the times are different than they used to be, and it's a great pity. It would be better if these women were reproved for their faults in front of everyone like they were in the old days.

I'll tell you more that I have heard from knights who knew the aforementioned Sir Geoffroy de Lyege. When he rode through the countryside and saw some place or manor, he would ask about it. If he understood that the lady of the manor or place was in any way disreputable, he would go out of his way to set a notice on the gate of the manor, and then ride away again. On the other hand, if he passed before the place of a lady of good reputation, he went to see her and said to her, "My good friend, I pray to God that he will keep you in this wealth and honor for ever and hold you among the number of good women."

Because of this the good women held themselves more firmly from doing anything that might cause them to lose their honor and reputation. I wish that time would come again, for I know many who should not be blamed and defamed as they are now.

Caxton's sensibilities may have matched our own in some ways, particularly here. In the French version of this story, the notice Sir Geoffroy de Lyege set on the gate of the disreputable lady was a fart. Caxton, like modern readers, might have wondered just how such behavior fit in a story ostensibly about how people used to be more honorable! However, Caxton seems as little bothered as Sir Geoffrey is about the double standard to which men and women are held. The men know that "such a man takes his pleasure" with a certain woman, but the woman alone is held culpable.

The next chapters give Jeanne and Anne de la Tour a different reason to behave themselves. Honor and reputation are important, and physical punishment of the kind that used to be practiced (or that's still used elsewhere) is to be avoided. But in the end, Sir Geoffrey returns to the place where he began: his daughters' relationship with God and the entrance into the Heavenly City of Jerusalem that he fervently desires for them.

How before this tyme men punysshed them that were diffamed
(How before this time men punished those who were defamed)

Women ought to think about the time before the coming of Christ, which lasted more than five thousand years, and how bad women, especially married women, were punished when they misbehaved themselves. If just two men could prove that a woman had had carnal fellowship with someone other than her lord, she was either burnt or stoned. No matter how noble she was, no gold or silver might save her, according to the law of God and of Moses.

I know of a few regions today outside of the realms of France and England and Low Germany where men still do justice when the certainty of the deed is openly known, and that is to say in Romania, in Spain, in Aragon, and in many other realms. In some places men cut their throats, and in some they are beheaded in front of the people. In other places they are immured between two walls. It's good for every woman to know this, because although this Roman justice is not carried out here, nevertheless women still lose their honor, the love of God and of their lord, of their friends and the world, too. I'll tell you a tale about this taken from the highest source: God told it from his own mouth, as it says in the holy scriptures.

How god compared the good woman to the precious Margaryte
(How God compared the good woman to the precious Margaret)

In the Gospels we are told how the sweet Jesus Christ taught the people about good women. He says, "Una Margarita preciosa comparavit eam." I tell you, our Lord said that a woman who is pure and clean ought to be compared to the precious Margaret. This was wonderfully spoken, for a margaret is a great pearl, round, bright, white and clean, without any mark. God showed the worth of the woman who is clean and without mark, that is to say, the unmarried woman who keeps her virginity, the married woman who holds herself pure within the holy sacrament of marriage, and the widow who keeps herself pure in her widowhood. These are the ones our Lord likened to the precious margaret. The holy scripture says nothing is as agreeable to God and his angels as a good woman. In some ways, God praises her more than a man, because she ought to have more merit since she has lesser spirit than a man has. Woman was made out of man's body so she is weaker than a man, and if she resists the temptations of the devil, of the world, and of the flesh, she gains greater merit than the man does—which is why God compares her to the precious margaret.

The commentary on the Scriptures also says that just as it's a foul thing to spill drops of ink in a dish of milk, it is equally foul when one who ought to be a good virgin spills her maidenhood to somebody other than her spouse. Likewise with the married woman who through falsehood and foul lechery spills or breaks her holy sacrament of marriage and forswears her faith to God, the Church, and her lord.

And finally, she who ought to bear herself purely in her widowhood yet who does the contrary—this kind of woman is like black ink on a white coverchief. They are in no way like the precious margaret, on whom there is no spot. Alas, a woman ought to hate herself and to curse her evil life when she is put out of the number of the good and true women. Then she should remember three things: first, how those who have not yet been married lose their marriage and their honor and acquire shame and hatred from their relations and friends in this world, and how every one points at them. Secondly, how married women lose all honor and the love of God and of their lord, their relations, and of all others, for God keeps them from having any wealth or success, and the foul and evil things which are said about them are too long to be rehearsed. People may have a good face in front of them but behind them they will scorn and mock them. Never after that will these women love their lord, for the devil will make them burn to have more delight in the damnable sin of fornication than in the deed of marriage.

In the deed of marriage there is no mortal sin because it's commanded by God, and the devil can have nothing to do with it; but he has great power with lechery and with deadly sin. He can incite the sinner to false delight, like a smith who puts coal in the furnace and then blows on it. The devil will wait a long time to serve people in their foul delight, and to keep continually within it, so that in the end he can carry their souls with him into the deep pit of hell. He takes great joy in that and considers himself as well paid as the man who hunts all day long and in the evening finally catches the beast and takes it. The holy scripture says that those who are warmed by the fire of lechery will be burnt in the fire of hell. For as God says, no good deed will go unrewarded, and no wickedness unpunished.

More than any other, this chapter sums up what Sir Geoffrey both fears and desires for his daughters. He fears stains on their reputations in this world, which could keep them from the honor, the good marriages, and the material success he believes they deserve. He fears the temptations of the devil, which could deny them heavenly bliss after their lives in this world have ended. Honor and reputation; God, the devil, and the world to come; marriage, material wealth, and success in this world—these are Sir Geoffrey's themes throughout his book. He expresses them with metaphors that may not be original—the pure round pearl, the drops of ink in milk, the devil as a smith—but that are evocative nonetheless. Whether virgins, wives, or widows, Jeanne and Anne's roles, like Katherine and Elizabeth Goodwyn's, are circumscribed by Church teachings and the established social order, rules their father hopes they will live by.

Sir Geoffrey's book doesn't actually end here. His final eight chapters tell the story of Cato's deathbed advice to his son, Cathonet, and how Cathonet ignored it, to his peril. The moral precepts attributed to the Roman writer Cato were popular in the Middle Ages, but in this version, Sir Geoffrey has attached a different story to a well-known name. The dying Cato gives his son three lessons: first, be self-sufficient, never desiring more than you need, so you won't attract envy; second, never reprieve a man who deserves to die; and third, test your wife to make sure she can keep a secret. It's not long before Cathonet forgets all three precepts. First greed overtakes him, then he tells his wife a great secret, and to top it off, he is almost hanged by the very thief whom he had reprieved. Fortunately for Cathonet, he's rescued just in time. Unfortunately for the reader, Cathonet repeats at length the entire story of the three lessons his father gave him, just to make sure we get the point. "Now you have heard what happened to me because I didn't believe the counsel of my father, who was such a wise and virtuous man," Cathonet says, reminding Jeanne and Anne to listen to their own father's counsel.

At the end of this long tale about the importance of obeying parental advice, Sir Geoffrey turns back to particulars. He reminds his daughters to keep their husbands' secrets, a topic he has thoroughly explored earlier in the book. But he adds a lovely metaphor, saying, "Just as the shaft which has departed from the bow must take her flight and never come again to the bow until it has hit something, so is the word which comes from the mouth. After it leaves the mouth, it may never be put back again, but it will be heard for good or evil."

Sir Geoffrey's final words to his *chiere filles* repeat the importance of not speaking evil of others or telling secrets. He reminds them once again of the eternal life that awaits them, and makes a final reference to his other book, the one he wrote for his sons:

> None is so wise that he can know what will come of him. And those who are full of discretion keep themselves from repeating any hearsay. He does well who opposes those who blame others in both right and wrong. Keeping secret the suffering and evil of others brings only good, as it is told in the book of my two sons, and also in the Gospel.

God, reputation, and family, Sir Geoffrey's overarching themes, coalesce in the last sentences of his book.

In the end, a father's desires were realized. Jeanne and Anne allied themselves with an important family and kept their own sororal alliance as well, when they married the Rochechouart brothers, sons of King Charles V's chamberlain. No stories of blame, shame, or defame have been attached to them, nor to their younger sister Marie, who grew up to marry Gilles Clérembault in 1391. No shame, perhaps, but great sadness when—four years before her father's death—Marie left this world and her family behind. And thus ends the history of Sir Geoffrey and his daughters.

Caxton's Epilogue

Yet there is more. As he did with most of the books he printed, William Caxton added a short epilogue to his edition of *The Book of the Knight of the Tower*, which Katherine and Elizabeth Goodwyn would have read once they had savored all of the stories therein. Caxton identifies himself as the book's printer and tells where he works, just outside of Westminster Abbey, the section of town where scribes copied manuscripts, the place where the book-trade flourished. Caxton also tells us the date the book was made. He finished translating in June of 1483 and printed the book on the last day of January. For Caxton, as for Katherine and Elizabeth, this was still 1483, since the new year began not on the first day of January but on Lady Day—March 25. The Feast of the Annunciation, when the angel Gabriel told the Virgin Mary that she was pregnant, marked the new year during the Middle Ages, emphasizing once again how deeply Christianity wound its way through all aspects of medieval European society.

> Here ends the book which the Knight of the Tower made for the instruction and teaching of his daughters, translated out of French into our maternal English tongue by me, William Caxton. This book was ended and finished the first day of June, the year of our Lord 1483, and printed at Westminster on the last day of January, in the first year of the reign of King Richard the Third.

Here the contents of *The Book of the Knight of the Tower* may close, but the book itself lives on. Perhaps Jeanne took the original manuscript with her as part of her dowry when, at around nineteen or twenty, she married. Did their father commission copies to be made of the manuscript for Anne and Marie, as well, so they could read them to their own daughters? Marie had no children, but her sisters' offspring may have made copies to take with them into their own new families. It's pleasant to imagine a scribe using Jeanne's manuscript as an exemplar as he creates the fifteenth-century manuscript that's now in the British Library—the one opening with the miniature of the Tour Landry family, the women arrayed in blue, pink, and scarlet gowns.

And what of the Goodwyn family's printed edition of the book? Perhaps it accompanied Katherine when she moved across London into the fine house her husband—an upstanding goldsmith who became an alderman of his guild—inherited from his father. There it remained as the house expanded. In the late sixteenth century we might imagine one of Katherine's great-grandsons making a room in the house into a library, since such a room would enhance his status. There the book remained. Except as a curiosity, however, no one read it once the Reformation made its Catholic sentiments seem odd and a little bit dangerous. Then, in the mid-seventeenth century, the book met its final fate: flames illumined its spine, then licked its covers, and greedily consumed its pages in the Great Fire of London, erasing forever all trace of Katherine's name, her sister's, and 200 years of their descendents.

Yet *The Book of the Knight of the Tower* survives in manuscripts, in translations, and in modern editions. And within the stories, Sir Geoffrey, his daughters, and the people he knew survive as well, opening a window into a distant era.

Notes

Chapter 1: The World of the Book

1. Pierre Boisard, "La vie intellectuelle de la noblesse angevine à la fin du XIVe siècle d'après le Chevalier de la Tour Landry," *La Littérature angevine médiévale. Actes du colloque, 21 March 1980, Angers*. (Hérault: *Université d'Angers, Centre de recherche de littérature et de linguistique de l'Anjou et des Bocages* 1981), p. 142 [135–154].

2. Bourmont, la Gallouère, Plessis de Coesmes, and la Cornuaille, according to M. Y. Offord, ed., *The Book of the Knight of the Tower*, Early English Text Society, Supplementary Series 2. (London: Oxford University Press, 1971), p. xxxvi.

3. Offord, *The Book of the Knight of the Tower*, p. xxxvi, fn. 2.

4. If the Arcades de la Tour of the historical record was indeed the son of Sir Geoffrey and Jeanne de Rougé. Offord, *The Book of the Knight of the Tower*, p. xxxvi.

5. In the earlier Middle English translation, Sir Geoffrey says that his wife is dead and that he has three daughters. However, neither the French manuscripts nor Caxton's translation report this. Thomas Wright, ed., *The Book of the Knight of La Tour-Landry*, rev. ed., Early English Text Society Original Series 33 (1906; repr. New York: Greenwood, 1969), pp. 1–2. This translation has given rise to an assumption that the knight's impetus in writing the book was to advise his motherless daughters, all three of whom are thus said to be portrayed in the manuscript miniatures. However, since unlike her youngest daughter, whose date of birth is unknown, Jeanne de Rougé was certainly alive in 1372, and since she plays a large role in the book itself, the miniature probably portrays a family grouping of husband, wife, and two daughters. Further evidence for this interpretation of the miniature can be found in the clothing; in at least two of the miniatures, the woman I identify as Jeanne de Rougé wears clothes that suggest she is married, and the color scheme and ornament matches that of her husband's clothing.

6. The manuscript is Paris, Bibliothèque Nationale ms. Fr. 1190, fol. 5. For a description of the miniature, see Roberta L. Krueger, " 'Nouvelles choses': Social Instability and the Problem of Fashion in the *Livre du*

Chevalier de la Tour Landry, the *Ménagier du Paris*, and Christine de Pizan's *Livre des Trois Vertus*," in *Medieval Conduct*, ed. Kathleen Ashley and Robert L. A. Clark (Minneapolis: University of Minnesota Press, 2001), pp. 61–62 [49–85].

7. Offord, *The Book of the Knight of the Tower*, p. xxxvii.

8. Ruth Harvey, "Prolegomena to an Edition of 'Der Ritter vom Turn,' " in *Probleme mittelalterlicher Uberlieferun und Textkritik* (Oxforder Colloquium 1966), ed. Peter F. Ganz and Werner Schröder (Berlin: E. Schmidt, 1968), p. 167 [162–182].

9. Offord, *The Book of the Knight of the Tower*, p. xxiii.

10. Harvey, "Prolegomena," p. 169.

11. Harvey, "Prolegomena," p. 169.

12. Harvey, "Prolegomena," p. 180. Boisard, "La Vie Intellectuelle," p. 149, claims Albrecht Dürer as the artist of some of the woodcuts.

13. Harvey, "Prolegomena," p. 177.

14. Offord, *The Book of the Knight of the Tower*, pp. xvii–xviii.

15. Description of London, British Library Manuscript Harley 1764, *A Catalogue of the Harleian Manuscripts in the British Museum with Indexes of persons, Places, and Matters*, vol. II. (Printed by Command of His Majesty King George III in pursuance of an address of The House of Commons of Great Britain, 1808), unpaginated.

16. Frieda Elaine Penninger, *William Caxton* (Boston: Twayne Publishers, 1979), p. 24; W. J. Blyth Crotch, ed., *The Prologues and Epilogues of William Caxton*, Early English Text Society, Original Series 176 (London: Oxford University Press, 1928), pp. 7–8.

17. London, British Library press-mark C.ii.c.6, which is not paginated.

18. Offord, *The Book of the Knight of the Tower*, pp xvii and xviii, fn. 1; Thomas Lane's signature is visible in Caxton's edition in London, British Library, press-mark IB. 55085.

19. On late medieval English girls' education, see Kim M. Phillips, *Medieval Maidens: Young Women and Gender in England, 1270–1540* (Manchester: Manchester University Press, 2003), pp. 66–67.

20. Richard W. Kaeuper and Elspeth Kennedy, *The Book of Chivalry of Geoffroi de Charny: Text, Context, and Translation* (Philadelphia: University of Pennsylvania Press, 1996). For Charny's advice to young ladies, see pp. 190–195.

21. *Menagier* can mean "householder," so the book is often called *The Householder of Paris*, but in their edition, Brereton and Ferrier explain that in the title, the word does not have this sense; rather, it means "book of housekeeping." Georgine Brereton and Janet Ferrier, eds., *Le Menagier de Paris* (Oxford: Clarendon Press, 1981), p. xxi, fn. 4. Power calls the author the Goodman of Paris, which is also the title of her translation. Eileen Power, trans. *The Goodman*

of Paris (1928; repr. Avon: The Bath Press, 1992). Crossley-Holland identifies the Householder as Guy de Montigny. Nicole Crossley-Holland, *Living and Dining in Medieval Paris: The Household of a Fourteenth Century Knight* (Cardiff: University of Wales Press, 1996), p. 7.

22. Christine de Pisan, *The Treasure of the City of Ladies, or The Book of the Three Virtues*, trans. Sarah Lawson (Harmondsworth: Penguin, 1985), p. 176.

23. John L. Grigsby "Miroir des Bonnes Femmes," *Romania* 82 (1961): 463 [458–481]; and 83 (1963): 30–51.

24. John L. Grigsby, "A New Source of the *Livre du Chevalier de La Tour Landry*," *Romania* 84 (1963), 187 [171–208].

25. Grigsby, "Miroir des Bonnes Femmes" (1961), 466.

26. Felicity Riddy, "Mother Knows Best: Reading Social Change in a Courtesy Text," *Speculum* 71.1 (1996): 82–85 [66–86].

27. Frederick J. Furnivall, ed., *Caxton's Book of Curtesye*, Early English Text Society, Original Series 3 (London: N. Trubner, 1868), p. 51. My translation.

28. Penninger, *William Caxton*, p. 73.

29. Penninger, *William Caxton*, p. 30.

30. N. F. Blake, *Caxton and His World* (New York: London House and Maxwell, 1969), p. 134.

31. Blake, *Caxton and His World*, p. 127.

32. Gertrude Burford Rawlings, *The Booke of Thenseygnementes and Techynge that the knyght of the towre made to his doughters by the Chevalier Geoffroy de la Tour Landry*, illus. Garth Jones (London: George Newnes, 1902) pp. 201–203.

33. G. S. Taylor, ed., *The Book of the Knight of the Tour-Landry*, intro. D. B. Wyndham-Lewis (London: John Hamilton, Ltd, 1930), p. xvi.

Chapter 2: The Prologues

1. Alfred T. P. Byles, ed., *The Book of the Ordre of Chyualry*, Early English Text Society, Original Series 168 (London: Oxford University Press, 1926), p. 121.

2. W. J. Blyth Crotch, ed., *The Prologues and Epilogues of William Caxton*. Early English Text Society, Original Series 176 (London: Oxford University Press, 1928), p. 99.

3. Crotch, *The Prologues and Epilogues of William Caxton*, p. 52.

4. N. F. Blake, "The 'noble lady' in Caxton's *The Book of the Knight of the Tower*," *Notes and Queries* 105 (1965): 92 [92–93].

5. Penninger, *William Caxton*, pp. 19–20.

6. London British Library Manuscript Royal 19 C vii, fol. 1r.
7. Offord, *The Book of the Knight of the Tower*, p. 195.
8. Anatole Montaiglon, *Le Livre du Chevalier de La Tour Landry pour l'enseignement de ses filles* (1854; repr. Nendeln/Liechtenstein: Kraus Reprint, 1972), p. xxix.
9. British Library Manuscript Royal 19 C vii, fol. 164.

Chapter 3: Turn Your Hearts to God—Prayer

Chapter 3 contains Chapters 1–5 in Offord, *The Book of the Knight of the Tower*; Montaiglon, *Le Livre du Chevalier de La Tour Landry*; and Wright, *The Book of the Knight of La Tour-Landry*.

1. Alison Hanham, *The Celys and Their World: An English Merchant Family of the Fifteenth Century* (Cambridge: Cambridge University Press), p. 27.
2. Christine de Pisan, *The Treasure of the City of Ladies*, p. 35.
3. Boisard, "La Vie Intellectuelle de la Noblesse Angevine," p. 145, my translation.
4. Boisard, "La Vie Intellectuelle de la Noblesse Angevine," p. 145.
5. The princess's schedule comes from Christine de Pisan, *The Treasure of the City of Ladies*, pp. 59–62, and the prayer is on p. 59.
6. C. M. Woolgar, *The Great Household in Late Medieval England* (New Haven: Yale University Press, 1999), p. 84. Woolgar takes this information for a collection of royal household ordinances kept from the reigns of King Edward III to the time of William and Mary. See p. 219, fn. 11.
7. Power, *The Goodman of Paris*, pp. 35–36.
8. I owe information about these phrases to Professor Joseph S. Wittig.
9. Clare Donovan, "Books of Hours" in *Medieval England: An Encyclopedia*, ed. Paul E. Szarmach, M. Teresa Tavormina, and Joel T. Rosenthal (New York: Garland, 1998), pp. 136–138.
10. Giovanni Boccaccio, *The Decameron*, trans. Mark Musa and Peter E. Bondanella (New York: W. W. Norton, 1977), pp. 3–17.
11. Hanham, *The Celys and Their World*, p. 61.
12. Antoine de la Sale, *Little John of Saintré (Le Petit Jehan de Saintré)*, trans. Irvine Gray (London: George Routledge and Sons, 1931), p. 75. The Latin verse reads: "Quando dives moritur, / In tres partes dividitur; / Caro datur vermibus, / Peccuniam parentibus, / Animam demonibus, / Nisi Deus miseretur."
13. Eamon Duffy, *The Stripping of the Altars: Traditional Religion in England 1400–1580* (New Haven: Yale University Press, 1992), pp. 308–309.
14. Duffy, *The Stripping of the Altars*, p. 369.
15. Montaiglon, *Le Livre du Chevalier de la Tour Landry*, p. xv.
16. Based on Hanham, *The Celys and Their World*, pp. 255–256.

Chapter 4: Driving the Devil Out—Fasting and Confessing Your Sins

Chapter 4 contains Chapters 6–9 in *The Book of the Knight of the Tower;* Montaiglon, *Le Livre du Chevalier de La Tour Landry;* and Wright, *The Book of the Knight of La Tour-Landry.*

1. Woolgar, *The Great Household*, p. 90.
2. Woolgar, *The Great Household*, p. 90.
3. Woolgar, *The Great Household*, p. 91.
4. Christine de Pisan, *The Treasure of the City of Ladies*, p. 169.
5. F. L. Cross and E. A. Livingstone, eds., *The Oxford Dictionary of the Christian Church*, 2nd ed. (Oxford: Oxford University Press, 1974), p. 503.
6. Robert C. Stacey, "Jews," in *Medieval England: An Encyclopedia*, pp. 380–381.
7. William Chester Jordan, "Jews," in *Medieval France: An Encyclopedia*, ed. William W. Kibler, Grover A. Zinn, John Bell Henneman, Jr., and Lawrence Earp (New York: Garland, 1995), pp. 496–497.
8. Power, *The Goodman of Paris*, p. 41.
9. Power, *The Goodman of Paris*, p. 43.
10. Macrobius, *Commentary on the Dream of Scipio*, trans. William Harris Stahl (New York: Columbia University Press, 1952), pp. 87–90.
11. Shinners reports the last sin, from Burchard of Worms' *Corrector*. John Shinners, ed., *Medieval Popular Religion 1000–1500: A Reader* (Peterborough, ON: Broadview Press, 1997), p. 455.

Chapter 5: Hearing God's Service—Going to Mass

Chapter 5 contains chapters 27–32 in Offord, *The Book of the Knight of the Tower*, chapters 28–33 in Wright, *The Book of the Knight of La Tour-Landry*, and Montaiglon, *Le Livre du Chevalier de La Tour Landry.* (In Caxton's version, no chapter break is made in the twelfth chapter, while the French and earlier Middle English versions split it into two chapters.)

1. Power, *The Goodman of Paris*, p. 38.
2. de la Sale, *Little John of Saintré*, p. 73.
3. Power, *The Goodman of Paris*, p. 39.
4. Cross and Livingstone, *Oxford Dictionary of the Christian Church*, p. 397.
5. J. H. Blunt, *The Myroure of Oure Ladye: Containing a Devotional Treatise on Divine Service*, Early English Text Society, Extra Series 19 (1873), p. 54, my translation.

6. Julian of Norwich, *Revelations of Divine Love*, trans. Clifton Wolters (London: Penguin, 1966), pp. 182 and 185.
7. Gillian Pritchard, "Religion and the Paston Family," in *Daily Life in the Late Middle Ages*, ed. Richard Britnell (Gloucestershire: Sutton Publishing, 1998), p. 73 [65–82].

Chapter 6: Taming the Sparrowhawk—Manners and Marriage

Chapter 6 contains chapters 10–12, 119–120 in Offord, *The Book of the Knight of the Tower*, 10–12 and 120–121 in Montaiglon, *Le Livre du Chevalier de La Tour Landry*. The text of the earlier Middle English manuscript ends near the end of chapter 119, and the rest is supplied from Caxton. Thus, only chapters 10–12 and 120 from Wright, *The Book of the Knight of La Tour-Landry*, appear here.

1. Krueger, " 'Nouvelles choses' " p. 51.
2. Phillips, *Medieval Maidens* pp. 36–43. For the daughters of English dukes, see p. 38.
3. Shulamith Shahar, *Childhood in the Middle Ages*, trans. Chaya Galai (1983, repr. London and New York: Routledge, 1984), p. 224.
4. Barbara Hanawalt, *Growing Up in Medieval London: The Experience of Childhood in History* (Oxford: Oxford University Press, 1993), p. 205.
5. Shahar, *Childhood*, p. 248 for peasant marriages.
6. Offord, *The Book of the Knight of the Tower*, p. 200, note 24/39–25/1.
7. This picture of a London neighborhood is based on Hanawalt, *Growing Up*, p. 31.
8. Offord, *The Book of the Knight of the Tower*, p. 208, note 44/31.
9. Offord, *The Book of the Knight of the Tower*, p. 245, note 160/13–14.

Chapter 7: Obey Without Complaint—Being a Wife

Chapter 7 contains Offord's chapters 15–18, 72, 74, 91, and 90—from *The Book of the Knight of the Tower*, and chapters 16–19, 72, 74, 92, and 91 in Wright, *The Book of the Knight of La Tour-Landry*, and Montaiglon, *Le Livre du Chevalier de La Tour Landry*.

1. Christine de Pisan, *The Treasure of the City of Ladies*, pp. 62–63.
2. Krueger, " 'Nouvelles choses,' " p. 52.
3. The proverb, found in French farces as well as medieval Latin satires, has its roots in Proverbs 19:13: "a wrangling wife is like a roof continually dropping through." Jerome also uses it in *Against Jovinian*, where he compares a nagging wife to a dripping roof. See Lisa Perfetti,

Women and Laughter in Medieval Comic Literature (Ann Arbor: University of Michigan Press, 2003), p. 170.

4. The source is not the *Gesta Romanorum* (which Sir Geoffrey calls the Chronicles of the Romans), but *The Mirror for Good Women*. Offord, *The Book of the Knight of the Tower*, p. 233, note 123/31.
5. Power, *The Goodman of Paris*, p. 113.
6. Power, *The Goodman of Paris*, p. 115.
7. Christine de Pisan, *The Treasure of the City of Ladies*, pp. 65–66.
8. Chapter 96 in Offord, *The Book of the Knight of the Tower*, Wright, *The Book of the Knight of La Tour-Landry*, and Montaiglon, *Le Livre du Chevalier de La Tour Landry*.

Chapter 8: Beat Them When They Deserve It—Raising Children

Chapter 8 contains Offord's chapters 84, 85, 89, and 92 from *The Book of the Knight of the Tower*, and chapters 84, 86, 90, and 93 in Wright, *The Book of the Knight of La Tour-Landry*, and Montaiglon, *Le Livre du Chevalier de La Tour Landry*.

1. Phillipe Ariès, *L'Enfant et la vie familiale sous l'ancien régime* (Paris, 1960); *Centuries of Childhood*, trans. Robert Baldick (New York: Knopf, 1962).
2. Laurence Stone, *The Family, Sex and Marriage in England, 1500–1800* (London: Harper and Row, 1977).
3. Shahar, *Childhood*, pp. 22 and 264, fn. 3.
4. Shahar, *Childhood*, p. 265, fn. 3.
5. Chapter 83 in Offord, *The Book of the Knight of the Tower*; Montaiglon, *Le Livre du Chevalier de La Tour Landry*; and Wright, *The Book of the Knight of La Tour-Landry*.
6. Shahar, *Childhood*, p. 184.
7. Christine de Pisan, *The Treasure of the City of Ladies*, p. 67.
8. Frederick J. Furnivall, *Robert [Manning] of Brunne's Handlyng Synne*, Early English Text Society, Original Series 119 (London: Oxford University Press, 1901), pp. 45–46.
9. Christine de Pisan, *The Treasure of the City of Ladies*, p. 67.
10. Christine de Pisan, *The Treasure of the City of Ladies*, p. 68.
11. Shahar, *Childhood*, p. 222. The two examples of recipes for the sick are from Power, *The Goodman of Paris*, pp. 192–193.
12. Phillips, *Medieval Maidens*, p. 87.
13. Nicholas Orme, *From Childhood to Chivalry: The Education of English Kings and Aristocracy 1066–1530* (London: Methuen, 1984), pp. 55–56.
14. Woolgar, *The Great Household in Late Medieval England*, p. 101.
15. Phillips, *Medieval England*, pp. 70–74.
16. Hanawalt, *Growing Up*, p. 83.

17. Phillips, *Medieval England*, p. 67.
18. Shahar, *Childhood*, p. 229.
19. Shahar, *Childhood*, p. 229.
20. Hanawalt, *Growing Up*, p. 129.

Chapter 9: I Tell You, I Must Have It—Medieval Fashion

Chapter 9 contains Offord, *The Book of the Knight of the Tower*, chapters 20, 48, part of 50, 51–54, 56, and 25. In Wright, *The Book of the Knight of La Tour-Landry*, these are chapters 21, 47–53, 56, 26; and in Montaiglon, *Le Livre du Chevalier de La Tour Landry*, chapters 21, 47, 50–53, 56, and 26.

1. Phillips, *Medieval Maidens*, p. 45.
2. 3/4 of an ell; an ell is 45 inches. Anne Sutton, "Dress and Fashions c. 1470," in *Daily Life in the Late Middle Ages*, ed. Richard Britnell (Gloucestershire: Sutton Publishing, 1998), p. 11 [5–26].
3. Sutton, "Dress and Fashions," p. 10.
4. Jean de Meun and Guillaume de Lorris, *Romance of the Rose*, trans. Harry W. Robbins, ed. Charles W. Dunn (New York: Dutton, 1962), p. 278.
5. Joan Evans, *Dress in Medieval France* (Oxford: Oxford University Press, 1952), p. 57.
6. Krueger, " 'Nouvelles choses,' " pp. 61–62; the manuscript is Paris, Bibliothèque Nationale MS Fr. 1190, fol. 5.
7. Krueger, " 'Nouvelles choses,' " p. 62.
8. Power, *The Goodman of Paris*, p. 37.
9. Krueger, " 'Nouvelles choses,' " pp. 62–63.
10. Sutton, "Dress and Fashions," pp. 11–14.
11. Sutton, "Dress and Fashions," p. 16.
12. Hanawalt, *Growing Up*, p. 204.
13. Evans, *Dress in Medieval France*, p. 35.
14. Krueger, " 'Nouvelles choses,' " p. 53.
15. Christine de Pisan, *The Treasure of the City of Ladies*, p. 133.
16. Evans, *Dress in Medieval France*, pp. 54–55.
17. Krueger, " 'Nouvelles choses,' " p. 58.
18. Offord, *The Book of the Knight of the Tower*, pp. 205–206, note 39/21.
19. Caxton does not include this paragraph; I've supplied it from Wright, *The Book of the Knight of La Tour-Landry*.
20. Hanawalt, *Growing Up*, p. 118; p. 37 for colors of clothing.
21. Offord, *The Book of the Knight of the Tower*, p. 205, note 38/36.
22. Chapter 59.
23. From "deer and unicorns" to the end of this sentence has been supplied from Wright, *The Book of the Knight of La Tour-Landry*, p. 63.

24. The explanation of deer putting their heads down to drink is supplied from Wright, *The Book of the Knight of La Tour-Landry*, p. 63.
25. The last paragraph, along with the next story, are taken from Offord, *The Book of the Knight of the Tower*, Chapter 50; Wright, *The Book of the Knight of La Tour-Landry*, and Montaiglon, *Le Livre du Chevalier de La Tour Landry*, Chapter 47.
26. Brereton and Ferrier, *Le Menagier de Paris*, p. xxxiv.
27. The story of the gallows adornment comes from Caxton's Chapter 50.
28. Quoted in G. R. Owst, *Literature and the Pulpit in Medieval England* (Cambridge: Cambridge University Press, 1933), p. 392.
29. Grigsby, "Miroir des Bonnes Femmes," p. 469.
30. The last paragraph has some additions—including the hair dyeing—supplied from Wright, *The Book of the Knight of La Tour-Landry*.
31. de Meun, *Romance of the Rose*, p. 278.
32. Chapter 55 in Offord, *The Book of the Knight of the Tower*, Wright, *The Book of the Knight of La Tour-Landry*, and Montaiglon, *Le Livre du Chevalier de La Tour Landry*.

Chapter 10: Hearts Set on This World—Acting Fashionably

Chapter 10 contains Offord, *The Book of the Knight of the Tower*, chapters 19, 14, 95, 21–24, 55, 49, and 33–34; Wright, *The Book of the Knight of La Tour-Landry*, and Montaiglon, *Le Livre du Chevalier de La Tour Landry*, chapters 20, 15, 96, 22–25, 55, 47 [48 in Montaiglon], and 34.

1. Eileen Power, *Medieval People*, 10th ed. (New York: Barnes and Noble, 1963), p. 91.
2. Power, *Medieval People*, p. 91.
3. David Farmer, *The Oxford Dictionary of Saints*, 4th ed. (Oxford: Oxford University Press, 1997), p. 310.
4. Woolgar, *The Great Household*, p. 78.
5. Offord, *The Book of the Knight of the Tower*, p. 202, note 31/6.
6. *3 Hen VI*, II.ii.144.
7. Offord, *The Book of the Knight of the Tower*, p. 207, note 40/35–36.
8. Jean Froissart, *Chronicles*, rev. ed., trans. and ed. Geoffrey Brereton (London: Penguin, 1978), pp. 131–136.
9. Froissart, *Chronicles*, p. 315.
10. Constance Bouchard, "Tournament," in *Medieval France: An Encyclopedia*, ed. William Kibler, Grover A. Zinn, John Bell Henneman, Jr., and Lawrence Earp (New York: Garland, 1995), pp. 915–916.
11. Keen, *Chivalry*, p. 134 for information about heralds.

12. Frederick J. Furnivall, *The Babees Book*, Early English Text Society, Original Series 32 (1868, repr. Bury St. Edmonds: Rowland Digital Printing, 1997), pp. 284–285.
13. For information about feasts, I am indebted to chapter 8 of Bridget Ann Henisch, *Fast and Feast: Food in Medieval Society* (University Park: Pennsylvania State University Press, 1976).
14. For information about jousts and tournaments, I have relied on chapters 5 and 9 of Maurice Keen's *Chivalry*.
15. Hanham, *The Celys and Their World*, pp. 311–314.
16. Chapter 55.
17. Furnivall, *Babees Book*.
18. Henisch, *Fast and Feast*, p. 188.
19. Christine de Pisan, *The Treasure of the City of Ladies*, p. 152.
20. Hanham, *The Celys and Their World*, p. 27.
21. William Melczer, *The Pilgrim's Guide to Santiago de Compostela* (New York: Italica Press, 1993), pp. 94–95.
22. Melczer, *Pilgrim's Guide*, pp. 119–133.
23. Sources for information about pilgrimages include the following: Hilda F. M. Prescott, ed., *Friar Felix at Large: A Fifteenth-Century Pilgrimage to the Holy Land* (Westport, CT: Greenwood Press, 1967), p. 124. Norbert Ohler, *The Medieval Traveller*, trans. Caroline Hillier (Rochester, NY: Boydell, 1995). John Capgreve, *Ye Solace of Pilgrimes* (1911; repr. New York: AMS Press, 1980), pp. 61–63. Margery Kempe, *The Book of Margery Kempe*, trans. Barry Windeatt (Harmondsworth: Penguin, 1985). Alison McHardy, "Pilgrimages and Pilgrims," in *Medieval England: An Encyclopedia*, pp. 601–602.

Chapter 11: As Fire Kindles Straw—Love and Its Games

Chapter 11 contains Offord, *The Book of the Knight of the Tower*, and Wright, *The Book of the Knight of La Tour-Landry*, chapters 122–133; the entire love debate is contained in chap. 124 in Montaiglon, *Le Livre du Chevalier de La Tour Landry*.

1. Andreas Cappellanus, *The Art of Courtly Love*, trans. John Jay Parry (New York: Columbia University Press, 1941), p. 186.
2. David F. Hult, "Courtly Love," in *Medieval France: An Encyclopedia*, pp. 267–269. Elizabeth S. Sklar, "Courtly Love," in *Medieval England: An Encyclopedia*, pp. 380–381.
3. Christine de Pisan, *The Treasure of the City of Ladies*, pp. 95–105.
4. Kaeuper and Kennedy, *The Book of Chivalry of Geoffroi de Charny*, p. 95.
5. Kaeuper and Kennedy, *The Book of Chivalry of Geoffroi de Charny*, p. 123.
6. See Joan M. Ferrante, *To the Glory of her Sex: Women's Roles in the Composition of Medieval Texts* (Bloomington: Indiana University Press,

1997) for a discussion of the ways (mostly early) medieval women and men cooperated with each other in the writing of texts, commissioning work, asking questions, and exchanging ideas that led to works composed by both sexes.

7. Kaeuper and Kennedy, *The* Book of Chivalry *of Geoffroi de Charny*, p. 169.

8. Kaeuper and Kennedy, *The* Book of Chivalry *of Geoffroi de Charny*, p. 32.

9. Kauper and Kennedy, *The* Book of Chivalry *of Geoffroi de Charny*, p. 25. For Augustine, see *Confessions* Book VIII, chapter 7. For Sir Bors, see Thomas Malory, *Works*, ed. Eugène Vinaver, 2nd. ed. (Oxford: Oxford University Press, 1971), p. 483: "And for all women sir Bors was a vergyne sauff for one."

10. Frances and Joseph Gies, *A Medieval Family: The Pastons of Fifteenth-Century England* (New York: HarperCollins, 1998), pp. 207–213; quotation is from p. 210.

11. Gillian Pritchard, "Religion and the Paston Family," pp. 72–73.

12. Hanham, *The Celys and Their World*, p. 315.

13. Thomas Frederick Simmons, ed., *The Lay Folks Mass Book or The Manner of Hearing Mass*, Early English Text Society, Original Series 71 (London: Oxford University Press, 1879), p. 298 (my modernization).

14. Shulamith Shahar, *The Fourth Estate: A History of Women in the Middle Ages*, trans. Chaya Galai (1983; repr. New York: Routledge, 1984), pp. 81–82.

15. "The Knight of Curtesy and The Fair Lady of Faguell," in Joseph Ritson, *Ancient English Metrical Romances*, 3 vols., rev. Edmund Goldsmid (Edinburgh: E. & G. Goldsmid, 1885), 3: pp. 172–188.

16. "Introduction" in Alice Kemp-Welch, *The Chatelaine of Vergi: A Romance of the XIIIth Century* (1903; repr. New York: Cooper Square, 1966), p. 3.

17. Kemp-Welch, *The Chatelaine of Vergi*. The moral is on page 57.

18. Quoted in de la Sale, *Little John of Saintré*, p. 17.

19. Caxton's text is confusing here; he may have misunderstood the French. I have tried to get at the gist of the section.

Chapter 12: The Devil's Subtle Craft—Vice and Sin

Chapter 12 contains Offord, *The Book of the Knight of the Tower*, chapters 37, 102, 135, 136, 35, 36, and 62; Wright, *The Book of the Knight of La Tour-Landry*, chapters 37, 104, 35, 36, and 62; and Montaiglon, *Le Livre du Chevalier de La Tour Landry*, chapters 37, 104, 126, 127, 35, 36, and 62. The Follies of Eve appear in Offord, *The Book of the Knight of the Tower*, chapters 39–47 and chapters 39–46 in Wright, *The Book of the Knight of La Tour-Landry*, and Montaiglon, *Le Livre du Chevalier de La Tour Landry*.

1. Offord, *The Book of the Knight of the Tower*, p. 227; the story is reported in chapter 73 in Offord, *The Book of the Knight of the Tower*, and Montaiglon, *Le Livre du Chevalier de La Tour Landry*, It is absent from Wright, *The Book of the Knight of La Tour-Landry*.
2. Translated by Elaine Treharne, *Old and Middle English: An Anthology* (Oxford: Blackwell Publishers, 2000), p. 319.
3. In Caxton's translation, the knight bows his head toward the crucifix. In the surviving French versions and in the other Middle English translation, the cross bows to the knight. See Offord, *The Book of the Knight of the Tower*, p. 238, note 137/20.
4. In Caxton, she is called "Cecyle of balleuylle." The name Olive is used in British Library MS Royal 19 C. vii and in Montaiglon, *Le Livre du Chevalier de La Tour Landry*. See Offord, *The Book of the Knight of the Tower*, p. 254, note 182/21.
5. Boisard, "La Vie Intellectuelle de La Noblesse Angevine," pp. 138–139.
6. Montaiglon, *Le Livre du Chevalier de La Tour Landry*, p. 274.
7. I am indebted to Professor Lisa Perfetti for help with this translation.
8. Chapter 70 in *The Book of the Knight of the Tower*; Montaiglon, *Le Livre du Chevalier de La Tour Landry*; and Wright, *The Book of the Knight of La Tour-Landry*.
9. T. Wright, *A Selection of Latin Stories from Manuscripts of the Thirteenth and Fourteenth Centuries* (London: Richards, 1842). See Notes, pp. 235–236, for the summary of the French version; pp. 83–84 for the Latin version and the English rhyme, which I have modernized.
10. Power, *The Goodman of Paris*, p. 58, my modernisation.
11. Hanawalt, *Growing Up*, pp. 38–39 for description of Midsummer Eve celebration.
12. Offord, *The Book of the Knight of the Tower*, p. 212.
13. From chapter 55 in Offord, *The Book of the Knight of the Tower*, chapter 54 in Wright, *The Book of the Knight of La Tour-Landry* and Montaiglon, *Le Livre du Chevalier de La Tour Landry*.
14. Katherine J. Lewis, "Model Girls? Virgin-Martyrs and the Training of Young Women in Late Medieval England," in *Young Medieval Women*, ed. Katherine J. Lewis, Noël James Menuge, and Kim M. Phillips (New York: St. Martin's Press, 1999), p. 28 [25–46]. Lewis discusses Sir Geoffrey's use of virgin martyrs in general and Saint Katherine in particular.

Chapter 13: True Women and Good Ladies—Virtuous Living

Chapter 13 contains Offord, *The Book of the Knight of the Tower*, chapters 86, 87, 110, 101, 94, 134, 111, 112, and 104; Wright, *The Book of the Knight of*

La Tour-Landry, and Montaiglon, *Le Livre du Chevalier de La Tour Landry*, chapters 87, 88, 110, 102, 95, 125 (this chapter is not in Wright), 113, 114, and 106.

1. Farmer, *The Oxford Dictionary of Saints*, p. 159.
2. The Middle English life was written for Lady Elizabeth de Vere by Osbern Bokenham. Mary C. Erler, *Women, Reading, and Piety in Late Medieval England* (Cambridge: Cambridge University Press, 2002), p. 22.
3. Ronald Baxter, "Bestiaries," in *Medieval England: An Encyclopedia*, p. 125 [125–126].
4. A. P. M. Orchard, "Isidore of Seville," in *Medieval England: An Encyclopedia*, p. 373 [373–374].
5. Baxter, "Bestiaries," p. 125.
6. Offord and Ferrier think Sir Geoffrey may have had access to a bestiary written in French verse. See Offord, *The Book of the Knight of the Tower*, pp. 200–201, note 25/5; p. 232, note 117/33; and Janet M. Ferrier, *French Prose Writers of the Fourteenth and Fifteenth Centuries* (Oxford: Pergamon Press, 1966), p. 11, note.
7. The shade is an addition from Wright's edition; Caxton omits it.
8. Benedicta Ward, *Miracles and the Medieval Mind: Theory, Record and Event 1000–1215* (Philadelphia: University of Pennsylvania Press, 1987), p. 3.
9. From *The City of God*, trans. H. Bettenson (London, 1972). Quoted in Ward, *Miracles and the Medieval Mind*, p. 2.
10. Jesus College. Farmer, *The Oxford Dictionary of Saints*, p. 422.
11. Christine de Pisan, *The Treasure of the City of Ladies*, p. 71.
12. Offord, *The Book of the Knight of the Tower*, p. 240, note 149/11.

Chapter 14: Praising Past Time

Chapter 14 contains Offord, *The Book of the Knight of the Tower*, chapters 114–118; and Wright, *The Book of the Knight of La Tour-Landry*, and Montaiglon, *Le Livre du Chevalier de La Tour Landry*, chapters 116–119.

1. Malory, *Works*, p. 649.
2. Byles, ed. *The Book of the Ordre of Chyualry*, p. 122.
3. Quoted in Barbara Tuchman, *A Distant Mirror: The Calamitous 14th Century* (New York: Knopf, 1978), p. 245.
4. Christine de Pisan, *The Treasure of the City of Ladies*, pp. 133, 153.
5. Evans, *Dress in Medieval France*, pp. 24–25.
6. Froissart, *Chronicles*, pp. 129, 140.
7. Kaeuper and Kennedy, *The Book of Chivalry of Geoffroi de Charny*, p. 21.
8. Offord, *The Book of the Knight of the Tower*, p. 242, note 152/38.
9. Offord, *The Book of the Knight of the Tower*, p. xxxv and note 152/36.

BIBLIOGRAPHY

Andreas Cappelanus. *The Art of Courtly Love*. Trans. John Jay Parry. New York: Columbia University Press, 1941.

Ariès, Phillipe. *Enfant et la vie familiale sous l'ancien régime*. Paris, 1960. Trans. Robert Baldick, *Centuries of Childhood*. New York: Knopf, 1962.

Ashley, Kathleen. "The *Miroir des bonnes femmes*: Not for Women Only?" *Medieval Conduct*. Ed. Kathleen Ashley and Robert L. A. Clark. Medieval Cultures Vol. 29 Minneapolis: University of Minnesota Press, 2001: 86–105.

Baxter, Ronald. "Bestiaries." *Medieval England: An Encyclopedia*. Ed. Paul E. Szarmach, M. Teresa Tavormina, and Joel T. Rosenthal. New York: Garland, 1998: 125–126.

Bennett, Judith M. *A Medieval Life: Cecilia Penifader of Brigstock, c. 1295–1344*. Boston: McGraw-Hill, 1999.

Blake, N. F. *Caxton and His World*. New York: London House and Maxwell, 1969.

———. "The 'Noble Lady' in Caxton's *The Book of the Knight of the Tower*." *Notes And Queries* ccx (1965): 92–93.

Blunt, J. H. *A Myroure of Oure Ladye: Containing a Devotional Treatise on Divine Service*. Early English Text Society, Extra Series 19. 1873. Millwood, NY: Kraus, 1973.

Boccaccio, Giovanni. *The Decameron*. Ed and trans. Mark Musa and Peter E. Bondanella. New York: W.W. Norton, 1977.

Boisard, Pierre. "La vie intellectuelle de la noblesse angevine à la fin du XIVe siècle d'après le Chevalier de la Tour Landry." *La Littérature angevine médiévale. Actes du colloque, 21 March 1980, Angers*. Hérault: Université d'Angers, Centre de recherche de littérature et de linguistique de l'Anjou et des Bocages, 1981: 135–154.

Boisard, Pierre and Daniel Régnier-Bohler. "Geoffroi de La Tour Landry." *Dictionnaire des Lettres Françaises: Le Moyen Age*. Ed. Robert Bossuat, Louis Pichard, and Guy Raynard de Lage. 1964. Rev. ed., Geneviève Hasenohr and Michel Zink. Fayard, 1992: 498–499.

Borstein, Diane. "Courtesy Books." *Dictionary of the Middle Ages*. Ed. Joseph R. Strayer. New York: Charles Scribners' Sons, 1983.

———. *The Lady in the Tower: Medieval Courtesy Literature for Women*. Hamden, CT: Archon Books, 1983.

Bouchard, Constance B. "Tournament." *Medieval France: An Encyclopedia*. Ed. William Kibler, Grover A. Zinn, John Bell Henneman, Jr., and Lawrence Earp. New York: Garland, 1995: 915–916.

Brereton, Georgine E. and Janet M. Ferrier, eds. *Le Menagier de Paris*. Oxford: Clarendon, 1981.

Byles, Alfred T. P., ed. *The Book of the Ordre of Chyualry*. Trans. William Caxton. Early English Text Society, Original Series 168, 1926. Millwood, NY: Kraus, 1971.

Capgreve, John. *Ye Solace of Pilgrimes*. 1911. New York: AMS Press, 1980.

A Catalogue of the Harleian Manuscripts in the British Museum with Indexes of Persons, Places, and Matters, vol. II. Printed by Command of His Majesty King George III in pursuance of an address of The House of Commons of Great Britain, 1808.

Cross, F. L. and E. A. Livingstone, eds. *The Oxford Dictionary of the Christian Church*. 2nd ed. Oxford: Oxford University Press, 1974.

Crossley-Holland, Nicole. *Living and Dining in Medieval Paris: The Household of a Fourteenth Century Knight*. Cardiff: University of Wales Press, 1996.

Crotch, W. J. Blyth, ed. *The Prologues and Epilogues of William Caxton*. Early English Text Society, Original Series 176. 1928. London: Oxford University Press, 1956.

de la Sale, Antoine. *Little John of Saintré (Le Petit Jehan de Saintré)*. Trans. Irvine Gray. London: George Routledge and Sons, 1931.

de Gendt, A. M. " 'Por ce a cy bon exemple': Morale et récit dans *Le Livre du Chevalier de la Tour Landry*." *Non nova, sed nova: Mélanges de civilisation médiévale dédiés à Willem Noomen*. Ed. Martin Gosman and Jaap van Os. Groningen: Bouma's Boekhuis, 1984: 67–79.

de Meun, Jean and Guillaume de Lorris. *Romance of the Rose*. Trans. Harry W. Robbins. Ed. Charles W. Dunn. New York: Dutton, 1962.

de Pisan, Christine. *The Treasure of the City of Ladies, or The Book of the Three Virtues*. Trans. Sarah Lawson. Harmondsworth: Penguin, 1985.

Donovan, Claire. "Books of Hours." *Medieval England: An Encyclopedia*. Ed. Paul E. Szarmach, M. Teresa Tavormina, and Joel T. Rosenthal. New York: Garland, 1998: 136–138.

Duffy, Eamon. *The Stripping of the Altars: Traditional Religion in England 1400–1580*. New Haven: Yale University Press, 1992.

Eckrich, Helen M. *An Edition of "Le Livre du Chevalier de La Tour Landry Pour L'Enseignment de ses Filles."* Diss., Fordham University, 1970. Ann Arbor: UMI 7020116.

Erler, Mary C. *Women, Reading, and Piety in Late Medieval England*. Cambridge: Cambridge University Press, 2002.

Evans, Joan. *Dress in Medieval France*. Oxford: Oxford University Press, 1952.

Farmer, David. *The Oxford Dictionary of Saints*. 4th ed. Oxford: Oxford University Press, 1997.

Ferrante, Joan M. *To the Glory of Her Sex: Women's Roles in the Composition of Medieval Texts*. Bloomington: Indiana University Press, 1997.

Ferrier, Janet M. *French Prose Writers of the Fourteenth and Fifteenth Centuries.* Oxford: Pergamon Press, 1966.

Froissart, Jean. *Chronicles.* Selected, trans. and ed. Geoffrey Brereton. Rev. ed. London: Penguin, 1978.

Furnivall, Frederick J., ed. *The Babees Book.* Early English Text Society, Original Series 32. 1868. Bury St. Edmonds: Rowland Digital Printing, 1997.

———, ed. *Robert [Manning] of Brunne's Handlyng Synne and Its French Original.* Early English Text Society, Original Series 119, 123. 1901. Millwood, NY: Kraus, 1973.

———, ed. *Caxton's Book of Curtesye.* Early English Text Society, Original Series 3. London: N. Trubner, 1868.

Gies, Frances and Joseph Gies. *A Medieval Family: The Pastons of Fifteenth-Century England.* New York: HarperCollins, 1998.

Godefroy, Frédéric. *Dictionnaire de L'Ancienne Langue Française et de Tous ses dialects du IXe au XVe siècle.* 10 vols. Paris, 1898.

Grigsby, John L. "A New Source of the Livre du Chevalier de La Tour Landry." *Romania* 84 (1963): 171–208.

———. "Wanted: An Edition of Marquard vom Stein's *Ritter vom Turn.*" *Archiv für das Studium der neueren Sprachen und Literaturen* 199 (114. Jahrgang, 1962): 325–329.

———. "Miroir des Bonnes Femmes." *Romania* 82 (1961): 458–481; 83 (1963): 30–51.

Hanawalt, Barbara. *Growing Up in Medieval London: The Experience of Childhood in History.* Oxford: Oxford University Press, 1993.

Hanham, Alison. *The Celys and Their World: An English Merchant Family of the Fifteenth Century.* Cambridge: Cambridge University Press, 1985.

Harvey, Ruth. "Prolegomena to an Edition of 'Der Ritter vom Turn.' " *Probleme mittelalterlicher Uberlieferun und Textkritik* (Oxforder Colloquium 1966, ed. Peter F. Ganz and Werner Schröder). Berlin: E. Schmidt, 1968: 162–182.

Henisch, Bridget Ann. *Fast and Feast: Food in Medieval Society.* University Park: Pennsylvania State University Press, 1976.

Henneman, John Bell. "Boucicaut." *Medieval France: An Encyclopedia.* Ed. William W. Kibler, Grover A. Zinn, John Bell Henneman, Jr., and Lawrence Earp. New York: Garland, 1995: 137.

Ho, Cynthia, "As Good as Her Word: Women's Language in *The Knight of the Tour d'Landry.*" *The Rusted Hauberk: Feudal Ideas of Order and Their Decline.* Ed. Cindy L. Vitto and Liam O. Purdon. Gainesville: University Press of Florida, 1994: 99–120.

Hult, David F. "Courtly Love." *Medieval France: An Encyclopedia.* Ed. William W. Kibler, Grover A. Zinn, John Bell Henneman, Jr., and Lawrence Earp. New York: Garland, 1995: 267–269.

Jordan, William Chester. "Jews." *Medieval France: An Encyclopedia.* Ed. William W. Kibler, Grover A. Zinn, John Bell Henneman, Jr., and Lawrence Earp. New York: Garland, 1995: 496–497.

Julian of Norwich. *Revelations of Divine Love*. Trans. Clifton Wolters. London: Penguin, 1966.

Kaeuper, Richard W. and Elspeth Kennedy. *The Book of Chivalry of Geoffroi de Charny: Text, Context, and Translation*. Philadelphia: University of Pennsylvania Press, 1996.

Keen, Maurice. *Chivalry*. New Haven: Yale University Press, 1984.

Kempe, Margery. *The Book of Margery Kempe*. Trans. Barry Windeatt. Harmondsworth: Penguin, 1985.

Kemp-Welch, Alice. *The Chatelaine of Vergi: A Romance of the XIIIth Century*. 1903. The Medieval Library. New York: Cooper Square, 1966.

Kermode, Frank and John Hollander, eds. *The Oxford Anthology of English Literature*. Vol. 1. New York: Oxford University Press, 1973.

Krueger, Roberta L. " 'Nouvelles choses': Social Instability and the Problem of Fashion in the *Livre du Chevalier de la Tour Landry*, the *Ménagier du Paris*, and Christine de Pizan's *Livre des Trois Vertus*." *Medieval Conduct*. Ed. Kathleen Ashley and Robert L. A. Clark. Medieval Cultures vol. 29. Minneapolis: University of Minnesota Press, 2001: 49–85.

———. "Intergeneric Combination and the Anxiety of Gender in *Le Livre du Chevalier de la Tour Landry pour l'enseignement de ses filles*." *L'Esprit Créateur* 33.4 (Winter 1993): 61–72.

Lewis, Katherine J., Noël James Menuge, and Kim M. Phillips, eds. *Young Medieval Women*. New York: St. Martins, 1999.

Leyser, Henrietta. *Medieval Women: A Social History of Women in England 450–1500*. New York: St. Martin's Press, 1995.

Macrobius. *Commentary on the Dream of Scipio*. Trans. William Harris Stahl. New York: Columbia University Press, 1952.

Malory, Thomas. *Works*. Ed. Eugène Vinaver. 2nd ed. Oxford: Oxford University Press, 1971.

McHardy, Alison. "Pilgrimages and Pilgrims." *Medieval England: An Encyclopedia*. Ed. Paul E. Szarmach, M. Teresa Tavormina, and Joel T. Rosenthal. New York: Garland, 1998: 601–602.

Melczer, William. *The Pilgrim's Guide to Santiago de Compostela*. New York: Italica Press, 1993.

Montaiglon, Anatole de. *Le Livre du Chevalier de La Tour Landry pour l'enseignement de ses filles*. 1854. Millwood, NY: Kraus, 1972.

Offord, M. Y., ed. *The Book of the Knight of the Tower*. Trans. William Caxton. Early English Text Society, Supplementary Series 2. London: Oxford University Press, 1971.

Ohler, Norbert. *The Medieval Traveller*. Trans. Caroline Hillier. Rochester, NY: Boydell, 1995.

Orchard, A. P. M. "Isidore of Seville." *Medieval England: An Encyclopedia*. Ed. Paul E. Szarmach, M. Teresa Tavormina, and Joel T. Rosenthal. New York: Garland, 1998: 373–374.

Orme, Nicholas. *From Childhood to Chivalry: The Education of the English Kings and Aristocracy 1066–1530*. London: Methuen, 1984.

Owst, G. R. *Literature and the Pulpit in Medieval England.* Cambridge: Cambridge University Press, 1933.

Penninger, Frieda Elaine. *William Caxton.* Boston: Twayne Publishers, 1979.

Perfetti, Lisa. *Women and Laughter in Medieval Comic Literature.* Ann Arbor: University of Michigan Press, 2003.

Phillips, Kim M. *Medieval Maidens: Young Women and Gender in England, 1270–1540.* Manchester and New York: Manchester University Press, 2003.

Piaget, Arthur. "Le Livre Messire Geoffroi de Charny." *Romania* 26 (1897): 394–411.

Power, Eileen. trans. *The Goodman of Paris (Le Ménagier de Paris).* 1928. Avon: The Bath Press, 1992.

———. *Medieval People.* 1924. 10th ed. New York: Barnes and Noble, 1963.

Prescott, Hilda F. M., ed. *Friar Felix at Large: A Fifteenth-Century Pilgrimage to the Holy Land.* Westport, CT: Greenwood Press, 1967.

Pritchard, Gillian. "Religion and the Paston Family." *Daily Life in the Late Middle Ages.* Ed. Richard Britnell. Gloucestershire: Sutton Publishing, 1998: 65–82.

Rawlings, Gertrude Burford. *The Booke of Thenseygnementes and Techynge that the knyght of the towre made to his doughters by the Chevalier Geoffroy de la Tour Landry.* Illus. Garth Jones. London: George Newnes, Ltd., 1902.

Riddy, Felicity. "Mother Knows Best: Reading Social Change in a Courtesy Text." *Speculum* 71.1 (January 1996): 66–86.

Ritson, Joseph. *Ancient English Metrical Romances.* Rev. Edmund Goldsmid. Vol. 3. Edinburgh: E. & G. Goldsmid, 1885.

Schofield, John. *Medieval London Houses.* New Haven: Yale University Press, 1995.

Shahar, Shulamith. *Childhood in the Middle Ages.* Trans. Chaya Galai. London and New York: Routledge, 1992.

———. *The Fourth Estate: A History of Women in the Middle Ages.* 1983. Trans. Chaya Galai. London and New York: Routledge, 1984.

Shinners, John, ed. *Medieval Popular Religion 1000–1500: A Reader.* Peterborough, ON: Broadview Press, 1997.

Simmons, Thomas Frederick. *The Lay Folks Mass Book or The Manner of Hearing Mass.* Early English Text Society, Original Series 71. London: Oxford University Press, 1879.

Singman, Jeffrey L. *Daily Life in Medieval Europe.* Westport, CT: Greenwood, 1999.

Sklar, Elizabeth S. "Courtly Love." *Medieval England: An Encyclopedia.* Ed. Paul E. Szarmach, M. Teresa Tavormina, and Joel T. Rosenthal. New York: Garland, 1998: 214–216.

Stacey, Robert C. "Jews." *Medieval England: An Encyclopedia.* Ed. Paul E. Szarmach, M. Teresa Tavormina, and Joel T. Rosenthal. New York: Garland, 1998: 380–381.

Stone, Laurence. *The Family, Sex and Marriage in England, 1500–1800*. New York: Harper and Row, 1977.

Sutton, Anne. "Dress and Fashions c. 1470." *Daily Life in the Late Middle Ages*. Ed. Richard Britnell. Gloucestershire: Sutton Publishing, 1998: 5–26.

Taylor, G. S., ed. *The Book of the Knight of La Tour Landry*. Intro. D. B. Wyndham Lewis. London: John Hamilton Ltd., 1930.

Thrupp, Sylvia L. *The Merchant Class of Medieval London (1300–1500)*. Chicago: University of Chicago Press, 1948.

Treharne, Elaine. *Old and Middle English: An Anthology*. Oxford: Blackwell, 2000.

Tuchman, Barbara. *A Distant Mirror: The Calamitous 14th Century*. New York: Knopf, 1978.

Vitto, Cindy. "Selections from *The Book of the Knight of the Tower*." *Medieval Literature for Children*. Ed. Daniel T. Kline. New York: Routledge, 2003.

vom Stein, Marquard. *Der Ritter Vom Turn*. Ed. Ruth Harvey. Berlin: Erich Schmidt Verlag, 1988.

Ward, Benedicta. *Miracles and the Medieval Mind: Theory, Record and Event 1000–1215*. Philadelphia: University of Pennsylvania Press, 1987.

White, T. H. *The Bestiary: A Book of Beasts*. 1954. New York: Perigee Books, 1980.

Woolgar, C. M. *The Great Household in Late Medieval England*. New Haven: Yale University Press, 1999.

Wright, T. *A Selection of Latin Stories from Manuscripts of the Thirteenth and Fourteenth Centuries*. London: Richards, 1842.

Wright, Thomas, ed. *The Book of the Knight of La Tour-Landry*. Rev. ed., Early English Text Society, Original Series 33. 1906. New York: Greenwood Press, 1969.

INDEX